EARLY METALLURGY IN NIGERIA

ADENIYI A. AFONJA

SineliBooks

3540 E Broad St. Suite 120-192
Mansfield, Texas 76063, U.S.A.

Committed to disseminating knowledge and promoting established and emerging authors in all major fields of academics.

© Adeniyi Ademola Afonja 2020

This publication is in copyright, subject to statutory exceptions and to the provisions of relevant collective agreements. No part may be reproduced without the written permission of SineliBooks.

ISBN 978-0-9985843-4-8

SineliBooks accepts no responsibility for the accuracy of information presented, the references cited, or the appropriateness, accuracy and persistence of the websites referred to in this publication.

If not for progress in metals technologies from early times, where would humankind development be today?

CONTENTS

	SOURCES OF IMAGES	vi
	PREFACE	vii
1	MATERIALS IN THE SERVICE OF HUMANKIND	1
2	HUMANKIND AND MATERIALS THROUGH HISTORY	13
3	METALLURGY OF MATERIALS OF ANTIQUITY	39
4	METALS TECHNOLOGY PROVENANCE THEORIES	65
5	EARLY METALLURGY IN AFRICA	83
6	EARLY COPPER AND IRON METALLURGY IN NIGERIA	107
7	BIBLIOGRAPHY	183
8	APPENDICES	191
	APPENDIX I DATING OF ARCHAEOLOGICAL OBJECTS	193
	APPENDIX II LOST-WAX (*CIRE PERDUE*) CASTING	197
	APPENDIX III BASIC METALLURGY OF METALS OF ANTIQUITY	201

SOURCES OF IMAGES

About four thousand of artifacts from Nigeria's rich Early Metals Culture are in museums and private collections all over the world. In the course of research for this book, details and the images displayed in Figures 6.7; 6;13; and 6.20-22 were obtained from websites and online databases of many museums, through visits to museums in Nigeria, Europe, and the United States of America where many of the artifacts are on display, and also through visits to numerous national and international exhibitions of Nigerian artworks. The main sources are listed below:

1. National Museum, Lagos, Nigeria.
2. National Museum, Benin City, Nigeria.
3. National Museum Ile-Ife, Nigeria.
4. National Museum, Owo, Nigeria.
5. The British Museum, London, United Kingdom.
6. Museum of London, United Kingdom.
7. Pitt Rivers Museum, Oxford, United Kingdom.
8. Ethnological Museum of Berlin, Germany.
9. Museum of Arts and Crafts, Hamburg, Germany.
10. Dresden Museum of Ethnology, Germany.
11. Museum of Ethnology, Leipzig, Germany.
12. Rautenstrauch-Joest Museum, Cologne, Germany.
13. Weltmuseum Wien, Vienna, Austria.
14. Museum of Ethnography, Leiden, Netherlands.
15. Metropolitan Museum of Arts, New York, U.S.A.
16. Metropolitan Museum, New York, U.S.A.
17. University of Pennsylvania Museum of Archaeology and Anthropology, Philadelphia, U.S.A.
18. Museum of Fine Arts, Boston, U.S.A.
19. Rietberg Museum, Zurich, Switzerland.
20. British Museum online database, britishmuseum.org.
21. "Kingdom of Ife: sculptures from West Africa". British Museum.
22. Frank Willett, The Art of Ife (CD Rom), The University of Glasgow, 2004. Bronzes from Ife and Benin, Peter Herrmann, Berlin, 2007.
23. Shaw. T (1977). Unearthing Igbo-Ukwu. Oxford University Press, Ibadan, Nigeria.
24. Public Domain.

PREFACE AND ACKNOWLEDGEMENTS

Humankind is believed to have existed in Africa for over 6 million years, based on the dating of excavated fossils. Transformations took place over time in response to severe climate changes and the Modern Human, believed to be the first to spread beyond Africa evolved only about 2 million years ago and did not move to other parts of the world until about 200,000 years ago. What is now known about ancient human history came from several sources: paleontologists excavate and evaluate human and article fossils dating back 2-3 million years; archaeologists excavate ancient sites and study recovered articles, mostly dating back 40-60,000 years; historians study oral and recorded history but the scope is limited to about 3,000 years when writing was invented. Archaeometallurgy evolved in the second half of the last century and has become a major tool for the study of ancient metals, metalworking structures, tools, waste products and finished artifacts, using techniques from the physical sciences. While this does not in anyway distract from the traditional approach of other archaeoscientists, it is a very valuable complement, since it provides in-depth information about ore and slag composition, furnace design, macro and micro analysis of objects, all of which give vital information about the probable production techniques. Materials have played a central role throughout human history, starting with stone, flint, wood, straw, and transitioning to metals around ten to twelve thousand years ago. In fact the major stages of historical evolution are delineated by the materials that were in prominent use: Stone Age; Bronze Age; Iron Age, etc.

I took my first course in metallurgy in 1962 as a mechanical engineering student at Kings College University of Durham, Newcastle Upon Tyne, United Kingdom. The course lecturer was Professor Ronald Frank Tylecote the world famous archaeometallurgist, widely regarded as the pioneer of the subject, although I did not know it then. I later came across one of his publications on the Nok Iron Culture located in modern North-Central region of Nigeria, and found that he had worked extensively on several other early metallurgy sites in Africa. I was fascinated by his conclusions that no one knew where the Nok Culture iron technology came from, arriving around 800 BC, and why it disappeared without trace after flourishing for about six hundred years. The first indication of its existence was from a terracotta figurine unearthed during open-cast tin mining in the area in the late 1920s, which eventually led to the discovery of ancient iron furnaces. Professor Tylecote described in detail several unique features of the thirteen furnaces found in Taruga near the state capital of Abuja which had not been found elsewhere in the early world, and the unusually high quality of the iron products. On my return to Nigeria in 1969, I took up a teaching position at the University of Ife, Western Nigeria and found that Ile-Ife too had a very rich Copper/Bronze Culture from around the 12th century AD, and it too disappeared some three hundred years later but this time leaving behind a very rich collection of internationally famous artifacts which are on display in British and Nigerian museums. I did more intensive search on the early metal history of Nigeria and found that an earlier Copper/Bronze Culture had flourished in Igbo-Ukwu, Eastern Nigeria some three centuries before Ife but also disappeared inexplicably although many for the outstanding artworks are also on display in British and Nigerian museums. A third Copper/Brass Culture also flourished in Benin from around 16th century AD and was prolific for about three hundred years before production was disrupted by foreign invasion in 1897 and around four thousand artworks were looted. However, the practice was revived and has been sustained to date. Some of the looted artworks of the Benin Copper/Brass Culture are on display in museums all over the world but many more are in private collections. The products of all the three Copper Cultures have been evaluated and described in superlative terms in numerous international art media and many are being copied and sold worldwide.

As at 1970, there was only one scrap metal processing plant in Nigeria, planning for the first integrated iron and steel plant had just commenced, and most people were oblivious of the rich early metal culture of the country. I therefore initiated a research project on early metallurgy in Nigeria, primarily to find out how the country had such a rich early metals culture and lost it all. The initial targets were the four identified early metal sites but I soon found that there were many more. Within a few years, every known site had been comprehensively evaluated, including extensive literature search, site visits, laboratory analysis of collected metal objects and slags, socio-ethnographic study of sites, interviews of current inhabitants of the areas, and visits to museums in Nigeria and the numerous foreign museums hosting Nigerian artworks. As the research progressed, it became clear that the scope needed to be expanded to early metal cultures of other African countries and Ancient Middle East (the apparent cradle of all early metal technologies) in order to place the Nigerian cultures in a proper perspective. Unfortunately, my primary academic teaching, research and administrative duties left little room for analysis of the very rich data collected, but I have had time since retirement in 2005 to update the data which has been greatly enriched by the extensive information and data on new discoveries that have been published in the last decade or so particularly on the Nok Iron Culture where over a hundred more furnaces have been found and many more potential sites have been identified and mapped.

I wish to dedicate this work to the memory of Professor R. F. Tylecote, a valued mentor and an accomplished scholar who introduced me to metallurgy in the first place, whose work has been a major inspiration to me and a rich source of data for this book. His personal contribution to the development of archaeometallurgy is unrivalled. As a Fellow of the British Institute of Metals, I had invaluable opportunities to interact personally with him at meetings and conferences on several occasions in the nineteen eighties and seek his views on this project. His comments and suggestions were very inspiring, helpful and are gratefully acknowledged. A book of this kind is never entirely the product of its author, but is dependent on the work of many scholars all over the world from whose works I have drawn extensively with due recognition. I also wish to acknowledge the assistance of Dr Ayo Olofinjana who worked with me at the early stages of the project. My wife, Professor Simi Afonja assisted with data collection and interpretation on the socio-cultural/ethnological aspects of the research and her immense contribution is gratefully acknowledged.

Adeniyi A. Afonja
Emeritus Professor of Materials Science & Engineering
Obafemi Awolowo University, Ile-Ife, Nigeria.

Chapter 1

Materials in the service of humankind

1.1 INTRODUCTION

Ample archaeological evidence suggests that anatomically modern humans originated from Eastern/Southern Africa around 200,000 years ago, based on the oldest skeletal remains that have been found, evaluated and dated (Chan *et al.*, 2019). However, they may have been around much longer, considering excavations in Kenya in 2015 which discovered primitive but shaped stone tools embedded in rocks dating to 3.3 million years ago (Encyclopaedia Britanica, 2019). However, the span of oral and recorded history is less than 5,000 years and what is now known about the pre-historic times was inferred from excavations of tools, implements, artifacts, etc. that were dated many thousands of years beyond recorded history. Most tools, implements, hunting gear and artifacts found were made from stone but some articles made from iron have also been found. Since iron does not normally exist in pure form and no evidence of smelting in this period has been found, it is safe to assume that they used meteoric iron. Ancient civilization which began around 3000-4000 BC is believed to have evolved in the final stages of the *neolithic revolution* (also known as agricultural revolution) which began 12 to 10,000 years ago when small agricultural communities began to form. These communities were small and moved constantly to find fertile land for farming or avoid extreme weather. From around 8000 BC, more stable communities began to form in many locations, mostly around fertile land. Settlements dating back to around 10000 BC have been identified in Asia, Africa and Central America. Communities began to develop crops, domesticate animals for use as food, for ploughing farmland and transportation. By 8000 BC the *urban revolution* had begun. Rudimentary governance structures, trading and urbanization had begun to emerge, and so were inter-community feuds.

Technology is as old as mankind because it has always been a survival tool: shelter had to be constructed, tools were required for hunting, energy was required for cooking and keeping warm, and as people migrated from indigenous communities, they took any available technological know-how with them. With the development of agriculture, farming tools had to be invented; as settlements became established, war between communities became a common occurrence and weapons had to be developed. From the earliest times materials have played a prime role in sustaining human life on earth, in fact, the history of civilization is synonymous with the history of materials. Wood, stone and clay, organic straw made possible construction of shelter; wood and flint provided heat for keeping warm and cooking and also were the main materials for the construction of hunting spears, traps, and farming implements. From the stone age around 9000 BC, fire had been invented and was readily made by rubbing flint stones. This development prompted the invention of stronger materials of construction - iron products were being forged from meteoric or ferrugenous sandstone using coal obtained from outcrops. Development soon progressed beyond tools for survival to ornaments, artifacts made from gold, copper, bronze. Mankind is even more dependent on materials today and progress in technology development is largely dependent on the materials available to meet the requirements. Many of the techniques used in the earliest times such as fiber-reinforced materials, sand casting, lost-wax casting and forging are still contemporary technologies in the modern industry.

1.2 MATERIALS THROUGH HUMAN HISTORY

Although humankind may have been in existence for 3 million years or more, written history began only about three thousand years ago when the first known type of coherent writing, cuneiform was invented in ancient Sumeria (WWU, 2017). Prior to this, humans were recording events by drawing pictures, and pictographs dating back to about 40,000 years have been discovered in southwest Africa, Australia and southwest Europe. Dated archaeological excavations put human existence on earth at around 60,000 years while fossils excavated recently in the Olduvai Gorge (now Tanzania) by paleoanthropologists indicate that humans may have existed from about 1.8 to 1.2 million years ago (Encyclopaedia Britanica, 2019). The history of materials dates back 40,000 to 60,000 years and there is extensive archaeological information on the types of materials that were in use, where and when. Human history has been divided into periods and classification systems are many. However, the most prominent is the definition of Periods, based on the dating of materials that were in use (Stone Age, Bronze Age, Iron Age, etc.). One major issue of contention is how the age of findings is determined.

1.2.1 Sources of human history

What is now known about ancient history came from several sources: paleontologists excavate and evaluate human and article fossils dating back 2-3 million years; archaeologists excavate ancient sites and study recovered articles, mostly dating back 40-60,000 years; historians study oral and recorded history but the scope is limited to about 3,000 years when writing was invented; while archaeometallurgists study the types of metals and other materials that were in use, including excavated furnaces and slags.

1.2.1.1 *Paleohistory*

Humans are believed to have existed in Africa for over 6 million years, based on the dating of excavated fossils. Transformations have taken place over time, in response to severe climate changes and the Modern Man, believed to be the first to spread beyond Africa evolved only about 2 million years ago and did not start to move to other parts of the world until around 200,000 years ago (Smithsonian, 2017). It is interesting to note that even the ancient man was making tools and implements from stone, based on dated tool excavations.

1.2.1.2 *Archaeohistory*

Archaeologists excavate and study artifacts, tools, inscriptions, physical remains of cultures, and other objects, the results of which they can use to interpret and reconstruct past human behaviour, ancient cultures, and the material cultures. Initially, archaeology was a branch of anthropology and it was basically a descriptive study of antiquities. However, the discipline has evolved over time and is now infused with scientific methods which include dating and elemental analysis of findings.

1.2.1.3 Archaeometallurgy (Historical or Early Metallurgy)

A major distinctive identity of past civilizations is the type of materials that were in use, which were mostly metals. While archaeologists are very good at excavation of ancient sites and describing findings, most do not have the competence to do in-depth scientific analysis, especially of metals and other materials. This has prompted the evolution of archaeometallurgy which may be described as a study of ancient metals, metalworking structures, tools, waste products and finished artifacts, using techniques from physical sciences (Tylecote 1972; 2002). While this does not in anyway distract from the traditional approach of archaeologists, it is a very valuable complement, since it provides in-depth information about ore and slag composition, furnace design, macro and micro analysis of objects, all of which give vital information about the probable production techniques. Archaeometallurgists use scientific methods to unravel the intricacies and complexities of early metallurgical practices, they use physico-chemical methods to identify, analyze and fully identify metals, determine metalworking structures, and types of waste products such as slags and crucibles, remnant furnaces found mostly in archaeological excavations, all of which give useful information on smelting processes adopted, types of ores used, and process thermodynamics. Finished objects are subjected to intensive microstructural analysis to determine method of manufacture (hot/cold forging, casting, drawing, welding, etc.), heat treatment processes used (annealing, quench-hardening, tempering). From the data they can determine the nature of manufacturing technologies used in the past as well as the socio-economic context. They can also reconstruct damaged excavations and produce models, and reconstruct ancient practices in the modern laboratory. Archaeometallurgical investigations also involve analysis of past metallurgical processes in relation to modern practices. Methodologies behind the production of ancient metals and metal objects and such details as main elemental composition of metals such as copper and iron, and alloying elements such as zinc, tin, lead, arsenic can be determined. Scientific analyses of antique metal objects can provide evidence for both the nature and scale of mining, smelting, refining and metalworking trades, and aid understanding of other structural and artifactual evidence. They can be crucial in understanding the economy of a site, the nature of the occupation, the technological capabilities of its occupants and their cultural affinities.

In view of the fact that the use of metals only became widespread in the last six thousand years or so (the beginning of the Bronze Age), the work of the archaeometallurgist covers this period to date. Much of the information available presently on the evolution of metallurgy has been as a result of extensive analytical studies by archaeometallurgists. Many difficulties faced by archaeologists such as distinguishing between metal alloys, method of smelting and working and heat treatment, probable ore chemistry, have been resolved by archaeometallurgists. (see Roberts and Thornton, 2014). For a long time, archaeologists had been perplexed by ancient swords which had been found, sections of which seemed to have been made from different metals. The structure and properties of the edge were different from the stem or the hilt. Archaeometallurgists have been able to determine from microstructural analysis that they were probably produced from the same material but different sections were given different heat treatment to obtain different properties.

Archaeometallurgy began to evolve in the nineteenth century when archaeological publications which were largely descriptive began to feature analytical data on metal artifacts. However, it was not until the mid-twentieth century that metallurgical study of ancient artifacts would become mainstream. By the early 1970s, a group of scholars in Europe who had combined training and competence in metallurgy and archaeology began to use extensive and complex metallurgical techniques to explain archaeological theories. They successfully combined archaeological fieldwork, scientific analysis and experimental reconstruction in order to promote understanding between ancient societies and their metallurgical technologies (Killick, 2001; Cleere, 1993).

1.3 DATING OF ARCHAEOLOGICAL EXCAVATIONS

There are many methods which paleontologists and archaeologists use in dating findings which can be classified into two groups: Style Analysis and Absolute Dating. While style analysis is based primarily on visual observations, absolute dating requires scientific analysis in specialized laboratories which use nuclear techniques to determine approximately the production date of an excavation. There are many variants of both techniques applicable to a wide range of objects but only those which apply to materials will be outlined here. A more detailed account is presented in Appendix I.

1.3.1 Relative/Stylistic Dating

The Style Analysis technique compares the shape and style of an object to another that had been dated on the basis of known progressive sequences. For example there is a rich database on the stylistic development of pottery, glass, stoneware over time and a newly excavated artifact can be easily placed. Relative dating involves the establishment of a date range outside of which an event would have been unlikely or impossible. Artifacts often have distinctive and stylistic design which developed over a period of time and some may have been dated by other means. It may be possible therefore to fix a typology into a chronological framework. The main weakness of the method is that it is imprecise.

1.3.2 Radiocarbon Dating

Carbon Dating technique is based on the fact the all living matter absorb carbon (C_{12} and radioactive carbon C_{14}) from the natural Carbon Cycle and when they die the carbon C_{14} begins to decay at a precise rate which has been established by other means. By determining the amount of C_{14} remaining in an object, the time it took to lose the missing amount can then be calculated fairly precisely. The main weakness of the method is that it is only applicable to organic matter. Since most Neolithic findings are made of inorganic stone, carbon dating cannot be applied. However, most rocks are formed by volcanic reaction or other cataclysmic event and contain a small quantity of radioactive substance, usually uranium or radioactive lead, which starts to decay immediately. By identifying the radioactive substance and determining the residual amount, the age of the rock can be determined from the known decay rate of the substance. The half-life of C_{14} is about 5,000 years, hence cannot be used to date accurately objects which are believed to be over 10,000 years old. On the contrary, isotope Potassium K_{40} has a half-life of 1.25 billion years and can be used to date articles which are several million years old. The problem with precise dating is that the object or part of it has to be destroyed. Also, the process is very expensive and often may not be justified except for valuable findings. Furthermore, the technique is in the process of continuous review and refinement, and recent review of some previously dated archaeological findings produced earlier dates, largely because of revision of earlier assumptions on the properties of cosmic rays and half life of C_{14} isotope.

1.3.3 Thermo-Luminescence Dating

Crystalline materials which include metals and rocks can be dated using luminescence techniques. The method is based on the fact that heated crystalline objects release electrons some of which are trapped inside the item. By heating the item in the laboratory, the trapped electrons become excited and they recombine with the parent material. This process frees energy in the form of light which can be measured. By repeating the process, the change in the amount of energy released over a known time frame can be used to estimate how much radiation the object has been exposed to over the years. Again, this method is expensive and requires that at least part of the object be destroyed.

1.3.4 Historical and archaeological dating styles

Archaeologists, paleontologists, and archaeohistorians attribute dates in the past to objects or events in order to place a new find in a previously established chronology. There is no consensus on the method of dating or classifying human history and many types of dating methods have emerged over time, which makes it difficult to reconcile dates quoted in different styles. Perhaps the most common is the division into three distinct ages or Periods: Ancient History, the Middle Ages, and the Modern Age. Another method involves division between BC/BCE. (Before Christ/Before Common Era) and AD/CE. (*Anno Domini/Common Era*). Other systems adopt the materials that were in prominent use in the period. The most prominent styles are listed in Table 1 (the dates quoted are typical, not absolute and there are many sub-divisions of the Periods).

1.4 EVOLUTION OF METALLURGY

Metallurgy is the study of the science and technology of metals and alloys, including extraction from natural ores, fabrication and production of a wide range of components. It also involves selection of materials for different applications and evaluation of behavior in service. Metals and alloys constitute by far the most important group of materials that drive technological and human development. Major attributes include ready availability, ease of fabrication, desirable mechanical, physical and aesthetic properties, good electrical and thermal properties, and versatility of applications. Metals are in two main groups - ferrous and non-ferrous. The ferrous group comprises cast iron, wrought iron, carbon steel and alloy iron and steel while non-ferrous materials include pure metals: copper, aluminium, lead, tin, nickel, zinc, and alloys: brass, bronze, cupro-nickel, aluminium-magnesium alloys, zinc alloys, etc.

Table 1. Typical methods of dating archaeological artifacts.

DATING STYLE	CHRONOLOGY
Stone Age	Before 10000 BC
Bronze Age	6000-2500 BC
Iron Age	2500 BC-800 AD
Pre-History	Earlier than 5000 BC
Ancient History	3600 BC - 500 AD
Middle Ages/Medieval Age	500-1500 AD
Modern Age	1500 AD-present
ante quem and *post quem*	A relative dating style which places the age of an object between the oldest and the most recent possible dates.
BC	Before Christ: the number of years an event occurred before Christ
AD	*anno domini* - In the year of our lord (AD 1).The number of years an event occurred after Christ
CE	Common Era (same as AD)
BCE	Before Common Era (same as BC)
BP	Before Present (present = 1950)

The history of metallurgy dates back to about nine millennium BC when humans began to acquire expertise in manipulation of naturally occurring metals for use. These included copper and gold whose occurrence in native form was fairly widespread. Techniques were developed to forge and cast both metals to produce artifacts, tools and weapons. Initially it was a purely selective process: deciding which of available materials was best suited to a given application, but with time they discovered techniques of altering and enhancing the properties of these metals through repeated hammering with intermittent heat treatment, progressing to the point where metals were being extracted from ores. Henceforth they developed expertise in alloying by combining several metals to produce an alloy or a composite with enhanced properties, casting and forging processes to produce intricate structures, tools, and artifacts, and differential heat treatment to achieve different properties in different sections of the same tool or weapon. This is the humble beginning of *process metallurgy*.

Of all known materials, none has been as important as metals in shaping the evolution of technology through time. Such advances as the Industrial Revolution, the invention of the automobile, electricity, weaponry, modern agriculture, telecommunication, and most of the domestic appliances we have come to take for granted would have been impossible without metals. Gold was the first metal to be discovered, it is not clear when or where and suggestions are many. There are several sources of gold in nature: it occurs in pure form embedded in solid rocks, and in stream beds probably through erosion of rock deposits. Although there is little archaeological evidence, it is possible that the Stone Age man had used gold picked up from streams because of its bright, gleaming appearance. Six other metals: copper, silver, lead, tin, iron and mercury were known and used in the Medieval Period. These seven metals now known as *Metals of Antiquity* dominated early metallurgy for nearly eight thousand years, to the end of the 17th century (Cramb, 2017). Only two of these metals (gold and copper) were used widely, due apparently to the relative scarcity of the others.

Five of the metals of antiquity (gold, copper, silver, iron and mercury) can be found in their native states. It is not clear how tin and lead were obtained but it is probable that they were impurities in copper ores. Furthermore, like gold, tin particles can settle in stream beds. Around 3000 BC, the Sumerians were known to be mixing different ores with copper ore to obtain a material which is stronger and more ductile than copper. Many artifacts have been found which were made from alloys of copper and zinc (brass). Heating a blend of malachite (copper ore) and calamine (zinc oxide) with charcoal could have produced brass while a mixture of copper ore with cassiterite (tin ore) could have yielded bronze, both of which are stronger, more malleable and castable than copper. It is unclear whether ore mixing was deliberate or incidental. The discovery of lead may have been accidental: the metal occurs in nature as galena (lead sulphide) and has low melting point of 327°C, low enough to be reduced to lead by wild fires. The beautiful, metallic look of lead which probably solidified in pools would have been found attractive and ancient Egyptians were using it as cosmetic eye paints around 3500 BC.

Detailed studies of articles, furnaces, slags, forges found in excavations showed clearly that the *early metallurgists* had the competence in many areas of modern metallurgy: they were aware of the versatility of carbon as an ore reductant in smelting; they were competent in complex casting techniques, in particular, *lost wax casting* which is still a vital production process in modern metallurgy; they were also competent in forging, shaping, and grinding all of which are modern production processes. They knew how to work metals to achieve desired properties and shape; they were familiar with heat treatment (quenching, annealing) as a means of obtaining metals of different strength and malleability; they combined different metals to make objects (composites in modern metallurgy); and analysis of excavated furnaces and slags showed clearly that they knew a lot about alloying and choosing the appropriate refractories that were resistant to the slag chemistry - furnaces have been found which had different refractory lining for different sections, a standard practice in modern ore smelting. Apart from metals, ores were being used extensively in the Neolithic Period: haematite (red iron oxide) was used extensively for wall and pottery decoration and in ritual and funerary practice. Green and blue copper ores were used extensively for cosmetics in ancient Egypt and Mesopotamia. Azurite, a blue copper ore was discovered in Crete in a habitation dating back 6000 BC (Coghlan, 1961).

Up to 1800 AD, only five more metals were in common use: platinum, antimony, bismuth, zinc and arsenic. In effect, the remaining 74 metals (there are currently 86 known metals) were discovered only in the last 300 years. Metallurgy remained essentially practical - development of larger and more efficient processes for smelting, melting and working of metals - until the 18th century when the science behind the practice began to develop. From then on, driven by the infusion of basic physical and chemical sciences, monumental progress has been made in the process of understanding how metals behave, why they behave the way they do, and what can be done to alter their behavior with a view to enhancing their technological properties. This has led to the development of thousands of metals, alloys and composites with specialized characteristics to meet the complex needs of modern technology. In fact, the profession has evolved to the point that a metal alloy can be designed from first principles to meet specific engineering requirements. Also, the scope of the subject has widened beyond metals to include non-metals (ceramics, glasses, polymers). Technology milestones of the late nineteenth and early twentieth centuries: telephone, phonograph, photography, electricity, steam and internal combustion engines, automobiles, aircraft, space exploration, biomedical implants, would not have been possible but for the emergence of appropriate materials.

Mankind has also learnt to understand metals' interaction with the service environment and to investigate failures in service, which led to further developments and innovations. For example, the sinking of the Titanic on its maiden trip in 1912 with the loss of about 1,500 lives was due to materials failure. The ship was designed to be unsinkable but no one knew at the time that the strength of steel could drop as much as 80% in freezing environment. The ship hit an iceberg and broke up. This disaster opened up a whole new area of metallurgy and material science – *fracture mechanics* which has become the prime basis for mechanical engineering high-integrity design and a major tool for investigating accidents caused by materials failure. The two most spectacular disasters in space exploration (Challenger, 1986, Columbia, 2003) were caused by materials failure and many other disasters have occurred in civil, mechanical and nuclear engineering structures as a result of materials failure, and are indeed occurring all the time. However, each event provides a new impetus for a greater understanding of the complex interrelationship between the structure, properties and service environment of metals and other materials.

Modern metallurgy has been infused with many engineering principles, especially design from first science and engineering principles. It is now also possible to design and engineer metals and other materials from basic principles to produce predetermined properties. There are now around three thousand different grades of iron and steel alloys to meet the very stringent environmental requirements - temperature, pressure, creep, fatigue stressing, impact, corrosive media, friction and wear, complex stress situations, etc. Developments in the non-ferrous field have also produced a wide range of aluminium alloys, brasses, bronzes, cupro-nickels, ferro-nickels, tungsten etc. The invention of silicon-based transistor around six decades ago marked the beginning of one of the most life-changing phases in technological development, but the proliferation into everything from cell phones, computers, medical equipment to aero-space equipment would not have been possible without the development of the technology for etching millions of electronic integrated circuits on a chip the size of a coin.

The close relationship between metals and other materials has also been realized from the earliest times. Archaeological excavations have found metal smelting furnaces with different clays for the shell and the lining, and wood, sand and clay were used extensively in the metal casting processes. The rapid development of iron and steel technology from the mid-seventeenth century propelled the development of ceramics and refractory technologies to produce appropriate high-temperature furnace linings for acidic and basic furnace environments, and many vital industrial components. Wood-based fibers have been used for reinforcement of clay for construction from the earliest times but the combination of metal and non-metals into composites to exploit the assets and compensate for the liabilities of the member materials has developed rapidly only in the last century or so. Ceramic and carbon fiber-reinforced metal composites are now vital materials in manufacturing technology. Many components of the modern airplane including the fuselage, aerospace crafts, sports equipment, are made from carbon fiber- reinforced aluminium. Up to the 18th century, metallurgy remained a practice and concerned traditional methods such as smelting, melting and working of metals. From this time, the basic scientific principles of thermodynamics, solid and fluid mechanics started to feature in the explanation of observed phenomena, not only in metallurgy but in all other branches of engineering, and, eventually, science became an indispensable design tool for all engineering, transforming metallurgy into *metallurgical engineering*. The study of mechanical, electrical and chemical properties of non-materials and composites is now a vital part of metallurgy and this development has changed the traditional scope of the study of metallurgy, and different names for the discipline have evolved over time: *metallurgy and materials science, metallurgical and materials engineering* or *materials science and engineering,* the last of which most appropriately identifies the current scope of the subject.

1.5 THE FAMILY OF MODERN MATERIALS

The history of civilization is the history of technology because technology has been the prime mover for development from the earliest times. On the other hand, the history of technology is synonymous with the history of materials since the pace of technological development is largely controlled by availability of appropriate materials. In fact and as discussed earlier, stages of civilization are usually demarcated by the major material in use - the stone age, the bronze age, the iron age. Materials: metals, alloys, rubber, glass, plastics, ceramics, concrete, wood, composites constitute an intimate part of human culture and feature very prominently in manufacturing and virtually every facet of our daily lives - transportation, communication, clothing, housing, food production and processing, recreation, medicare. From the earliest times, development and advancement of civilization have depended on the ability of humans to produce and manipulate materials to meet their needs. The development of many new technologies that we depend on so much today has been made possible primarily because suitable materials became available, but also, many of the inventions created a need for the development of new, appropriate materials. For example, paper technology as we know it today evolved from papyrus technology which was developed in ancient Egypt (the oldest known civilization) around 3500 BC; evolution of electricity depended critically on the development of copper and ceramic technologies; the development and proliferation of the automobile was only made possible by availability of cheap steel in abundance. The modern computer, smart phone and so many other electronic instruments that have become part of our everyday lives would not have been possible without the semiconducting materials (transistors) and integrated circuits of today. Advancement in medicare would have been a lot more difficult but for the availability of suitable biomedical materials - metal and non-metal implants, heart pacemakers, artificial organs, cosmetic surgical materials, dental materials.

There are three basic components of the family of materials: ceramics, metals and polymers. In prehistoric times, stone (a ceramic) was the dominant material for tools and weapons. From about 6000 BC metals became the preferred materials and this remained so until about sixty years ago when polymers became available in commercial quantities. Wood is often considered a distinct member of the materials family but, technically, wood, like rubber is a monomer and belongs to the polymer family. Henceforth, the interrelationship between the three major materials have become very strong. Metals cannot be produced without the appropriate ceramics (refractories) for lining the furnaces and ladles while the group of metal-ceramic and metal-polymer composites has emerged and is now considered the fourth member of the materials family, and a modern metallurgical engineer needs a good foundation in ceramic and polymer science and engineering. Also, with developments in nano science and technology, a new group of materials is emerging: nanomaterials, with unusual and exceptional characteristics which make them potentially suitable for a very wide range of new applications, from electronics to medical implants. Furthermore, the traditional trial-and-error process of choosing materials for applications has given way to a more scientific approach, and it is now possible to design and engineer a material to meet desired application specifications. These developments have resulted in the transformation of the traditional discipline of metallurgy to materials science and engineering (Figure 1.1).

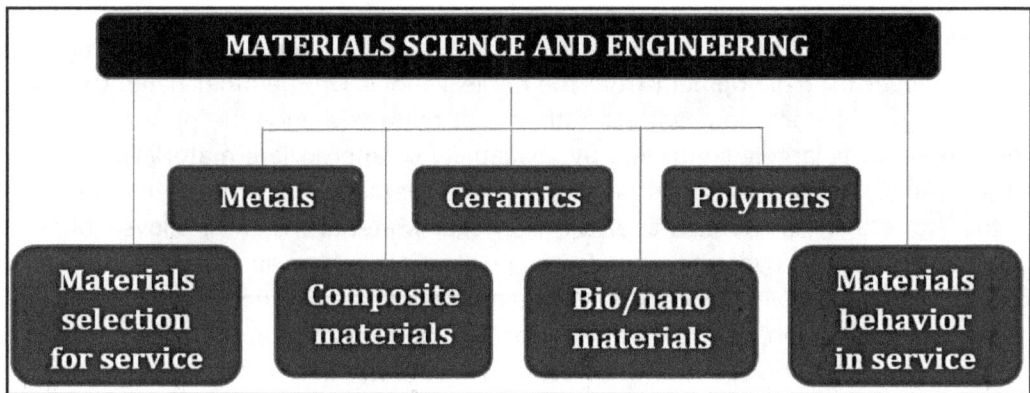

Figure 1.1 Main areas of materials science and engineering

Chapter 2

Humankind and materials through history

2.1 INTRODUCTION

There are many definitions of periods of history but the most common used by archaeohistorians, archaeologists and archaeometallurgists is the division of human history on the basis of the materials that were in use at the time. There are basically six divisions: Prehistoric Stone Age (dating back to around 3.3 million years), Neolithic Age (12000-5000 BC), Copper/Bronze Age (4000-1000 BC), Iron Age (1000-600 BC), Post Medieval Age (600 BC-1500 AD), and Modern Age (1500 AD-date). Humankind appears to have evolved through these stages over a period of 2 to 3 million years, and most civilizations seemed to have progressed from the stone age in sequence - through the Bronze Age and the Iron Age, separated by several thousand years in some areas of the world. It should be noted however that this categorization is somewhat arbitrary because each of the metals was probably already in limited use much earlier. Furthermore, proliferation of any of the metals did not arrive in different societies at the same time, or in the same order, due probably to the diffusion processes at play. For example, Africa progressed from the Stone Age to the Iron Age, and then the Bronze Age, while in most other regions, Bronze Age preceded Iron Age. The Copper/Bronze Age also needs some clarification: copper had been in limited use since about 9000 BC, produced in small quantities mainly for ornaments and artifacts, while the discovery of true bronze came around five thousand years later (low-tin copper alloys which proliferated between 5000 and 3000 BC were erroneously classified as bronzes and have been reclassified as tin-, zinc-, arsenic coppers since the emergence of archaeometallurgy). However, bronze use spread very rapidly from around 3000 BC primarily because tin, the main alloying element became widely available, probably through intra- and inter-regional trading, and also because of its wide range of unique properties which made it superior to copper for many applications that included artifacts, tools and weaponry.

2.2 EARLY WORLD METALLURGY

There is evidence that some native metals: gold, copper and iron have been in use since Neolithic times. Gold was used for ornaments while copper and iron were worked to produce small objects like hand tools and spear tips. However, these metals are very rare and use must have been very limited, although some items evidently produced by working native copper and dated 9000-7000 BC have been found in Iran and Anatolia: pins, beads, awls. Also, lithic peoples were using metallic materials like red oxide of iron (haematite) in funerary and ritual practice, and in wall and pottery decoration as early as 4000 BC. Copper ores (green and blue) were in common use as cosmetics in the Middle East as early as 6000 BC. Native iron and copper are not only scarce, they are difficult to cold-work, and no evidence of hot-working in this period has been found. It is widely accepted that the experience gained from the use of metallic materials was largely responsible for the eventual emergence of metallurgy. For example, while red iron ores are stable, copper ores oxidize and turn black on heating in air. The early people must have learnt the value of creating reducing conditions in closed kilns in order to retain the beautiful colors of copper ores. It is possible that metallic lead and copper were produced by accident in the process of making glazes under such conditions. In spite of the long history of use of metals, the practice was rare and archaeometallurgists regard the emergence of melting native copper

16   Early metallurgy in Nigeria

and smelting copper ores when use of metals became common as the beginning of metals history.

2.2.1   Ancient Middle East: cradle of metallurgy

The pre-history of the Middle East is hazy but it is believed that the earliest migrants from Africa may have settled there, attracted by the fertile land, abundance of water around the Red and Mediterranean seas (particularly around many rivers like the Tigris, the Euphrates and the Nile), and an ideal climate for the introduction of agriculture. Throughout the history of migration, only the most enterprising and daring embarked on the very risky task of exploring unknown territories. Also, necessity is often a major driving force that motivates such people to be inventive and innovative. This may explain why the ancient Middle East hosted the world's earliest civilizations believed to have flourished from around 3500 BC, starting from Mesopotamia (modern Iraq) occupied by the Sumerians and spreading to Anatolia, Babylon, Phoenicia and Assyria (Figure 2.1).

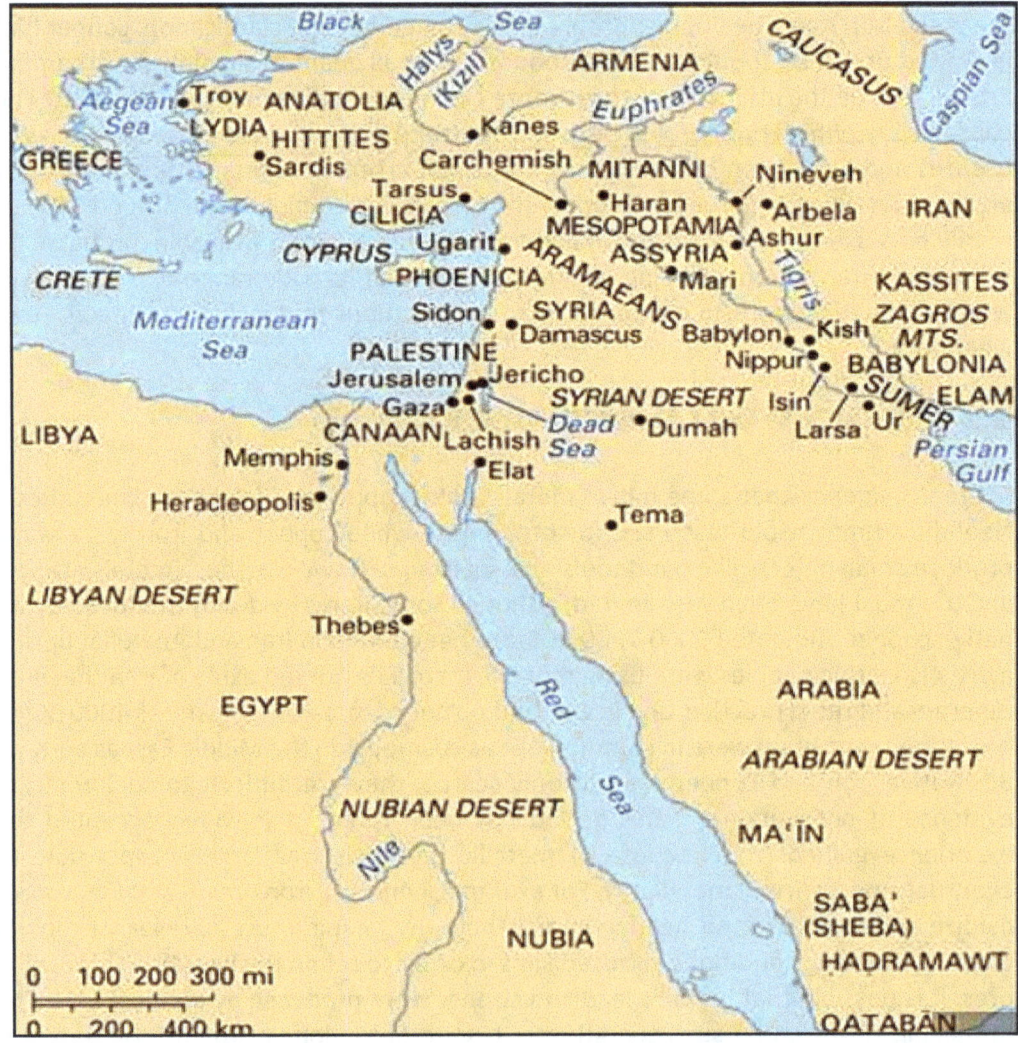

Figure 2.1   Ancient Middle East   *(Encyclopeaedia Britanica)*

Most of the earliest developments in metallurgy (and indeed many other technologies: paper, writing, irrigation, socially stratified society, literate culture, city states, weaponry) are believed to have emanated from the region: gold, iron, copper, bronze technologies, lost-wax casting technology, heat treatment metallurgy, trading in metals. It is interesting to note that two of the major religions of the world (Christianity and Islam) also have their roots in the ancient Middle East. Although there is evidence of significant trading between the different cultures in the region, it was mostly along the rivers and oceans and was largely confined to the region for thousands of years, until other cultures who were ardent traders migrated into the region, notably the Phoenicians, a group of independent city-states that flourished along the coast of the Mediterranean from about 3200 BC. The Phoenicians were prolific traders using horses by land and boats and ships on the oceans and rivers. They were highly skilled in commercial and maritime trading, ship-building and the manufacture of a wide range of goods including artifacts, exquisite glass products, dyes, luxury products, etc. which they traded across the ancient Middle East, and, eventually to Europe, Asia and Africa. They established harbours, trading posts and settlements throughout the Mediterranean basin. They are believed to have pioneered the inter-regional spread of ancient metallurgical skills and products.

2.2.2 Archaeological evidence of Metal Age

Archaeologists and archaeometallurgists look for several indicators that help identify the extent of metallurgical practice in a location or region: preponderance of crucibles, furnaces and accessories, slags, unburnt charcoal, and other remnants of smelting processes, sources and types of ores, as well as significant volume of tools, implements, artifacts, construction components made from the metal. Crucibles and furnaces give valuable information about the smelting technology adopted, temperatures which could have been achieved, blowing and slagging systems adopted, types of furnace construction materials and lining used, the melting atmospheres used (oxidizing or reducing). Ceramics and clays can be dated fairly accurately by thermoluminescence techniques especially when not vitrified, while unburnt charcoal is extremely useful in radiocarbon dating techniques. From the analysis of slags, it is possible to distinguish between melting and smelting processes, the probable smelting technology and slagging techniques, ore and slag composition, operating temperatures, etc. The phases identified in a slag found at an ironmaking site not only reflect the chemical composition of the slag but can also provide crucial information regarding the reconstruction and interpretation of the metallurgical operations, such as the prevailing redox conditions in a furnace at the time of cooling. Free iron oxides, such as hematite, magnetite and wüstite, are important indicators of these redox conditions. The bloomery process adopted in producing wrought iron produces bloomery slag as well as cinder which is produced at a particular temperature during furnace operation as a result of reaction between molten smelting products and the furnace lining. Cinder is infusible or partially fusible and, although it is similar to slag in chemical composition, it differs significantly in chemical appearance. In effect, slag evaluation can distinguish between melting, smelting, bloomery slags and cinders. Useful information can also be obtained from evaluation of products to determine chemical composition. Microstructural analysis gives information about the forming and working processes, the amount of hot work and/or cold work, intermediate or finishing heat treatment, etc. The main problem is that it is not always possible to take representative sample without destroying the object and surface chemical analysis can be erroneous because of segregation which was a very common feature of ancient castings. In effect, published chemical composition can only be taken as very approximate since there can be substantial segregation within an object in terms of composition and structure

2.2.3 The Prehistoric Stone (Paleolithic) Age [12000-4000 BC]

The earliest humans of the Old Stone Age were few and scattered, and development of small settlements and communities dates back only about 10 to 12,000 years. They were migrant hunters and fishers, they utilized whatever materials were available in their environment to survive and, through skill, established supremacy over the numerous, much stronger and faster wild animals. They found, collected and shaped stones and wood for hunting, plucking fruits, and providing shelter huts and caves. Later, they graduated into using hammer-stone to work flint, stone and wood to produce cutting edge, spear tips, stone axe, and other desired shapes; they learnt to start fire and burn coal and wood. The dominance of stone in their daily lives explains why this period is often referred to as the Stone Age. Other materials, wood in particular, were also very prominent but since they were perishable, they did not get handed down through generations as stone implements and artifacts were. Archaeologists are still discovering stone artifacts and tools dating many thousand years, possibly several million years BC. Palaeoanthropologists have found human fossils, stone implements and artifacts in Africa dating back to around 2-3 million years. These collections serve as a major means to determine human existence, activities and existing technologies in the Period. Progressive improvement and sophistication in choice of stone and shaping methods are evident in the excavated stone tools and implements, and are often used to sub-classify the Stone Age. Initial technologies involved striking a stone with another until a sharp edge was achieved at one end which was probably used for cutting while the blunt end was used for crushing and smashing (see Figure 2.2).

Figure 2.2 Paleolithic stone tools *(shortstreet.net)*.

Many of these tools also known as choppers have been found in different parts of Africa. Flint was the initial favourite stone for making choppers but tools made from quartz, quartzite and other rocks have also been found.

2.2.4 The Neolithic (New Stone Age) [4000-2000 BC]

Phasing out of stone tools and implements persisted until around 4000-2000 BC depending on local availability of metal substitutes. Before 4000 BC, people were nomads and hunters but transited gradually into farming communities. Domestic livestock flourished, hunting and fishing became more organized and such crafts as pottery and weaving became widespread. A wider range of stone tools was developed and harder stones were shaped by grinding and polishing rather than chipping softer stones as was the practice in the Old Stone Age (see Figure 2.3).

Figure 2.3 Neolithic stone age tools *(wikipedia.org)*.

The Stone Age is believed to have ended in most early regions of the world between 12000 BC and 2000 BC when metals and metalworking became widespread. The stone age civilization was not restricted to the use of stones alone but also practiced some of the rudiments of metallurgy. Iron oxide, also called red oxide was probably the first mineral in common use in the Neolithic period. It was used widely for wall decorations and in ritual and funerary practice. There is ample evidence that the mineral was being used to burnish pottery in Eridu and Susa as early as 4000 BC (Tylecote, 1992); green and blue copper minerals were in wide use as cosmetics in Egypt and Mesopotamia; in Crete; azurite, commonly called azura (a blue-green basic carbonate of copper) was in use by about 6000 BC. Although there is evidence that glazes were being used on pottery in Egypt as early as 5000 BC, copper minerals were apparently not ingredients until around 1600 BC (Tylecote, 1992). The delay in the use was due probably to the fact that, unlike the red iron oxides, copper-base minerals turn black and unattractive when heated under oxidizing conditions. The eventual use in glazing implies that the potters managed to solve this problem by creating reducing conditions in the glazing oven.

2.2.5   The Copper Age [5000-2000 BC]

No evidence of wide use of any metal earlier than around 7000 BC has been found but it is widely believed that metals, in particular, gold, copper and iron all of which occur naturally, have been in use much earlier. Copper was probably the first metal to be used by man and modern metallurgical analyses of many of the artifacts have shown that smelted copper was long in existence before bronzes became common, although there was an overlap between the two metals in most areas. The origin of the use of copper metallurgy is unknown but it is believed that it may have originated from Anatolia (part of modern Turkey) or Iran where it was in use as early as the 9th to 7th millennium BC, spreading slowly to China and Europe through the south-east by the beginning of the 2nd millennium. (Smith, 1965, Mellink, 1965). Substantial evidence supports the thesis that the Neolithic people were working native copper. The discovery of copper artifacts dated between 7000 and 6000 BC in Catal Huyuk, a very large Neolithic and Chalcolithic proto-city settlement in southern Anatolia, is perhaps the oldest clear evidence of copper use anywhere in the world. There is considerable debate on how the objects were made. Apparently, native copper was cold-forged and, although the material work-hardens rapidly (and in any case much of native copper is already work-hardened), it is possible to reduce small pieces by up to 96% by cold forging, provided hammering is continuous and incipient cracks are immediately removed. In spite of the long history of copper, use was severely restricted because of difficulties in forging native copper. Native copper can be extremely heterogeneous, associated with arsenic, nickel, silver, lead, antimony, iron, and several other elements. Comprehensive investigation of early copper objects showed no evidence of any heat treatment or hot working, but practice cannot be ruled out.

It has been suggested also that some of the artifacts may have been made from melted native copper or in fact smelted from ore. For example, it was clear that the beads found in Catal Huyuk were produced from vitrified copper but analysis of the associated slaggy material could not determine whether it was a crucible melting or ore smelting process. Crucible slags result from the reaction between the alkali in the fuel ash and silicates from the fabric of the crucible, typified by large amounts of entrapped copper. Smelting slags are usually predominantly ferrous silicates with only small amounts of copper. It is possible that small particles of original pure copper are left behind in the crucible and may become oxidized as a result of weathering. No major chemical and morphological analyses of the Catal Huyuk slags have been carried out but available chemical analysis indicates the absence of ferrous silicate which in turn indicates that it may be neither a crucible melting nor ore smelting slag. It is possible that the beads were produced from hammered native copper. However, another discovery of a large number of crucibles in Anatolia and Iran, dated to the same period and analysis of slags found on site are evidences that the people were also smelting copper ores to produce almost pure copper (Caldwell, 1967; Melleart, 1967). As discussed earlier, slag chemistry is a reliable distinguishing feature between melted native copper and copper smelted from oxide ores. Analysis of slags found on site confirmed the presence of substantial traces of arsenic or nickel in some of the early copper objects which strongly indicates that they were made from copper ore by smelting (not by melting native copper). The transition from use of flint in the Stone Age to native copper, melted native copper and copper smelted from ore for knives, sickles, arrow tips, etc. was gradual and the use of both materials co-existed for a very long time, leading archaeologists to classify this period as Chalcolithic Period (Chalcos is the Greek word for copper and lithos means stone).

It is unclear how copper ore smelting was discovered, by who or when but it may have been by accident. Production of lead glazes under reducing conditions was already well-established in places like Egypt by 5000 BC and the fact that they were able to create reducing conditions for lead smelting by using enclosed kilns suggests that they may have been able to melt heavily oxidized native copper ores in similar kilns if they used enough charcoal to achieve a higher temperature. Trial of the same process with copper ore would have been unsuccessful but probably inspired the emergence of crucibles which could provide a sufficiently reducing atmosphere for copper ore smelting. A laboratory experiment has shown that copper can be obtained from pure oxide minerals in a crucible by direct reduction with excess charcoal (Tylecote, 1974; 1982). Many native copper pieces are heavily oxidized and if they were melted mixed with charcoal in closed kilns, it is possible that the atmosphere could have been sufficiently reducing to produce more copper than expected, which would probably have prompted processing of copper oxide ores which are more common than sulphide types in a similar manner. All that would have been needed was to increase the fuel:ore ratio and use several blowers to achieve the required temperature of around 1100°C.

The quick exhaustion of native copper deposits probably promoted the development of complex extraction technology of the metal from its ores. It was quickly learnt that, in order to free copper from its native partners, it must be substituted with another partner and carbon plays this role pretty well in many cases. It was also realized that heat was needed to effect this substitution and this was provided by burning charcoal. It is not clear how this technology developed but there are speculations that it was probably accidental. Malachite (green copper carbonate ore) was widespread in the Middle East and was being used as a cosmetic for painting the eyelids as early as the fifth millennium BC. Copper carbonate is an easily reducible ore of copper and a drop of the ore on hot burning wood fire produces a bead of copper. This could easily have happened and initiated the extraction of copper and other metals from ores. The smelting of copper ore in the early times was probably carried out by burning ore-wood piles in several stages to obtain copper of about 95% purity. The metal was then heated with charcoal in kilns supplied with a blast of air for further purification (Derry and Williams, 1960). Extracted copper was either hammered into desired shapes or re-melted and cast into pre-shaped sand moulds. Lead was often added to improve fluidity and castability. Also, evidence has been found showing that the early smelters processed sulphide ores which would have required preliminary roasting to convert to oxide before smelting. However, there has been a lot of speculation on the ability of the early people to carry out this tedious and dangerous two-stage process (many sulphide ores contain arsenic which produces toxic fumes during roasting). However, new evidence has emerged that they probably cosmelted mixed copper oxide and sulphide ores in a single stage. Laboratory tests have shown that this is in fact possible (Lechtman and Klein 1999). (See also Appendix III).

The copper artifacts found in Tepe Yahya in Iran, dated 3800 BC were indisputably products of copper ore smelting and many other sites mostly in the near East - Egypt, Israel, Iran, Syria, Palestine Mesopotamia - dated between 2800 and 4000 BC have been found (Tylecote, 1972). The objects were mainly small items - pins, small tools, chisel, spatula, saw, axe, spear head, vessel. They were mostly made of pure or arsenal copper and associated slags contained ferrous silicates, confirming that they were by-products of copper ore smelting processes. There have been speculations as to whether these artifacts were made locally or imported in view of the of the fact that Near East was very active in trade. However, furnaces, crucibles, moulds, slags have been found in some of the excavated sites indicating that the objects were locally produced.

In archaeometallurgy, the Age of a metal is considered to have begun when evidence of smelting from ore was found. It is safe to assume therefore that the Copper Age had in fact begun by 6000 BC. However, while it was probable that the technology spread quickly within the region, it was confined within the region for around 4,000 years until the technology is believed to have been spread by diffusion from the Near East to Europe through Greece, and also to Russia, China, and India, all areas of active production of copper artifacts by around 3000 to 2000 BC. The proliferation beyond the Middle East is believed to have been propelled by the emergence of inter-regional trade routes from around 3000 BC, in particular the Silk Route which had become well-established around 2000 BC. The practice reached Africa possibly through Egypt or through the Trans-Saharan Trade Route. The Copper Age evolved very slowly and must have overlapped with the Neolithic period and even the Iron Age in many places, possibly until around 200 BC in some places.

The conclusion that may be drawn from these findings is that the period that is often classified as Early Bronze Age was in fact Copper Age, it extended to around 2000 BC when the use of bronze became common, and, in some areas, there was an overlap between the two metals, with copper still being used widely around 1500 BC. Many of the objects were made of almost pure copper while others had substantial amounts of arsenic or antimony. While copper products may have been made from melted native copper and smelted oxide ore for the previous 3000-4000 years they must have been in very small quantities in a few locations. This very long period of transition between the Neolithic Age and true Copper Age is often referred to as Chalcolithic or Eneolithic Age. The true Copper Age is believed to have begun when the technology for smelting copper from ore became widespread across regions and well-crafted objects were being produced in large quantities, around 3500-3000 BC. Numerous objects that were products of melted native copper and copper smelted from ore, dated to the same period have also been found in Mesopotamia. Examination of the worked objects showed clear evidence that they were made from solid native copper by hammering and some of the larger objects like axes and hammers were cast in native copper. Clearly, the producers had mastered the art of annealing between workings. Without this knowledge, it would not have been possible to produce the objects which include spears whose sections showed different degrees of cold work and annealing and others which were in fully annealed condition. In some, the tips were lightly cold-worked after annealing to improve strength. The crystal structures of some of the objects also show that annealing must have been carried out at temperatures as high as 800°C. Many other copper objects dated between 4000-3500 BC have also been found in Iran and Egypt, most of them probably produced by melting and casting native copper in small crucibles. The first discovery of large quantities of well-crafted copper objects found in the Lake Superior region of North America were dated between 3000 BC and 1400 BC (Muhly, 1984; Rothenberg, 1966).

Another interesting aspect of copper objects dated to the Copper Age is the presence of arsenic in significant amounts. It is not clear whether smelted copper ores were deliberately mixed with arsenic ores such as arsenic sulphide at the melting stage , or copper ores rich in arsenic were selected purposefully. Neither option was likely unless the smelters were already aware of the positive benefit of arsenic on castability of copper (it acts as a mild deoxidant and lowers the melting point of copper, thereby improving fluidity but its presence can also cause problems in casting) or were able to take advantage of its effect on workhardenability to make strong objects like spear and arrow tips from copper, especially as they were also already familiar with the moderating effect of intermediate heat treatment. (Copper containing 8% arsenic worked to 50% reduction in thickness is twice as hard as pure copper worked to the same level). It is probable therefore that people of the period preferred to stick with the well established copper working technology. The well-known segregation of typical copper ore deposits could also account for the widespread use of arsenal copper, even when the Bronze Age had already taken off. The chemical composition of sulphide copper deposits tends to change with depth: the upper layers are usually oxidized and low in copper content because of the presence of many other minerals like iron oxides and some precious metals. Because of the relative solubility of copper, lower layers would have higher copper content, along with arsenical and antimoniacal minerals which are also relatively soluble. In effect, the presence of arsenic and antimony in many copper objects may have been incidental and a consequence of the exhaustion of the upper oxidized layers or the desire to use richer copper ores in smelting.

2.2.6 The Bronze Age [4000-1500 BC]

Bronze is primarily an alloy of copper and tin, but may contain some zinc as well as several other elements. Several other bronzes containing antimony, arsenic, zinc and other metals are known to have been common in early times but it is not clear whether these elements were introduced deliberately or occurred as impurities from the ores. However, the presence of each element even in small quantities has a significant influence on the technological properties of bronze. For example, tin and arsenic confer on hammered copper objects considerable additional strength as a result of relatively rapid work-hardening. Perhaps an even more valuable effect of these elements is the improvement of castability as well as conferment on copper objects considerable additional strength in the cast state. This discovery probably opened the doors for the very wide range of low-alloy copper and bronze castings found in antiquity, in a very diverse range of structural applications. It is difficult to quote a precise period for the arrival of the Bronze Age characterized by widespread use of tin bronzes largely because of the major overlap with the Copper Age in many places, but also because its arrival in different places was not universally synchronous. For example, the Middle East and parts of Asia had arrived at the Bronze Age by 4000-3500 BC while some parts of Europe did not reach the Age until around 1800 BC. Furthermore, until archaeometallurgy emerged a couple of hundred years ago, archaeologists had no way of distinguishing between low-alloy coppers, brass and bronze and simply classified all as bronzes.

24   Early metallurgy in Nigeria

The discovery of bronze may have been purely accidental, probably through the smelting of copper ores contaminated with tin minerals, although tin ores are not often found in association with copper ores. The fact that the development appears to have nucleated in the Near East and proliferated to other areas of the world by diffusion is baffling, since tin ores have not been found in the area. The excellent artistry that had been acquired working with stone, wood and ivory in the earliest times was easily transferred to metalworking and some of the finest bronze artifacts ever found were being produced in ancient Mesopotamia and Egypt as early as 3000 BC (Figure 2.4). It is possible that, at least in the earlier times, some of the copper ore deposits in the Near East were contaminated with tin ore in a similar manner to copper ores found in Cornwall, U.K.

Figure 2.4   Bronze tools and artifacts from the Bronze Age
(historyrocket.com; bbc.co.uk).

There is evidence also that tin was being produced in Europe by the second millennium and exported to the Near East where it was used extensively for bronze production. Prior to these trade links, tin content of bronzes had fluctuated quite widely, usually below 4% (bronzes contain at least 7% of tin). During this period, arsenal copper was also in common use. The establishment of a reliable trade link with the sources of tin apparently made it possible to standardize the tin content of bronzes at 10%. It is not clear whether metallic tin was used in the alloying process but it is possible that pieces of tin and copper metal were heated together covered with charcoal in a crucible. The tin would melt (mp. 232°C), and diffuse into the copper, bringing its melting point down from 1083°C to 850°C with 10% tin content. See Appendix III). This practice would have been uncommon in view of the rarity of metallic tin. A more probable practice would have been to add the tin as oxide, heat the mixture covered with charcoal to create reducing conditions under which pure tin would be produced for further reaction with the copper to produce bronze.

Diffusion of bronze technology is believed to have flourished through trade until the Greeks and Romans in succession overthrew the ancient civilizations of the Near East and, although they destroyed much of the fine technical achievements of earlier ages, they acquired metalworking skills and, through trade, spread the Bronze Age across the eastern Mediterranean in all directions. The Greeks mastered metalworking techniques and produced bronze coins which they used extensively in their trading. The development of standard grade of bronze and precision casting techniques led to the gradual phasing out of arsenical copper and low-tin bronzes which required considerable forging and hammering to give them the final shape. Split-mould casting technology became common and castings were being produced which carried very fine detail and needed little if any finishing. Also, the effect of lead in increasing fluidity of bronze and improving casting quality appeared to have been widely exploited.

The Bronze Age is often considered synonymous with Bronze Metallurgy Age. However, In the early stages, bronze was not produced because of the non-availability of tin, the main alloying element. This has prompted the sub-division of the period to Early Bronze Age (EBA) in which pure and arsenical coppers were the primary metals in use, the Middle Bronze Age (MBA) which was a transitional period before the Full Bronze Age (FBA) when the use of copper had ceased and bronze technology had spread to many regions. While there was little change in bronze technology throughout the FBA, there were substantial increases in the scale of operations and ingots weighing more than 30 kg were being produced in China and India. Also, casting became the preferred production method for better finish and accuracy compared with forging and hammering which were dominant in the earlier Bronze Periods.

Another problem with the proper identification of the arrival of the Bronze Age arose from the fact that many archaeologists could not distinguish between copper and bronze, especially when the object is heavily weathered or contains arsenic or antimony which are common impurities in copper ores. Furthermore, any object that was not made of pure copper was classified as a bronze irrespective of the level of tin content. However, developments in metallurgical analysis in the 19th century have made it possible to re-classify and re-date earlier copper objects. True bronze is an alloy of copper and tin (minimum, 7-10% Sn) with properties that are superior to pure copper which has low work-hardenability. Furthermore, bronze has significantly higher strength in the as-cast state without the necessity for cold-working. While this was without doubt a major discovery, it is not clear when or where it happened, but access to tin ore which is relatively rare must have been a major factor. Unlike copper ores, tin ore deposits are relatively rare because deposits, mainly cassiterite (SnO_2) are associated with certain types of granite and deposits are a rarity. Even today, tin ores are found in less than ten locations in the world.

The regions that first developed bronze technologies either had access to local deposits of both ores or were able to import tin from neighbouring regions. However, some copper ores have been found to contain some tin, notably in Cornwall, South Wales, in the

United Kingdom which is also famous for tin deposits. There is evidence that the tin deposits have been worked extensively for many centuries, dating back to at least Roman times, and possibly as early as the Full Bronze Age (2100-1500 BC). Also, smelting tin-rich copper ores found in the same location could have yielded true bronzes. For example, some of the copper ores smelted in South Wales in the 19th century contained 12.3% copper and 0.94% tin. This translates to a ratio of copper:tin of 93:7 which falls within the range of standard bronzes. The possibility of occurrences of similar deposits elsewhere, especially in the Ancient Middle East cannot be ruled out.

The Full Bronze Age is believed to have emerged first in Sumeria around 3000 BC, following several millennia of working and melting native copper and smelting copper ores probably obtained from many deposits which have been found in the area. Some of the deposits may be similar to the tin-rich Cornwall deposit and are either yet to be discovered or evidence has been destroyed by earth movements. Also, the common assumption that tin deposits had not been found anywhere close to the region may not be correct. For example, tin deposits have been discovered in Afghanistan, Turkey and Egypt, all within easy reach of Anatolia (Muhly 1985). Also, in view of the Silk Route which was already emerging in the region from around 3000 BC, tin could have been imported from as far away as Malaysia, China or Nigeria. The emergence of the Full Bronze Age is believed to have been very gradual, possibly through experimentation over several thousand years, spread within and across regions by diffusion through trade. It is also possible that bronze technology emerged independently in several different locations, as is being speculated for Cornwall, England.

The benefits of adding tin to cast copper in order to improve strength and eliminate the need for cold-working may have been known for a long time prior to around 3000 BC when the practice became common. One major reason may have been the scarcity of tin, found in only a few locations in the world. It is possible that bronze was discovered by accident in the process of smelting copper ores containing some tin. Although this is very rare, a few deposits of mixed tin and copper ores like the Cornwall deposit discussed above have been found and may have been the sources of early bronzes. However, the true Bronze Age only arrived when sources of tin were found and smelters were able to consistently produce bronzes containing optimum tin (7-10%) and the practice became widespread. While the superior properties of bronze compared with copper, particularly in terms of workability had been known apparently for a long time, the scarcity of tin ores probably precluded the proliferation of the technology, possibly until inter-region trade began to flourish and tin ores could be imported. It became possible to import bronze ingots and re-melt to make castings of artifacts and tools or heat and shape into implements. This theory is strengthened by a shipwreck found off the coast of Southern Turkey dated 1200 BC which carried tin, bronze and copper ingots and scrap metal. The ship was believed to have been traveling from Cyprus to Crete or Greece. It was clear that the materials were not from anywhere in the area and must have been part of wide-spread inter-regional trade. The oldest full bronze objects have been found mostly in the Middle East (Iran, Iraq, Turkey, Egypt dating back to 3900-1800 BC, but some have also been found in England dated 1800-1700 BC.

The increasing scarcity of tin and the emergence of iron technology largely determined the end of the Bronze Age around 1800-1000 BC. The Bronze Age was marked by major advances in technology in several regions of the early world, including highly refined complex casting and shaping techniques (Figure 2.5).

Figure 2.5 An elaborate set of Chinese ritual bronze castings consisting of an altar table and thirteen wine vessels, products of complex casting, with intricate design and surface decorations *(metropolitan museum; metmuseum.org).*

Communities and farming settlements developed, animals were domesticated, ox-drawn ploughs were invented, textile and pottery industries flourished weaponry - swords, daggers, arrowheads body armour etc. were invented. Also, one of the most important technologies: writing developed during the period in Egypt, Sumeria, China, Mesopotamia. However, even after the use of true bronze became widespread, tin contents were hardly more than 4% and arsenal coppers were still used extensively, due possibly to uncertainties and interruptions in tin supply. The quick spread of the bronze technology to Asia was probably through trade. It is not surprising that bronze culture arrived in Europe as early as 2000 BC since the continent has a few tin deposits, notably the Cornwall deposit in England. Egypt was also producing bronzes around the same time. However, it is possible that any of these developments may have been local inventions since there were local or within-reach tin-rich copper ore deposits which may have been worked in early times.

2.2.7 Bronze-Iron Age Transition (Early Iron Age) [2000-1000 BC]

The Bronze Age (Early, Middle, Late) dominated the world's materials scene for thousands of years before the Iron Age started to phase in, gradually in some places, fast in others. Bronze was reserved initially for precious products, probably because of the scarcity of tin but the emergence of iron which is stronger and cheaper would have been a significant force in the demise of the Bronze Age especially in areas which had no ready access to tin but had local deposits of iron ores. Various theories have been propounded to explain the rise of the iron age. One school of thought believes that the Hittites of Anatolia had mastered iron technology to the extent that they produced a wide range of weapons which gave them military superiority over their neighbours. They kept this knowledge much to themselves until the empire was broken up by wars towards the end of the Bronze Age after which the technology started to spread throughout the East Mediterranean as a result of their migrations. Another theory gives the collapse of the Hittite empire and the consequent disruption of the traditional routes of tin supply as the main reason for shortage of bronze, a development which gave impetus to the exploitation of the more abundant iron ores. Neither theory is supported by any reliable archaeological or historical evidence. The most probable reason is the poor quality of weapons and tools made from bronze and the consequent constant search for stronger materials. As discussed earlier, meteoric and native (telluric) iron had been worked into tools and implements from pre-historic times and native iron is sometimes found in sulphide ore deposits hence, it was only a mater of time that the early people would have tried to smelt iron ores, particularly the sulphide types which were common and relatively easy to reduce with charcoal. They probably already had substantial experience in smelting copper ores. However, translating from copper smelting to iron smelting would have required a more sophisticated furnace technology capable of temperatures sufficiently high (an additional 50-100°C) to release the carbon monoxide needed to reduce iron ore in the solid state and produce wrought iron. This could have been achieved either by increasing fuel:ore ratio and/or developing more powerful blowing systems. Once the technology was perfected and production of wrought iron (and ultimately cast iron) on a substantial scale became more widespread, it was inevitable that the Iron Age would have grown very rapidly, considering that most of the early societies were involved in one war or another and weapons were vital possessions.

The production of non-ferrous metals continued throughout the early Iron Age, the only major milestone being the appearance of brass, an alloy of copper and zinc, in proportions which determine the mechanical and electrical properties of the alloy. Other elements notably arsenic, lead, phosphorus, manganese, aluminium, silicon may be present in minor quantities depending on the chemistry of the copper ore deposit but most of the elements are also added to obtain specific properties. The presence of zinc (up to 45%) improves malleability of copper significantly and brass can be cold-worked extensively unlike copper or bronze. The presence of zinc greatly improves corrosion resistance and lowers the melting temperature of copper by around 150 decrees centigrade, making the alloy much more fluid and castable (Appendix III). Furthermore, brass has a very attractive, distinctively golden colour when polished, making it very attractive for the production of a wide range of products: coins, musical instruments, bells, door knobs, ammunitions, pipe fittings. The earliest low-zinc copper objects dated around 3000 BC have been found in the East Mediterranean: on sites in Iran, Iraq and several other locations and the technology is believed to have spread to Western Asia, notably India, Uzbekistan around 2000 BC. Most of the objects contained 5-15 % zinc, which suggests that they were produced from zinc-rich copper ores which are fairly common, probably by redox processing using charcoal. It is also possible that copper and zinc ores were deliberately mixed to obtain the higher zinc concentrations of 12-15% which is required to confer the golden colour. However, true brass containing at least 15% zinc was first produced only at the close of the first century BC.

Copper produced in the early Bronze Age often contained small quantities of arsenic and zinc. This was probably incidental because both elements are often present in copper ores. The typical zinc content in copper ores is usually no more than a few percent, too low to produce brass. Brass first appeared in Egypt around 30 BC and quickly spread throughout the Roman world. It was made by the calamine process, in which additions of zinc carbonate or oxide were made to copper and melted under reducing conditions by covering the ore with a layer of charcoal, and alloys produced contained 25-30% zinc. Silver was also produced by the Greeks around 600-25 BC by smelting lead-silver ores by the cupellation process, and used extensively for coinage which had become widespread in Europe and the Near East by the seventh century BC. Lead was produced and used to clad ship bottoms, for ship anchors, water pipes, etc. Copper and tin were also being produced in large quantities, based on ingot found in a ship wreck off the French coast dated to around 600 BC. Some of the copper and tin ingots weighed up to 100 kg and 25 kg respectively. Neither the source of the tin nor its destination has been positively identified but it was clear that inter-regional metal and ore trading had been well-established at this time.

Coins, made of non-ferrous metal emerged from Greece around 600 BC and quickly spread to most parts of the Middle East and Europe. Initially, silver was the primary metal for coinage but the first gold coins appeared in Macedonia around 350 BC. Apart from the fact that gold was expensive, it was too soft, hence alloying elements, mainly copper were added to improve hardness and wear resistance, and typical coins contained between 10 and 40% copper although gold coins containing up to 40% silver were also in common use. Low value coins were made from brass and bronze and use was widespread in Europe and Asia. Stamping was the primary process used for making coins but some, especially brass and bronze coins were also produced by casting. Development of non-ferrous metallurgy continued throughout the Iron Age, particularly in Roman times from around 29 BC when copper and silver were being produced and traded extensively.

2.2.8 The Iron Age [1200-500 BC]

As discussed earlier, meteoric and native iron had been worked into tools and implements by cold hammering in the Neolithic period but wrought iron emerged around 2000 BC, believed to have been an accidental discovery in the process of copper and bronze smelting from a mixture of copper ores and iron ore fluxes. It is possible that temperatures were high enough for some of the iron ore to be reduced by carbon to produce almost pure iron which settled mixed with slag at the bottom of the furnace. Some may have contained enough ductile iron to be picked out hammered. It was not possible to achieve high enough temperatures to produce molten iron but smelters were able to produce iron by reducing ore with charcoal in the solid state, and this practice did not become widespread until around 1200-1000 BC, the real beginning of the Iron Age. Again, the Iron Age arrived at different times in different regions but, for most, it had ended by around 600 BC. The origin of systematic production of iron is unknown but there is evidence that the technology had been established in Asia Minor by the Hittites in Anatolia-Iran axis by around 2000 BC. One of the earliest man-made iron daggers has been found at Alaca Huyuk. Clearly use was restricted initially to small items, due apparently to the scarcity of the metal. However, by around 1200 to 1000 BC, iron weapons and implements had become quite common. In the next five hundred years or so the technology spread rapidly across parts of Europe, Asia, North and West Africa. The Philistines had iron weapons in the 11th century BC and iron culture is believed to have spread to Egypt through Greece or Mesopotamia by the 9th century BC. The Phoenicians are believed to have spread it to Western Mediterranean and Carthage from where it probably spread to Nigeria around 800 BC, from where it probably spread to the rest of Africa.

Iron smelting technology may have been another accidental discovery, possibly in the process of using iron oxide fluxes in smelting copper ores. Hot and cold forging of meteoric/native iron in the solid state was common in the Early Iron period, a process which persisted for nearly 3,000 years due primarily to the inability to achieve a high temperature necessary to melt pure iron (1538°C), a feat achieved only in the latter part of the 19th century AD. However, It is possible that temperatures in the copper smelting furnaces were high enough to cause reduction of some iron ore by charcoal. The slag at the bottom of the furnace may have contained substantial iron mixed with slag and, if worked would have produced wrought iron. This could have happened in any location where copper ore was being smelted, and explains why there is some disagreement about the origin of the technology. Another complication is the use of meteoric iron from the early times, especially when they were being melted and cast into products. Until the analytical metallurgical techniques matured, it was difficult to distinguish between copper objects made from melted native copper and those from ore-smelted copper. It is probable that iron technology first flourished in Asia Minor around 2000 BC or even earlier, based on dating of iron daggers found in the area, but there is no evidence that iron was being used on a large scale until 1200-1000 BC. Even with this development, bronze was still the preferred metal for many applications, mainly because *wrought iron* which was being produced at this time was considered too soft for some applications. However, it did not take very long to find solutions to this problem, for example by producing bronze-hilted, iron-tipped swords combining bronze and iron. Also, the practice of strengthening wrought iron objects by heating in a charcoal bed to improve strength (carburization) soon became common.

Wrought iron was produced in the solid state by chemical reduction of iron ore to solid, almost pure iron at about 1150°C by heating a mixture of iron ore, charcoal and flux (crushed seashells or limestone) in a pit furnace also known as *bloomery* which had air bellows used to force air through the ore/fuel/flux pile. If fuel:ore ratio was high and powerful bellows were deployed, the furnace temperature may have been high enough to produce carbon monoxide which reduced the iron oxides to metallic iron in the solid state but too low to melt the iron. Some of the slag formed from silicates in the iron ore would drip out but much of it would be trapped in the pasty mass of low carbon iron. The product of the bloomery was a porous mass of slag-coated fused granules of refined iron, known as *sponge iron*. It was removed from the bloomery, reheated and worked (wrought) with a hammer into coherent bars known as blooms. The hammering (shingling) process expelled excess slag and also shaped the remaining slag into thin fibers finely disseminated in the iron matrix. Reheating and shingling may have been repeated several times to achieve the desired shape and quality. The bloom was reheated to soften the iron and melt the slag, and then repeatedly hammered to break it up into pieces and force out the slag so that the relatively ductile pieces of iron could be separated. The pieces were reheated and welded together into bigger lumps by hammering in the hot state. The process was laborious and time consuming but it produced fairly soft wrought iron, a malleable but soft iron which contained some carbon. Although, throughout the Iron Age it was not possible to achieve the high temperature required to produce molten iron, wrought iron became a very versatile metal used for a very wide range of applications. Iron ore is the world's fourth most abundant element and makes up more than 5% of the Earth's crust, hence it is widely available, making it possible for wrought iron technology to spread quickly to most regions of the world. Local inventions can also not be rule out. The combination of low carbon and fibers of silicon oxide conferred exceptional properties on wrought iron, in particular, high strength, malleability, corrosion resistance and high fatigue strength. The material was used for a very wide range of products and structures throughout the Iron Age, the Roman times right to the end of the nineteenth century when mild and structural steel became readily available (Figure 2.6). Incidentally, this material is still being produced today in much the same way for many applications, including fences, gates, railings, statutes and many complex products. Wrought iron began to replace bronze around 3000 to 2000 BC. The technology is believed to have started in Asia Minor but it spread quickly to China and India and became the choice material for a wide range of products including tools, implements, rails, weapons, etc. Even when the Iron Age ended, the use of wrought iron remained widespread up to the 1800s and was used for buildings and railroads.

One major problem with wrought iron is that the production is a batch process and the quality of the product very much depends on the skill of the producer. Furthermore, it is too soft for some applications, in particular, railroads. Iron smelting technology spread to many parts of the world from about 1000 BC, reaching Europe, Asia and North Africa over the next five hundred years or so. Even though the popular view is that the technology diffused through trade, the possibility of local invention was real, and there were clearly many significant local innovations. For example, there is no substantial evidence that China produced wrought iron on any significant scale, instead, more powerful, water-driven blowers were developed which made it possible to achieve higher furnace temperatures necessary for producing molten, high-carbon iron (cast iron containing carbon of around 4.5% melts at about 1150°C). This is the first evidence of molten iron production, and the forerunner of the modern iron blast furnace.

Cast iron products were in common use in Asia by about 1000-500 BC but use was restricted to cast products because of the brittleness due to the very high carbon content. Iron working and smelting may have begun in India as early as 1800 BC based on the dating of some recent excavations and had become fairly widespread by the 13th century BC. It may have reached China around the same time but there is no credible evidence that India produced cast iron before China. India also introduced important innovations by producing steel around 300-200 BC either by heating (carburizing) sponge/wrought iron mixed with charcoal and glass to increase carbon content to optimum levels and improve strength (cementation) or by de-carburizing high-carbon cast iron to reduce brittleness (fining). The product called wootz steel was widely exported and traded throughout ancient Europe, China and the ancient Middle East. Daggers produced from the steel (Damascus daggers) were exported to many parts of the world including Europe for hundreds of years.

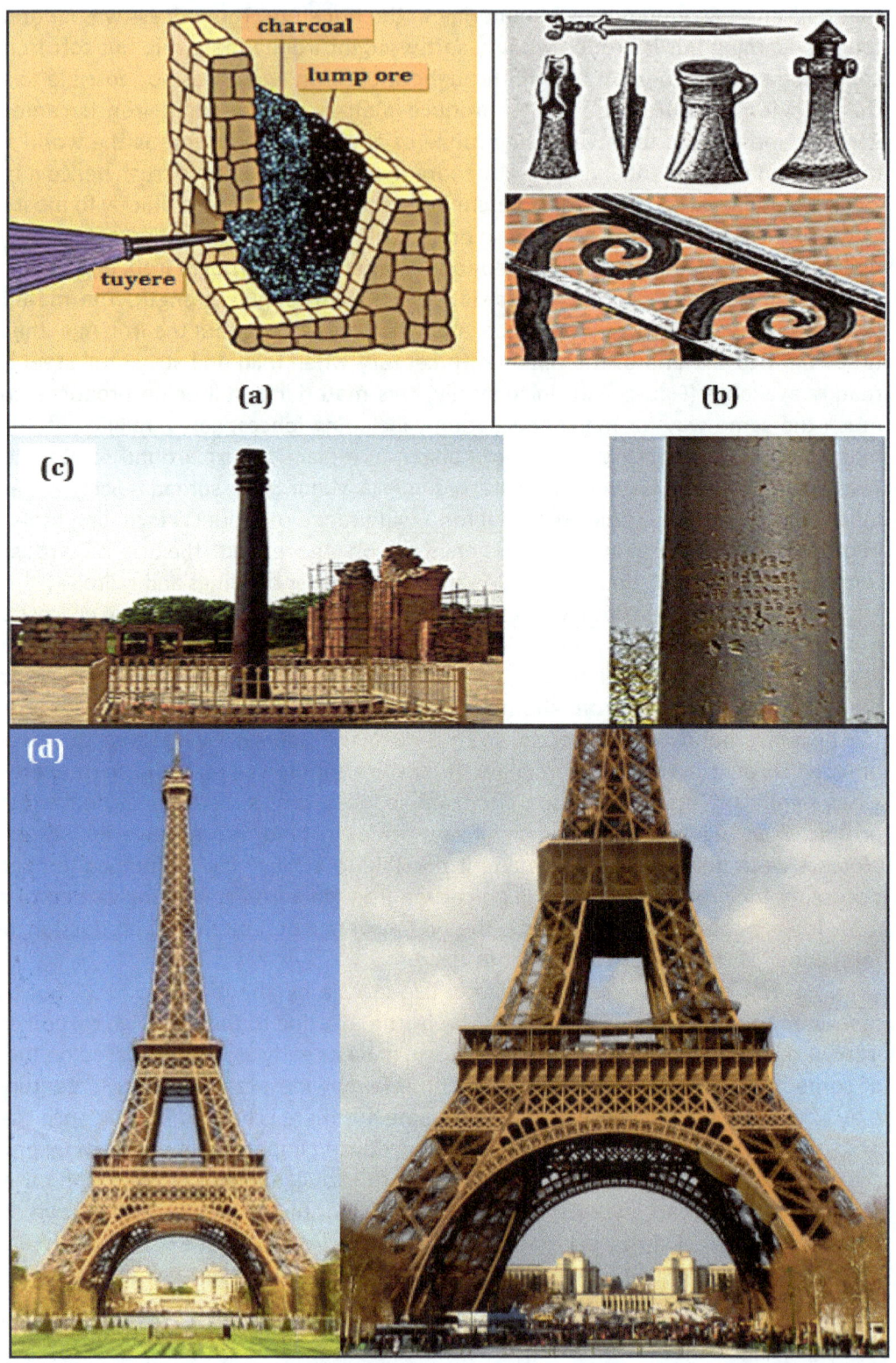

Figure 2.6 (a) A bloomery (b) Wrought iron products (c) The Iron Pillar of Delhi, built from wrought iron around 300 AD, weighs more than 6 metric tons (d) The Eiffel Tower, Paris, built in 1889 from 7,300 metric tons of puddled wrought iron, and 3000 metric tons of non-metal.

2.2.9 Medieval Period

Historians often classify the end of the Roman Empire in 476 AD to the beginning of the Renaissance in the 14th century as the "Middle Ages" or "Medieval (Migration) period." The fall of ancient Rome is believed to have marked the beginning of the end of the Iron Age, although it ended at different times in different countries and regions, for example, around 43 AD in Britain. Events in the period, particularly the first part, largely shaped the evolution of metallurgy for the next one thousand years or so. The ancient Roman Republic was founded in 509 BC and, until its collapse in 29 AD, the Republic had established itself as a major power of the ancient world, and was involved in wars which extended its territory to much of Europe, Asia Minor and North Africa. The 1st century BC was a period of unrest and civil wars which eventually led to the fall of the Republic and establishment of the Roman Empire in 27 BC. The first Emperor, Augustus Caesar embarked on massive development projects including extensive construction projects and rebuilding the army. The booming economy and arming of the military pushed up demand for all metals, in particular, iron and, although his reign was short (he died in 14 AD), his influence on the empire's economy, prosperity, political, and cultural life was profound, sustaining peace for the first two hundred years or so. Many of the new territories already had long experience in non-ferrous and iron metallurgy (be it on small scale), notably Asia Minor which is credited with the invention of copper and iron smelting technologies. Copper technology had flourished by 3500 BC and one of the earliest iron daggers dated to 2000 BC was found in the area. By 1000 BC, bronze-hilted iron blade daggers were being produced on a large scale. It is not surprising therefore that Rome quickly acquired non-ferrous and iron technologies from its new territories. The booming Roman economy fueled the demand for metals and advanced iron technologies quickly spread to many parts of the Middle East, Europe, Asia and North Africa.

Perhaps the most important contribution of the Romans (from 29 BC) to the Iron Age was the scale-up and proliferation of iron technologies available in the empire to Europe and other regions through trade. While pre-Roman and non-Roman Iron Age world used induced-draft shaft furnaces and small bowl furnaces, the Romans had developed large, bellows-blown and bowl-type furnaces and set up large-scale iron and non-ferrous production facilities to meet the increasing military and civil needs of the empire. Large amounts of copper-based alloys were used in coinage and lead was used extensively in plumbing. The widespread trade within the Roman empire fueled the demand for coins and many mints were established. Brass (copper containing 20-25% zinc) appeared to have been reserved for coins while copper-zinc-tin alloys (gun metals) were used in castings, apparently because they are better casting alloys. The demand for iron was particularly high because of its extensive use in construction and military Hardware. An extensive range of weaponry was developed and traded with neighbours in exchange for ores which the empire lacked, and ores were imported from as far as North Africa. One of the major reasons for the decline and eventual collapse of the empire was the development of strong ethnic, tribal, religious and regional groupings within and around the empire, and the emergence of conflicts, fueled by the proliferation of arms facilitated by the Romans. Production facilities were disrupted and development declined. In effect, the Romans were largely responsible for the supply of arms that were eventually used to bring down the empire. The decline and break-up of the Roman Empire induced massive migration, and with it, an extensive proliferation of ferrous, and non-ferrous technologies, welding and casting skills, and weaponry design and production throughout Western Europe. Although there was little change in the non-ferrous and iron technologies for over a thousand years, there were many notable innovations, including adoption of water power to work the blowers, bigger and more efficient furnaces.

2.2.10 Post-medieval Period

It is clear from the account in the last section that there was no significant development in metals technology for over a thousand years after the fall of the Roman Empire. However, advances were made in scaling up of technologies for the production of non-ferrous metals, wrought and cast iron in Europe and Asia, including the introduction of water power which was already in use for other purposes such as corn grinding. Blast furnaces fitted with water-driven blowers emerged and production of molten cast iron proliferated throughout Europe from about 1350 AD although the Chinese had apparently developed water-driven piston-blowing machines for their iron furnaces and were producing cast iron over a thousand years before. Adoption of this technology by the Chinese made it possible to achieve high enough temperatures required to produce molten iron, and the ancient Chinese iron blast furnaces are considered the forerunners of the modern steel blast furnace. Silver and brass largely replaced gold in coinage and trade in metals across nations and regions flourished. Casting technology was upgraded and cast products including bells and statutes weighing over hundred metric tons were common, cast in sections in such a way that the last piece interlocked the previous piece. Germany was particularly famous for copper production and the emergence of the banking system helped the country to assist other countries including Britain in exploiting their mineral resources. However, from about 1500 AD, the beginning of the Renaissance in Europe, technology, in particular metals technologies took a significant leap forward. Prior to this period, artisans had no formal education and there had been little awareness on the need for and potential of technology. There was a surge of interest in education and technology, a development which led to monumental inventions like paper and printing, and laid the foundations for the Industrial Revolution which started in Europe in the 17th century.

2.2.11 The Industrial Revolution

Prior to around 1600 AD, metals were being produced in batches of small quantities, wrought and cast iron technologies had been mastered, but steel could not be mass-produced because the necessary temperature above the melting point of pure iron (1538°C) could not be achieved. Small quantities were being made from wrought iron by cementation (carburization) or fining pig or cast iron (decarburization) which had been practiced in Asia since around 500 BC but did not reach Europe until about the 13th century AD. Many variants of the fining process evolved in Europe over the next two hundred years, notably the *puddling process* carried out in water-powered bloomeries, making it possible to mass-produce malleable wrought iron and mild steel from molten cast iron by creating a turbulent oxidizing atmosphere in the furnace which decarburized the iron. The blast furnace fitted with water-powered blowers which had been in operation in Asia from about 300 BC spread to Europe and made possible mass production of pig iron. Large furnaces that operated continuously (unlike the bloomery batch process) became common all over Europe, producing molten pig iron for the foundry or for refining to produce steel. However, the furnaces were fired with charcoal and large quantities were required to produce relatively small quantities of cast iron. Charcoal was becoming increasingly scarce and expensive, and there were concerns about massive deforestation. This changed with the development of commercial coal mines in the 16th century and widespread use of coal in many metallurgical applications by the beginning of the 18th century. Coke (carbonized/degasified coal) was first used as a substitute for coal or charcoal in 1709 by Abraham Darby in England and the effect on the blast furnace process was dramatic: it brought about the release of ironmaking from the inhibition caused by persistent shortage of charcoal making it possible to scale up furnaces to almost any size. It also stimulated the development of coal carbonizing technologies (coke ovens) which mass-produced coke ready for use in blast furnaces. Further improvements included the use of hot blast in which waste heat was used to pre-heat incoming air blast, greatly improving efficiency, cutting coke consumption by a third and coal consumption by two-thirds. This technology remains a prominent feature of modern blast furnace technology. Sintering was another important technology that emerged in this period: it involves pre-roasting of iron ores mixed with limestone and coke breeze to reduce gangue and elements such as sulphur associated with the ore, thereby greatly reducing consumption of expensive coke in the blast furnace and increasing efficiency significantly, another important feature of modern blast furnace practice. Not much else has happened in the iron and steel industry, except that blast furnaces have become bigger: today's furnaces are up to forty meters high and 15 meters in diameter compared with the 3-meter tall furnaces of the 18th century. Blast furnaces now operate continuously for up to five years before they are shut down for relining, with a daily production of about 10,000 metric ton of pig iron.

Pig iron which is the primary product of the modern blast furnace is very brittle because of the very high carbon content and many impurities (typically 3.8–4.7% C and many impurities, notably silica), and is of little direct use as a cast or structural metal. However, cast iron is produced from molten pig iron by heating with coke in a hot air blast usually in a cupola, a process which reduces the carbon content to about 3% and removes much of the silica and other impurities. Different grades of cast iron (white, gray, malleable, ductile) are produced by adjusting the carbon and silicon contents, and adding alloying elements. Steel is also produced by refining molten pig iron in an open-hearth furnace or an oxygen converter, by reducing carbon content to less than 1% (mild steel) to a maximum of 2% (high-carbon steel) depending on the desired grade, reducing silica content as desired, and alloying with some elements to produce the thousands of grades of steel that are available today. Pig iron produced in the early part of the Industrial Revolution was either processed in fineries to produce wrought iron, or in open-hearth furnaces to produce steel. The emergence of open-hearth furnaces, and, ultimately oxygen converters capable of reaching around 1600°C opened up the possibility for the production of a very wide range of steel alloys because higher temperatures produced relatively ductile, lower-carbon, lower-silicon steel. Also, alloying with elements, notably manganese, nickel, chromium, molybdenum, tungsten, columbium, made possible the production of a wide range of high-strength, heat and corrosion-resistant steel grades, required by many industries that were emerging around the same time, notably the chemical, machine-building and construction industries. The emergence of the blast furnace did not render wrought iron obsolete because of its malleability and wide range of potential use, hence bloomeries developed in parallel with blast furnaces for a very long time and new processes of producing wrought iron from molten cast and sponge iron emerged. However, demand for the metal began to decline with the wide availability of low-carbon steel which has similar properties and is relatively easy to produce on a large scale, and wrought iron is no longer produced commercially today, except in some developing countries. Many products such as gates and fences which are advertised as wrought iron today are in fact produced from malleable or ductile cast iron.

The production of non-ferrous metals especially copper, bronze, lead, zinc and tin remained active and proliferated extensively from the Medieval Period to the Industrial Revolution especially for the use of coins, jewelry and ornaments. Demand for copper, aluminium, tin also grew rapidly and provided the impetus for the development of the non-ferrous industry. A wide range of copper and aluminium alloys emerged for many applications particularly in the chemical, food and electrical industries. The ceramics industry developed in parallel largely because different types with varying thermochemical properties were required for lining furnaces, ladles, apart from increasing use in construction. Up to 1600 AD metallurgy remained essentially practicing the traditional methods of smelting, melting and working of metals and the practice was not universal. While there was proliferation in some regions, the technology was virtually non-existent in others. Trade in primary metals grew between countries and regions and so did trade in raw materials and finished products.

2.2.12 Emergence and development of metallurgy, materials science and engineering

Prior to the Industrial Revolution, metallurgy was primarily an art largely sustained by traditional practices, but with constant infusion of innovations. The early metallurgists were basically empiricists, with little knowledge of science, but even then, they were very familiar with many *physical/mechanical metallurgy* phenomena that are now backed by science: like assessment and alteration of malleability of metals, alloying, heat treatment, hardening, tempering, carburizing, de-carburizing, and working to change mechanical properties. They also practiced the rudiments of *chemical metallurgy* like roasting of copper sulphide ores to make smelting easier, creation of oxidizing and reducing atmospheres for different ore smelting processes, choosing appropriate furnace and ladle lining ceramics, etc. In effect, they knew a lot about what to do but very little about why. For example, the practices of producing wrought iron, cast iron, or even steel had been firmly established for nearly two thousand years and the unique properties of each were well known, but no one could explain the reason for the difference in properties of the three types of ferrous metals. The firm establishment of science started from the 17th century, with the emergence of a significant pool of active scientists, astronomers, mathematicians. The microscope was invented in 1600 and the Royal Society (England), was founded in 1662, followed closely by the French Academie des Sciences in 1666. *Metallography* was perhaps the first beneficiary of these developments. Polished samples of metals were being observed under the microscope and microphysical structures described. By the early 1700s, properties of ferrous metal were being discussed in terms of grain structure, and even microscopic hardness indentation tests, and mechanical testing to determine dead-load fracture and bending strength tests became common practice, a development which firmly established *physical metallurgy* as a core subject. There was also substantial contribution to *chemical/extraction metallurgy* by science: scientists began to study the blast furnace process and to document accurately the changes in the burden as it descended down the furnace. This made possible the adjustment of material and operating parameters to optimize production processes. The explanation for the differences in the properties of wrought iron, cast iron and steel eventually emerged from the work of the Swedish chemist, Torbern Bergman (1735-1784). After a long series of experiments by fusing iron ore with different ferrous metals in sealed crucibles and determining the amount of smelted product, he concluded that ductile (wrought) iron contained almost no reductant (carbon which he named plumbago), while steel contained lesser amount and cast iron was saturated with it, thus laying the foundation for *thermochemistry*.

The Industrial Revolution also inspired a cooperation between industrialists and scientists. Prior to this time, industrialists were only interested in the profitability of their operations and a scientific basis was of little interest. However, by the late 1700s, metallurgical problems emanating from industry began to inspire chemists and physicists, forging a close cooperation between industrialists and scientists. The physical and chemical properties of most existing metals as well as about a thousand alloys were determined and documented by 1788: density, melting point, mechanical properties including hardness and tensile strength. Over the next hundred years or so, extensive work was done by analytical chemists on the chemistry of ferrous and non-ferrous ores, and physico-chemical studies of important metallurgical processes such as blast furnace smelting, metal casting, rolling, forging and drawing. Various microstructures in iron and steel, like ferrite, austenite, martensite and cementite, troostite, sorbite, eutectics which were identified, characterized and documented, made possible by developments in etching technologies and photomicrography. By the beginning of the twentieth century, a largely correct iron-carbon equilibrium diagram (phase diagram) had emerged, so had detailed crystallographic description of the phase constitution of alloys and the structures of alpha, beta, gamma and delta iron, and dislocation mechanisms, made possible by the emergence of X-ray diffraction technology, the humble beginning of modern *metallography and phase transformations*.

There were also very important contributions by scientists in non-ferrous metallurgy, for example, age-hardening of aluminium alloys which led to the invention of *duralumin*. Previously, aluminium alloys containing copper, zinc, magnesium had been mostly used in the cast state but, by accident, it was found that when heat-treated aluminium-copper-magnesium alloys are quenched, the product is soft but becomes much harder after a few days of undisturbed storage, a phenomenon which came to be known as *age-hardening*. For an alloy containing 4% copper and 0.5% each of magnesium, manganese, iron and silicon, the strength doubles, elongation is reduced by half, while density is only 5% higher compared with high-purity aluminium. Duralumin quickly emerged as a metal of choice for applications where strength-to-weight ratio is important, such as aircraft frames, aerospace structures, high-performance automobile components, and a very wide range of other applications. Similar properties have been found in copper-beryllium alloys and high-strength (maraging) steels containing nickel and cobalt. Extensive studies on age-hardening by X-ray crystallographers have attributed this behavior to changes in solid solubility but, with the emergence of the electron microscope in the 1950s, it was possible to establish an optimum time beyond which strength starts to decrease with time due to precipitation of a second phase. These studies have led to the establishment of optimum heat treatment temperatures before quenching and age-hardening temperatures and times for a very wide range of age-hardening alloys and many more are still being characterized today.

Perhaps the most important outcome of the work of scientists of the period of Industrial Revolution was the realization of the profound influence of physical properties on the mechanical and other engineering properties of metals. Early solid-state physics was based on idealized-perfect structures and did not recognize any relationship between structure and properties. However, observations of defects and solid-state diffusion in physical metallurgy opened up new cooperation between metallurgists and solid-state physicists, who have worked jointly to document the phenomena of dislocation structure and movement during deformation of metals, a major work which helped to explain the basis of the long-established practical knowledge of work-hardening and heat-treatment. The cooperation between science and metallurgy has led to many important milestones like the evolution of atomic theory and structure, deformation mechanics, and other very important phenomena such as magnetism and radioactivity. The metallurgist now has a good working knowledge of ferromagnetism and can create different types ferromagnets for different applications.

In summary, the period of Industrial Revolution was one of scale-up of metallurgical processes, invention of new alloys, and infusion of metallurgy with scientific principles. Without the major advances in metallurgy, monumental inventions and developments such as civil and mechanical construction, electrical, electronic, telecommunications, chemical, automobile, aircraft and aerospace industries would not have been possible. The increasing importance of ceramics in metallurgy, the prime role of science and engineering principles, the emergence of polymers, the transistor and composite materials in commercial quantities in the mid 20th century, and developments in bio- and nano-materials technologies have also changed the traditional scope of metallurgy considering the close interrelationship between metals and non-metals, and the most appropriate name for the profession is now *materials science and engineering*.

Chapter 3

Metallurgy of metals of antiquity

3.1 INTRODUCTION

Metallurgy is basically the process of extraction of metals from ores, the design of metals for specific applications, and shaping into forms required by other technologies. Most ores are oxides, sulphides and other complex chemical compounds mixed with many undesirables (clay, sandstone, etc.) collectively known as gangue, and are upgraded by hydrological or thermal processing (*mineral beneficiation*) before extraction which may also be by hydrological, chemical or thermal processing (process/*extraction metallurgy*). It requires the application of principles of chemistry, fluid mechanics and thermodynamics. The metal extracted is alloyed (with the addition of various elements in relatively minor quantities) in the molten state to obtain desired properties and the molten metal is cast into ingots or blooms for further processing. Mechanical processing (*mechanical metallurgy*) starts with casting of molten metal into semi-finished products, followed by rolling, hot and cold forging, drawing, stamping, welding, all of which are sensitive to chemical composition. Worked products may need intermediate or final heat treatment to optimize properties or surface protection such as plating, coating, tinning. Desired mechanical and environmental properties of products are achieved by manipulation of the microstructure through heat treatment and evaluated by physical testing (*physical metallurgy*)

The rudiments of mechanical metallurgy were practiced by the early humans: they forged and shaped meteoric iron and native copper to make small tools and implements; they worked other naturally occurring metals, in particular, gold and silver. However, these operations were on a very small scale. There is also some evidence that they were melting and casting native copper from the Neolithic Age, again apparently on a very small scale. However, extractive metallurgy really began in the Copper Age when smelting of copper from ore became common, with the subsequent evolution of other metallurgical techniques, including slagging, alloying, heat treatment, casting and working. Primary metals were cast, hot or cold-forged, drawn, and heat-treated to obtain desired shapes, all elements of *mechanical metallurgy*. From then on, and until the 16th century, the evolution of metallurgy was largely about scale and scope.

3.2 BRIEF HISTORICAL METALLURGY

Some metals which occur in nature, also known as metals of antiquity have been known and used since the early human times and little is known about when and where they were first used, or how use spread to different parts of the early world. Gold, copper and iron were the earliest metals in use but there is ample evidence of use of four other metals that were often components of ores of these three major metals: tin, lead, silver and mercury. These seven metals dominated the world from the early times until the last two or three centuries when most of the other metals were produced in commercial quantities. The number grew to twelve by the end of the 17th century and twelve more were added over the next hundred years. In effect most of the 86 currently known metals were discovered from the 19th century when science had become very active. Iron ore is the fourth most abundant mineral in the Earth's crust and deposits are very widely distributed in all regions of the world. Copper ores are also abundant and available in all regions, yet, the smelting technologies of these two metals were the last to emerge in terms of quantities and scope of use in early times. Clearly the delay was due to the long process of surmounting the

3.2.1 Gold and Platinum

Gold is widely distributed in the Earth's crust in very low concentrations (0.005 ppm), either in solid rock (lode deposits), which can be retrieved by normal mining techniques, or as tiny granules (gravelly deposits) in stream beds, which are the products of erosion of lode deposits by streams. It is conceivable that a Stone Age hunter found a small piece of metal (native copper, gold, ironstone) and tried to shape it into a tool or an ornament. Copper artifacts such as beads, pins and awls, dated 9th-7th millennium BC have been found in parts of Iran and Anatolia, but no gold artifacts dated earlier than 5th millennium BC have been found. However, archaeologists believe that gold was in fact in common use much earlier, probably as early as 6000 BC but was considered too precious to put in graves and was retained in circulation.

Gold almost entirely occurs in impure, native metallic form containing about 10% silver and up to 1% copper. Although large nuggets are found occasionally which goldsmiths collect and weld together into larger lumps by hammering, it is mostly in fine dust-like particles collected by washing stream beds. These particles are neither easy to retrieve nor to consolidate by melting. Furthermore it is difficult to separate gold from silver and, quite often, the minerals are processed together to obtain a wide variety on gold products, from pure gold, through electrum to white gold, ranging in colour from pale yellow to amber to white, depending on the silver content. The high luster of gold, high environmental stability, coupled with the scarcity of naturally occurring concentrations, and difficulty of recovery and processing, probably conferred on it the pride of place as a valuable (noble) metal. Also, the high malleability which enables it to be formed into extremely thin wire and sheet precluded its use for any utilitarian applications and restricted it to jewelry and ornaments. In the early Egyptian civilization, gold was considered divine and was the material of choice for moulding the gods they worshipped.

Platinum also occurs in nature in the form of water-borne grains in alluvial gravel like gold. It usually is impure, containing 50 to 80% platinum, the balance being made up of other metals in the platinum group and some base metals. Platinum was discovered officially in the 16th century and it is not thought that the metal was recognized as a separate entity by the early people, although artifacts containing large amounts of platinum have been found in South American countries, in particular, Columbia and Ecuador. Since this region has significant amounts of platinum ore deposits, it is thought that these artifacts were made by melting a naturally occurring mixture of precious metals recovered from alluvial deposits. The fact that some of the objects were made by combining thin sheets of platinum and gold welded together by hammering may also suggest that gold and platinum were first separated before use.

3.2.2 Lead

Lead does not occur in nature in native form but as Galena (lead sulphide). This ore was used widely in ancient Egypt as an eye paint, due probably to its metallic appearance. With a low melting point of 327°C, lead was probably smelted accidentally as a result of the reduction of Galena in camp fires. At the typical fire temperatures, molten lead would probably flow to the lowest point of the fireplace and collect in a pool where it eventually solidified. The ability of lead to flow and separate is an important concept in modern extractive metallurgy, as reduction reactions are only useful when the metal can separate from the gangue. The relatively easy transition of lead between liquid and solid phases also probably gave the early people their first introduction to casting technology - melting metal, pouring it into moulds of pre-determined shape and cooling. The high malleability of lead and the fact that it does not work-harden on hammering greatly restricted its use initially for structural objects. However, the development of casting technology provided a new method of producing non-corrosive pipes and containers which were in wide use in Ancient Middle East from around 3500 BC.

3.2.3 Tin

Tin is not found in uncombined form in nature but in the oxide form - *cassiterite.* Deposits of the ore are relatively rare and are often associated with certain types of granite which occur in a few locations around the world - Malaysia, China, Bolivia, Cornwall, Saxony-Bohemia, and Nigeria. The ore is white in pure state but may be brown or black due to contamination with varying amounts of iron. It may occur in mined deposits or, because of its high stability and specific gravity, may collect in the beds of streams through erosion of deposits or in gravels and sands like gold. There is no evidence to show that tin was ever used by itself in antiquity but it is probable that it has been recovered for as long as gold but discarded as worthless. Many castings of the Early Copper Age contained minor quantities of tin but this was probably incidental since it is a common impurity in copper ores. However, by around 2500 BC the Sumerians had recognized the versatility of blending different ores to obtain metals of desired quality. By blending copper and tin ores they produced a different material *bronze* - which flowed more easily on hammering, was stronger after forming by forging or casting, and was easier to cast than copper. This made the material versatile for the production of tools and weapons. An axe head dated at this period contained 11% tin and 89% copper. This development may have been purely accidental since some natural deposits of copper ores have been found to contain tin in sufficiently high proportion to produce bronze (7% tin or higher depending on the relative concentration of copper in the ore). Tin ores were reduced by charcoal and the metal was initially thought to be a form of lead, hence the classification of both metals as *plumbum:* lead as *plumbum nigrum* and tin as *plumbum candidum* in Roman times.

3.2.4 Silver

Silver is found uncombined in nature but occurrences are very rare. Silver usually occurs with lead and sulphur (galena) in nature and the art of silver extraction appears to have originated from the north-east Asian Minor. The ore was roasted to remove some of the sulphur, then melted by heating using charcoal which produced the desired non-oxidizing atmosphere. The silver-lead alloy which would have separated at the bottom of the melt was recovered and melted in a porous clay crucible called the cupel through which air was blown. It is possible that the lead oxide was mixed with bone ash, in which case, the lead oxide would have been adsorbed and a large amount of material could have been processed to obtain silver. The lead content would have been oxidized and, being of lower density, acted as a flux, removing impurities, it would have been decanted, leaving relatively pure, shinny silver in the cupel. This process known as the *cupellation process* was in wide use in the Near East as early as 3000-2500 BC, and is believed to have been used extensively to refine gold as well by deliberately mixing gold and lead ores. Silver is a soft and reactive metal, second only to gold in ductility and malleability. It is stable in pure air but tarnishes when exposed to ozone, hydrogen sulphide or sulphur. Pure silver was used primarily in jewelry and ornaments and, like gold, it was a symbol of wealth. Silver, like lead, is a very soft metal, easily damaged when used by itself. It was therefore often alloyed with other metals, notably a small amount of copper to increase its hardness, and used extensively for ornaments and coins from the early times. An alloy of gold and silver, called *electrum* was often regarded as more valuable than pure gold or silver.

3.2.5 Mercury

Mercury also known as *quicksilver* occurs in native state, although rare. It is also found in such ores as calomel, livingstonite, corderite, and is the only metal known to occur in liquid state at room temperature. Mercury compounds decompose at moderate temperatures, hence pure mercury is obtained easily by distillation. It has been found in tombs as far back as the 16th to 15th century BC. It is believed also that the metal was revered and possibly worshiped by some early civilizations. Mercury dissolves silver and gold to form an amalgam a process which formed the basis for early plating technologies.

3.2.6 Copper, brass and bronze

Copper was the earliest metal smelted, followed by bronze and, ultimately brass. There is a lot of confusion about the differences between copper and its two major alloys (brass and bronze), especially in archaeology, largely because of lack of knowledge of metallurgy but also because most excavated artifacts are in various stages of degradation and it may be difficult to differentiate visually between copper and its alloys, although the difference is visually evident in fresh metals (Figure 3.1). The emergence of archaeometallurgy in the later part of the 19th century has helped to resolve this problem and many objects characterized earlier have been re-classified.

Figure 3.1 Visual differences between copper, brass and bronze.

3.2.6.1 *Copper*

Native copper was apparently used to some extent in the Neolithic period but it came into common use between 4000 and 6000 BC. The main problem with use would have been its extreme heterogeneity, containing grains varying from very large to very small, interspersed with gangue (unwanted minerals such as calcite). Silver may be present up to about 0.6% and other metals such as arsenic, nickel, lead, antimony and iron may also be present. There is no evidence that the technology of smelting copper from ore had been developed in this period, hence copper objects found in places like Iran, dating back to the 7th millennium BC, and those found in large quantities in the Lake Superior region of North America (3000 to 1500 BC) must have been produced from unmelted copper by hammering and smithing. Native copper is difficult to work because it work-hardens quite quickly. Furthermore, depending on the original grain size, cracks can propagate quite rapidly along the grain boundaries, but it was apparent that the Neolithic people were aware that working could be extended considerably by intermittent re-heating, and as long as the cracks are immediately removed during forging, reductions of up to 100% can be achieved on native copper, and small objects such as beads and ornaments can be produced. This process is the forerunner of the modern heat treatment/annealing technology. Many of the archaeological objects found clearly had undergone some heat treatment: some were in the soft, annealed state while others were finished by a final light cold working. The microstructures of some of the objects also show that the annealing process was below about 600°C in view of the segregation of impurities at the grain boundaries, typical of native copper. Above this temperature the impurities tend to dissolve and diffuse away from the boundaries.

Arsenic featured prominently in most of the copper artifacts found in the Near East, as high as 7%, although some contained up to 24% arsenic. The presence of this element in the objects and indeed in many other objects found in other sites elsewhere has generated considerable debate. It is not clear whether smelted copper ores were deliberately mixed with arsenic ore such as arsenic sulphide at the smelting stage, or copper ores rich in arsenic were selected purposefully. In fact, both could be right: many copper ore deposits contain some arsenic, and tin may also be present in small quantities. Arsenic has low melting point of 613°C, and the oxides and sulphides melt at even much lower temperatures, hence the element should volatilize well before copper melts at 1083°C. However, many arsenical copper ores were oxidized and would have had to be smelted under reducing conditions, like in closed crucibles. In such situations, loss of arsenic would be minimized or in fact eliminated, especially when present below 7% (see Tylecote, 1992). Many copper deposits are stratified due to long-term weathering, with the initial copper sulphide and associated ferrous sulphide near the surface of the deposit being converted to oxide. Some native copper and some precious metals may also be found mixed with the sub-surface copper ore. Copper concentration in this layer is usually low, no more than about 5%. Because of the relative solubility of copper, lower layers would have higher copper content, along with arsenical and antimoniacal minerals which are also relatively soluble, Copper concentration in this enriched layer could be as high as 25%. From this level, copper concentration decreases and could be as low as 0.3% in the bottom layers. Ore retrieved from the top layers would be mainly in oxide form (copper and iron) and would have been easy to smelt: the iron oxide reacts with silica in the ore to form ferrous silicate (fayalite) slag which is removed to retrieve pure copper. However, the copper/iron sulphide ore mixture in the rich middle layer of the deposit would have had to be roasted, mixed with silica slag at temperatures up to 800°C to convert both copper and iron sulphides to oxides. Copper oxide would then be further reduced to copper and the iron oxide removed in the slag. Some archaeologists question the ability of the early copper smelters to carry out this tedious two-stage process while risking poisoning by arsenic trioxide released during roasting. Recent in-depth laboratory studies suggest the probability that the smelting was carried out in a single stage called *cosmelting*. This issue is discussed in some depth in Appendix III. In effect, the presence of arsenic and antimony in many copper objects may have been incidental or deliberate, the later being a consequence of the desire to use richer copper sulphide ores in smelting. The ore deposit stratification described above may also explain the common chronological sequence of archaeological copper and bronze objects: copper to copper-arsenic to copper-arsenic-tin. It should be noted however that not all copper ores conform to the stratification described above and some contain antimony or tin rather than arsenic.

Even if the presence of arsenic or tin in early copper objects was incidental initially, it would not have taken the smelters long to appreciate its significantly positive effect of the two elements on the mechanical properties of copper, even in small quantities. This would have provided the incentive to deliberately mix ores of different chemical compositions. As has been discussed earlier, the early metallurgists had considerable difficulty producing structural materials from pure copper by cold-hammering and smithing because of its ductility and low work-hardening characteristics. Attempts to produce arsenical copper objects by casting would have yielded similar results because the element is of little or no benefit to the mechanical properties of cast copper (see Appendix III). However, the effect on cold-worked copper could be substantial since arsenical or tin copper work-hardens much faster than pure copper (Copper containing 8% arsenic worked to 50% reduction in thickness is twice as hard as pure copper worked to the same level. See Figure 3.2).

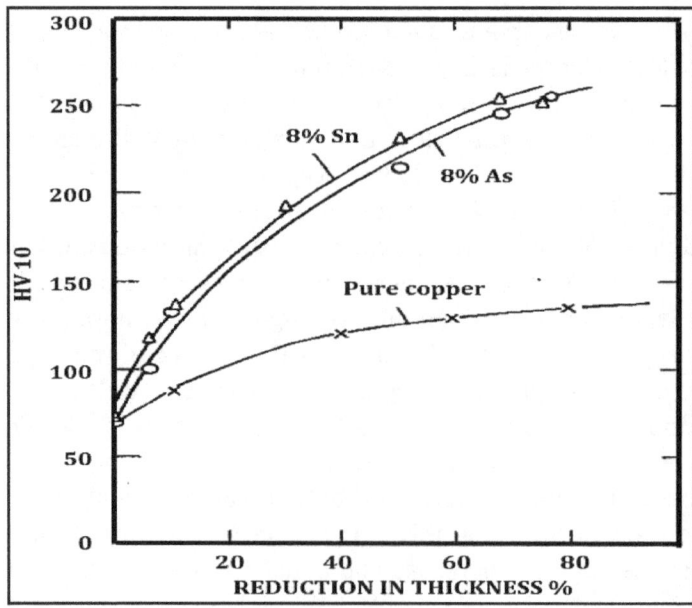

Figure 3.2 Effect of tin and arsenic addition to copper on the hardness after cold working. *(Tylecote, 1974).*

When hot-forged, copper will lose most of its arsenic content but, cold-forging combined with intermediate anneals could produce very strong material for making tools and weapons. Since antimony hardens copper to the same extent as arsenic, its presence in copper would have been just as desirable. The presence of tin has a similar effect on copper and discovery of this fact, whether by accident or deliberate experimentation, would have heralded the beginning of the bronze age. The effect of tin and arsenic on the mechanical properties is more or less additive and copper ores that already contain these elements (about 1-2% and 1-4% respectively) yield material that is stronger than pure copper and has better work-hardening characteristics. They are commonly called arsenical or tin bronzes but they are in fact low alloy coppers. Copper alloys constitute one of the most important groups of materials that have dominated the materials scene from the earliest times to date. It is important to understand the metallurgical principles behind these alloys as discussed briefly below and in some depth in Appendix III in order to appreciate the reason for their dominance. In modern engineering, copper is used in a wide range of products due to its excellent electrical and thermal conductivity, good strength, good formability and resistance to corrosion. Pipe and pipe fittings are commonly manufactured from these metals due to their corrosion resistance.

3.2.6.2 *Brass*

Brass is an alloy of copper and zinc but may contain small amounts of arsenic, lead, aluminium, manganese, silicon, phosphorus. By varying the amount of zinc content, a wide variety of alloys with different mechanical, electrical properties and colours can be made. Increased amounts of zinc provide the material with improved strength and ductility. Brass can range in colour from red to yellow depending on the amount of zinc added to the alloy. Zinc content may vary from around 30% to almost 70%. The relatively low melting point compared with copper (900-940°C depending on composition) and its good flow characteristics make it a good casting material. Also, the muted yellow colour of brass (similar to gold), and its resistance to tarnishing make it very attractive for decorative objects, artifacts, musical instruments, coins, etc. The standard 60:40 brass has good hot-workability while higher zinc content (Muntz metal) increases strength but lowers room-temperature ductility. Addition of tin inhibits dezincification in hostile environments. Tin brass alloys containing small amounts of tin are perhaps the most versatile grades of brass, combining moderate strength with high corrosion resistance and excellent electrical conductivity, and good hot and cold working properties. They are used extensively as fasteners, pump shafts, and for marine hardware. Addition of nickel increases thermal stability and corrosion resistance. They are used extensively for musical instruments and buttons because they can be polished to a very high degree of finish. There is ample evidence that brass has been produced since early times, (brought to prominence by the Romans around 30 BC) by smelting mixtures of copper ore and calamine (a mixture of zinc carbonate and zinc silicate). Artifacts of brass: coins, polished brass mirrors have been discovered in some ancient Roman settlements, and it is believed that many archaeological objects classified as bronzes were indeed brasses (or arsenical copper), since the term 'bronze' has become the common name for virtually all types of coppers and copper alloys.

3.2.6.3 *Bronze*

Bronze is an alloy of copper and tin but may also contain other metals in small quantities, such as manganese, nickel, aluminium or zinc. A minimum of about 7% tin content is required to classify a copper-tin alloy as bronze, and tin content may be up to 12%, but bronzes with tin content as low as 4-5% and around 1% of zinc are used in coinage. Bronze is much harder than copper and elements such as phosphorus, manganese, silicon, aluminium confer different properties on the alloy. Phosphorus content (1-2%) increases wear resistance and stiffness and these properties make the alloy an excellent material for bearings, bushings, pump plungers, valves (phosphor bronze). Bronze is also more fusible (i.e., more readily melted) and is hence easier to cast. It is also harder than pure iron and far more resistant to corrosion. Bronze became the prime metal in the last two millennia BC and was used extensively for making tools and weapons. The displacement of iron by bronze from about 1000 BC was probably the result of iron's abundance compared with copper and tin rather than any inherent advantages of iron. While many copper ores contain arsenic and, to a lesser extent, antimony, tin is not often found together with copper, although there are a few exceptions such as the copper deposit in Cornwall, England which has significant tin content relative to copper concentration. Tin occurs in nature mainly as oxide SnO_2, also known as cassiterite or, less commonly, as sulphide (stannite), and there are only a few deposits in the world. This explains why it took so long for bronze use to become widespread. While copper and low-tin copper had been in use for around five millennia BC in Asia Minor, the earliest date for the use of standard bronze (7-10% tin) coincides with the establishment of inter-regional trade links from about 2500 BC, and tin was probably imported from Turkey, Malaysia, China, Bolivia, Cornwall or Nigeria.

Bronze can be made in two ways, either by smelting mixtures of copper ore and cassiterite (or copper ore with high tin content), or dropping pieces of tin into molten copper. In early times, the copper-tin ore and charcoal mixture would have been smelted probably in an externally-heated closed crucible to create a sufficiently reducing atmosphere and achieve the melting temperature of bronze. The cassiterite (or stannite) would be reduced to tin which would be absorbed by the copper. The second option assumes that metallic tin is available, which was not common in early times. However as discussed earlier, evidence of substantial inter-regional trading in tin and copper dating 3-2 millennium BC has been found: several sunken ships carrying tin and copper ingots have been found and dated to the True Bronze Age.

3.2.7 Iron

Meteoroids are solid debris originating from space, mostly from asteroids but some are believed to come from comets, the moon and mars. The debris glows as it enters the Earth's atmosphere due to tremendous pressure, friction and heat. It is the familiar *shooting star* also known as *meteors*. The extreme heat and pressure cause major physico-chemical changes in the material which eventually falls on the Earth's surface and is known as *meteorite* (Figure 3.3(a). There are many types of meteorites classified on the basis of physical and chemical properties and sizes range from very small to very large. In the early times, meteorites were melted with coal to produce iron which was worked into farming implements and war weapons. In some cultures it was revered as *sky iron* and made into religious statutes.

Figure 3.3 (a) a meteorite (b) a statute carved from meteorite
(Source: thehistoryblog.com)

Iron meteorite contains mainly iron but also typically contains about 10% nickel and some cobalt, which makes it very hard and difficult to work. When hammered the material tends to crack along well-defined crystal planes. Figure 3.3(b) shows a statute carved from iron meteorite around the 11th century BC. Geochemical analysis and archaeological dating showed that the artifact weighing about 10 kilograms was carved from a piece of iron meteorite believed to have fallen to the Earth's surface between Mongolia and Siberia around 15,000 years ago. There is some indication that man-made iron was available as early as 2500 BC but it took over a thousand years for the technology to spread and become common practice in different regions of the early world . The initial spread of iron use was also restrained by the inability to obtain high temperatures of around 1150-200°C, required to produce useful iron. The relative rarity of meteoric iron and difficulties with processing made iron about five times more expensive than gold in the Neolithic times and this restricted its initial use to ornaments.

There is little doubt that meteoric iron had been cold-worked from Neolithic times to produce small pieces of tools but, considering its scarcity, use was probably rare and on a very small scale. Early iron technology is believed to have evolved by accident from the smelting of copper, but it is also possible that operators of early copper furnaces deliberately tried to smelt iron ore which was in common use as flux in copper smelting, and found a way of obtaining sufficiently high temperature and reducing conditions that produced iron. There are also speculations that iron may have been invented by a completely new group who did not even know the technique of smelting copper. Pure iron has a melting point of 1538°C which could not be achieved in any of the early furnaces, hence early iron was produced in the solid state by chemical reduction of iron ore with solid charcoal to produce solid, almost pure iron at about 1150°C. As much as possible of the slag had to be removed from iron by liquidation, hence the smelting process must have taken place at or above the temperature of around 1150°C at which the slag would become sufficiently fluid to drain away from the solid iron. While this temperature is well above the temperature at which iron oxide can be reduced to iron by carbon, it is substantially below the melting point of the metal, hence iron was produced in the solid state, as a sponge or bloom from which slag partially drained away. The trapped portion was expelled by gentle hammering while the slag was still in fluid state. The product, a mixture of solid iron, slag and pieces of unburnt charcoal known as wrought iron bloom was treated in one of two ways: in one method, the product was broken up by hammering. Because iron is more ductile than the other components, it would flatten as a result of hammering and could be easily identified and separated. The pieces were then welded together to produce larger pieces by heating them in a smith's fire followed by hammering. In the second method, the bloom was smithed in one piece or, if too large, cut into smaller pieces which were individually smithed.

The product of the bloomery process could be very heterogeneous depending on the chemical composition of the iron ore which often contained elements like phosphorus and arsenic both of which have a marked hardening effect on the object produced. Furthermore, carbon concentration in the product could vary significantly from point to point. It would have been possible to sort the products into soft (low-carbon) and hard (high-carbon) pieces for different applications. Clearly, the early iron producers knew that they could produce either type by simply adjusting the fuel : ore ratio. Smithing was carried out by heating the bloom in a forge which contained a heap of charcoal with air supplied through a tuyere by a bellows, very much like primitive forges that are still operating in many parts of the developing world today. Temperatures as high as 1150°C could be achieved easily, and annealing at around 700°C between step reductions would have made possible the production of complex-shaped objects. With wrought iron, most of the work could have been done cold with intermediate annealing. The earliest iron object found in Gizeh, Egypt in 1837 was dated 2750 BC (Tylecote, 1974). The structure was well stratified and typical of wrought iron which emerged over a thousand years later. It is unclear whether the object was produced locally or acquired through trade with the Middle East or Asia.

The Chinese are believed to have received iron technology from Asia Minor around 600-400 BC, or may have invented the technology independently much earlier. Although the more common assumption is that iron technology originated in Asia Minor and spread to other parts of the world, some archaeometallurgists believe that ferrous metallurgy evolved independently in China. This is possible considering the high degree of sophistication of non-ferrous technologies that had flourished in the region for centuries. It was probably relatively easy to infuse the numerous innovations that have come to be associated with early Chinese ferrous metallurgy. They apparently skipped wrought iron technology and succeeded in producing molten high-carbon iron (cast iron) by designing more efficient furnaces with powerful water-driven, double-acting, forced-draft air-blowing bellows and were able to achieve furnace temperatures as high as 1200°C. The cast iron technology required large amounts of charcoal compared with the amount of iron being melted, and carbon monoxide produced diffused into the iron, lowering the melting temperature. The same sort of accident that produced recognizable ductile iron at the bottom of a copper-smelting furnace could, under certain conditions, have produced cast iron. There is some evidence that this may have occurred occasionally in Asia Minor and Europe but it was China that seemed the first to have appreciated cast iron technology.

The cast iron produced in early China contained about 96% iron and 3.5-4% carbon. The first blast furnace for producing cast iron was in operation from around 200 BC but did not spread to Europe until the post Medieval Migration period. Several large blast furnaces whose air bellows were powered by water wheels, producing several metric tons of iron a day were built and cast iron was used extensively for structural components that were subjected to compressive stresses, but the metal was too hard and brittle for other applications that required ductility. However, the Chinese found a way of producing wrought iron from cast iron either by decarburizing the metal in a smiths fire, or using lower fuel: ore ratio. They produced a wide range of types of iron including wrought iron, though not by the typical bloomery process but by decarbonizing molten cast iron, they were also able to induce some ductility in cast iron objects produced by casting by reheating object to 800-900°C in air and burning off some of the carbon. Oxygen penetrates and decarbonizes the skin of the casting, thereby inducing some ductility. The Chinese also learnt to improve the mechanical properties of cast iron which was considered brittle, by heating it in air for several days, a process which significantly decarburizes the iron and produces steel (fining process, or by heating it with charcoal under reducing conditions to produce wrought iron. The products were used mainly for weapons and other applications that required high tensile strength. This was apparently the way the Chinese produced wrought iron objects that have been dated 403-221 BC since no evidence of the alternative bloomery method has been found in the area.

The Chinese cast iron making process is considered the forerunner of the modern blast furnace, a development that did not reach Europe until late medieval times. Apparently the Chinese were able to produce cast iron in the blast furnace by choosing appropriate ore:fuel ratios and residence times that allowed enough of carbon and impurities such as silica to be removed. Modern blast furnaces produce pig iron which contains more carbon and impurities and have to be remelted and refined in cupolas with scrap metal and alloying elements, notably manganese to produce cast iron. The proliferation of large blast furnaces producing several tonnes of iron a day in China caused severe deforestation as a result of the felling of trees to make charcoal and adequate supplies were major constraints to the scale-up of the iron blast furnace. However, the Chinese were able to replace charcoal with coal which was abundant and were the first to substitute coal for charcoal in iron smelting.

The contribution of India to the early development of iron and steel technology has been widely acknowledged. Archaeological sites in India and Sri Lanka show iron implements dated 1800 to 1200 BC. These included knives, daggers, spikes, bowls, spoons, axes, chisels, iron chains, etc. As early as about 300 BC, high quality steel was being produced in southern India by a process called *crucible technique*. The Indians had developed a complicated alloy called *wootz or Damascus steel*, a mixture of iron, some trace elements, precipitates of carbides and cementite which had been flattened into fine fibers through hammering. In the process, high-purity wrought iron, charcoal, other carbonaceous materials and glass were mixed and heated in a hearth with a forced draught for about four hours, producing a homogeneous steel with carbon content of about 1.8-2% carbon. The product was annealed to reduce the carbon content to about 1-1.6%, compared with around 0.08% for wrought iron, then hammered into bars from which a wide range of finished products were made. This process, the forerunner of the modern surface hardening technologies, is solid state carburization of wrought iron in an atmosphere which promotes diffusion of carbon into the iron and prevents oxidation.

The quality of this material was legendary and the technology became very popular in the international market especially Europe, spread by the Dutch through trade with southern India. It was used widely to make swords with quench-hardened and tempered, durable edges, capable of cutting very hard materials due to the presence of carbide precipitates, and at the same time retaining some toughness and flexibility as a result of the low carbon steel matrix. It is interesting to note that this technology did not reach Europe for a thousand years even though the products were used widely in the region for hundreds of years - it arrived in Northern Europe around 800 AD, probably through trade with the Middle East. The steel technology was eventually refined in Europe and, for several hundred years, small quantities of steel products were being produced by this process now known as *cementation process*. Clearly the Indians had mastered many of the fundamental principles of metallurgy including heat treatment, tempering, quench-hardening and thermo-mechanical treatment. One famous symbol of the superiority of Indian iron technology is the Delhi iron pillar which stands some seven meters high and weighs about six metric tons. The pillar is made from 98% wrought iron of pure quality and has withstood atmospheric corrosion for over 1600 years (Fig. 2.5c). Many archaeometallurgists believe that modern iron and steel technology originated from India and was diffused by the Persians to the Arabs who in turn spread it through the Near East and Europe. The Indians were also believed to have pioneered several other technologies including tanning, dyeing, soap making, glass and cement technologies, all of which were also spread to the Near East and Europe by the Moslems.

In spite of the fact that iron and steel technologies seemed to have spread by diffusion through many parts of the world, there were apparently many local innovations. For example, Sri Lanka replaced the bellows-driven blast furnace with a previously unknown and advanced technique which utilized winds driven through the furnace by natural draught. The furnaces were trenches which were dug into the crest of hills, with air vents designed and strategically placed to produce a pressure differential which drew air into the furnace through the vents. The temperatures achieved were sufficiently high to produce iron of better quality than bellows-driven furnaces. Japan probably acquired both bronze and iron technologies from neighbouring China between 600 BC and 200 AD. Bronze artifacts including arrow heads, mirrors, bells dating to this period have been found, many of them very similar to designs found earlier in China. The Japanese were particularly famous for the very large bronze castings produced from complicated cupola-type furnaces which adopted advanced blowing technology. It is believed that this technology was also probably acquired from China.

Iron technology reached Central Europe around 8th century BC from Asia Minor, probably first to Austria through Danube, then to Switzerland. Iron objects were found in a grave in Hallstart in Austria and La Tene in Switzerland but they appeared to have been modeled on the earlier bronze objects produced in the area. Iron remained a luxury material for several hundred years, reserved mainly for the production of artifacts. By 500 BC production had become more widespread in Northern Europe and Britain, and eventually in Central and Western Europe as a result of Celtic expansion. Iron military weapons were being produced by the Romans and probably accounted for their long-term military superiority in the region. Although iron metallurgy had emerged in the ancient Roman Republic by the latter part of the first millennium BC, the major innovations emerged only after its fall and the establishment of the Roman Empire in 27 AD. While there were few new metal technologies that could be attributed to the Empire, the military and civil needs of the Romans created considerable demand for ferrous and non-ferrous metals. Production facilities spread and more than enough metal was being produced to meet internal needs, hence international trade grew rapidly. Silver and copper-based alloys were being produced for coinage and artifacts. Although brass was being produced in the Bronze Age by heating copper alloys with calamine ($ZnCO_3$) the amount of zinc absorbed was too low (less than 10%) to qualify the product as brass, hence it was called calamine copper, and when it also contained some tin it was known as gunmetal. True brass containing 20-30% zinc was first made by the Romans around 45 BC and it was used almost exclusively for coinage.

It is unclear how and when iron technology reached Africa but iron objects dated to around 2750 BC have been found in Egypt. It is possible that they were imported from neighbouring Anatolia region which is believed to have been producing iron by that time. It is also possible that they were produced locally but no clear evidence of smelting dated to the same period has been found. Evidence of iron smelting has been found in several other parts of Africa, the oldest being the Nok area of the Middle Belt of Nigeria, dated to around 700 BC. There is considerable controversy about how Africa acquired the technology: many archaeologists believe it came from the ancient Middle East probably through the trade routes while others suggest local inventions. This issue is discussed inconsiderable depth in a later chapter.

Wrought iron dominated the Early Iron Age for several hundred years, and, by 1000 AD had emerged as a material of choice for daggers which had previously been made from cast tin and leaded bronzes, both of which are not sufficiently ductile to survive extensive hammering. China is credited with the invention of cast iron technology around the fifth century BC because the oldest cast iron artifacts dated to that period have been found in the region. There is also ample evidence that the Chinese used the material extensively for weapons, agriculture and architecture. In early times, the material quickly replaced wrought iron in many products including stoves, pots, fireplace, bells, cannon, cannonball. However, the technology did not appear to have spread beyond Asia for over a thousand years. The blast furnace technology is believed to have been introduced to Europe through Sweden around 1100 AD, possibly from China through strong trade ties between the two countries facilitated by the Volga river. However, the furnace produced mainly wrought iron and another which was installed in Italy in the 15th century produced granulated cast iron.

In spite of efforts to operate and improve the blast furnace, cast iron could not be produced in large quantities well into the 15th century. The products were limited in terms of quantities and were used mainly for weaponry, in particular, cannon balls. However, nothing much happened in terms of innovation for another three hundred years or so, largely because of increasing scarcity and rising cost of procurement of charcoal. However, the invention of the coke-fired blast furnace in England in 1709 was a major turning point. The development made it possible to produce pig iron on a very large scale for further refinement to cast iron or steel, and widened the scope of applications of both metals. It also led to the development of the puddling process towards the end of the 18th century AD for making wrought iron from molten cast iron. The process was similar to the Chinese process invented more than two thousand years earlier but, while the Chinese decarburization process involved heating small quantities of molten metal in air for several days, the English puddling process involved agitating molten cast iron in a hollowed hearth with a bar so that the carbon in the molten metal was removed by the oxidizing gases of the furnace. The product was cast and rolled in a rolling mill powered by a steam engine, to produce rolled lengths of wrought iron bars, angles and other profiles. This development made it possible to produce wrought iron on a mass scale and expanded the scope of applications. Cast iron became a major structural metal in applications requiring high compressive strength such as building structures, bridges and machinery components, while wrought iron was used in applications that required malleability, ductility and high tensile strength.

Further advances in cast iron technology produced malleable (ductile) cast iron by heat treating which transforms the microstructure into spheroidal aggregates of graphite embedded in ferrite or pearlite matrix. This microstructure confers significant ductility and the development opened up a very wide range of applications for soft-grade cast iron beyond cast products. Malleable cast iron is believed to have been produced in China as early as 4th century BC, based on worked cast iron artifacts discovered in the region and dated between 4th century BC and 9th century AD. However, production was probably limited to small quantities because of the rigorous technology involved. A French scientist took out a patent in England for malleable iron in 1720, produced by a method similar to the Chinese technology. However, the real breakthrough came in the United States in 1826 when a foundry was established by industrialist Boyden that produced malleable iron in large quantities. Today, different types and grades of malleable (nodular) cast irons are produced for different applications, notably small castings that require some ductility: machine components, hand and bench tools, structural and powerline fittings, etc. The cast iron technology has changed very little over time, the most important being the development of coke-fired cupolas capable of producing large volumes of molten metal for casting large shapes in foundries.

The modern blast furnace technology has changed only in size and charge composition (apart from more powerful electrical blowers and injection of supplementary fuels) since the Chinese iron era. Most furnaces produce 5 million metric tons or more of pig iron a year and coke is charged instead of charcoal or coal. Blast air is pre-heated and supplementary fuels such as coke breeze and natural gas are injected to optimize production parameters. The pig iron produced is too crude for any application and is either refined into cast iron or steel which is basically decarbonized cast iron (reduction of carbon content from over 4% to 2% or less). Technologies emerged in Europe in the 17th century for producing steel by heating and agitating pig iron in an oxidizing atmosphere. The emergence of mild, low-carbon steel marked the beginning of the demise of wrought iron as a material of choice in any but ornamental applications such as gates and fences. A very wide variety of alloys of cast iron or steel may be produced by varying the levels of carbon and silicon contents of molten pig or cast iron and addition of small quantities of some elements (manganese, nickel, chromium, molybdenum, tungsten, columbium, etc.) and thermochemical heat treatment to achieve desired microstructures and engineering properties (some elements may remain in solution while others form precipitates). The emergence of alloying technologies has extended the range of steels to around 3000, including corrosion, creep, fatigue resistant alloys, high-temperature alloys, high-strength alloys, as well as a wide range of cast irons for different applications. Steel now accounts for about 95% of all metals used by modern industrial society. Iron and steel became widely available beyond Europe by the 18th century and marked the beginning of closure of the Early Iron Age in some regions, although it persisted in some developing nations until around 1900 when scrap steel became widely available.

3.3 BRIEF HISTORY OF METALLURGICAL TECHNIQUES

The evolution of metallurgy has been very gradual, starting from around 5000 BC when smelting of ores to obtain metals became widespread. However, many of the modern metallurgical techniques of today are upgrades of practices dating back thousands of years.

3.3.1 Ores

Local availability of mineral ores was perhaps the greatest stimulant for the development of early metallurgy, since local people were very likely to experiment with any materials available locally. This probably explains why gold, silver, mercury, lead, none of which are structural metals were discovered and in common use from lithic times. However, emergence of three metals: copper, tin and iron had the greatest impact on the emergence of early metallurgy as a source of metals for structural use such as manufacture of tools, implements and weapons.

3.3.1.1 *Copper ores*

It is well established that native copper was being cold-hammered, probably with intermediate annealing, to produce small objects such as arrow tips and axe heads from Neolithic times. Native copper is extremely heterogeneous and may contain a lot of gangue such as calcite, alumina, silica, magnesia. It can also be heavily oxidized. Most copper ore deposits contain small bits of native copper which may have been collected, melted in closed crucibles and cast into more homogeneous ingots for further working. Although no significant evidence has been found, it is possible that Neolithic people were also melting and casting native copper. Strong evidence of smelting copper ores began to appear in Asia Minor after 3500 BC, and seemed to have spread through the region rapidly. Most ores were different grades of oxides, but sulphide ores were also used, probably roasted at around 800°C prior to smelting to convert to oxides, although evidence has emerged showing that it was more likely they cosmelted mixtures of copper and sulphide ores in a single process (see Appendix Iii). The main copper sulphide minerals are chalcopyrite ($CuFeS_2$ 34.5%Cu) chalcocite (Cu_2S 79.8%Cu), covellite (CuS 66.5%Cu), bornite ($Cu_2S.CuS.FeS$ 63.3%Cu), malachite ($CuCO_3.Cu(OH)_2$ 57.7%Cu), azurite ($2CuCO_3 \cdot Cu(OH)_2$ 55.1%Cu), cuprite (Cu_2O 88.8%Cu). Other copper ores include oxidized copper ore, gossan (CuO often enriched with iron hydroxide, limonite), copper-arsenic-antimony sulphides: fahlerz $(CuFe)_{12}$ $(AsSb)_4S_{13}$), or solid solutions of tetrahydrite $(CuFe)_{12}Sb_4S_{13}$), and tennantite $(CuFe)_{12}As_4S_{13}$). The best ores for smelting are cuprite and chalcocite. The green and blue copper ores (malachite and azurite) were used as cosmetics by the Egyptians as early as 6000 BC.

Most natural copper ores are sulphides but chemical composition can change due to weathering. Several types or copper ores can be found in the same deposit depending on depth (Figure 3.4). Copper sulphide in the surface layers is oxidized to form various miner-

56 Early metallurgy in Nigeria

als including copper oxides, sulphates, carbonates (when limestone is present). Native copper may also be present in the outermost layers. Some of these compounds (sulphides of copper, arsenic, antimony) are water soluble and get leached, sinking into lower layers and precipitating to form richer ores. At the lowest levels where reducing conditions prevail, copper ores are mainly in the form of sulphides. This may explain why artifacts dated to the Copper Age had very variable compositions.

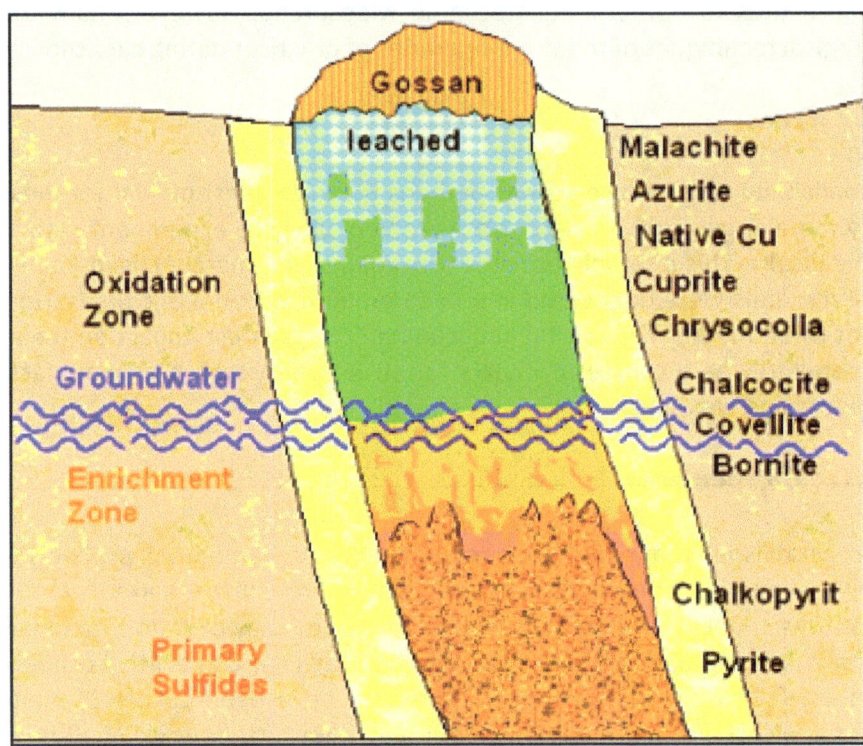

Figure 3.4   Distribution of copper ores *(Pernicka/Weisgerber 2001)*

3.3.1.2 Tin ores

The only evidence of tin smelting and use in lithic times was in ritualistic context, and the metal did not become important until the Copper Age, when it was realized that even small quantities in copper improved work-hardenability significantly. This probably made copper ore deposits containing tin (or arsenic or both) very popular. However, very few such deposits contain enough tin required for true tin bronze (7-10%). Tin is hardly used by itself, except perhaps in corrosion-resistant tin plating of steel for food packaging, but it is a valuable alloying element. Apart from use in making bronzes from copper, tin is also alloyed with lead (usually 60:40) in solders, and in the manufacture of transparent, electrically conducting films for optoelectronic applications. Tin occurs in nature mainly as oxide (cassiterite or SnO_2), but there are also small deposits of complex sulphides. The best cassiterite deposits contain only 1% or less of tin oxide, and there are less than ten known significant deposits in the world. It is estimated that, at the current rate of exploitation, the world could run out of tin ores in 20-40 years but secondary sources from recycling are becoming increasingly important. The relative rarity of tin ores is the main reason for the late arrival of the Full Bronze Age in some places and regions. The earliest widespread use of bronzes and displacement of copper occurred in places and regions such as England and South America which had tin ore or tin-rich copper ore deposits. Furthermore, it stimulated a very strong and wide inter-regional trade in tin ingots, and this possibly explains why ancient Asia Minor (Anatolia region) that had no significant tin deposits was where the Full Bronze Age was first established.

3.3.1.3 *Iron ores*

Meteoric iron (native iron from space meteorites) was in common use by the lithic people, forged to make simple tools and implements. However, the nickel content which varies from about 10% to 26% makes cold-working difficult. Furthermore, meteorites are heated and heavily strained during travel in space and are very hard by the time they land on the Earth's surface. However, Neolithic people probably tried intermediate annealing or hot-forging although most objects found were probably cold-worked with intermediate and final annealing. Iron ranks fourth in abundance in the Earth's crust, and is the major constituent of the Earth's core but only those deposits that are near the surface are mined and processed for iron and steel production. Every region of the world has a wide range of ore deposits of different qualities: magnetite (Fe_3O_4, 72.4%Fe), haematite (Fe_2O_3, 69.9%Fe), goethite (FeO(OH), 62.9%Fe), limonite $FeO(OH).n(H_2O)$, 52%Fe, n=1), siderite ($FeCO_3$, 48.2%Fe). Most iron ore deposits are associated with other undesirable minerals and need to be upgraded by beneficiation or sintering before use in modern iron smelting. However, some magnetite or haematite ore deposits may contain iron greater than about 60%. These are known as natural iron ores and can be fed directly into modern blast furnaces without beneficiation, but such deposits are relatively rare. Every type of iron ore can be smelted to produce iron and would probably have been tried in early times. However, magnetite is the richest and best ore, especially because it can be upgraded by simple magnetic technologies, but the ore is relatively rare. Haematite is the next richest ore and the most common in modern iron production technologies. Because of its red colour, it has been used in ritual and funerary practice, for decorating walls and burnishing pottery across regions from the earliest times. Iron ore deposits are very widespread and have been found in virtually every country of the world. It is conceivable that the early people would have experimented with any local ore deposits in many ways, and this explains why many archaeometallurgists believe that iron technology could have been invented anywhere in the world.

3.3.2 Melting and smelting technologies

In Neolithic times, probably as early as 8000-6000 BC, native copper and meteoric iron were cold-worked to produce tools and weapons. Native copper was probably melted in bowls or crucibles heated with charcoal and the molten metal was cast into small ingots for further processing by forging or small finished cast products. However practice must have been on very small scales in view of the scarcity of native cooper and iron and difficulties in working them. The true Metal Age began when copper or iron was being produced directly by smelting ores and production and use became common.

3.3.2.1 Copper ore smelting

By 5000-4000 BC copper was being produced from ores, with or without the use of complex slags. Many copper ores contain iron oxides, or silicon dioxide or both. Ores that contained both oxides would have been relatively easy to smelt without further addition of slag since iron oxide would react with silica at high temperatures to form complex ferro-silicate slag, and smelting of the ore mixed with charcoal was probably carried out in covered, externally-heated crucibles or crucibles placed below a bed of hot charcoal which provided sufficiently reducing atmosphere for the required chemical reactions to occur. Air would have been supplied from hand bellows through clay tuyeres, or by natural draught (Figure 3.5).

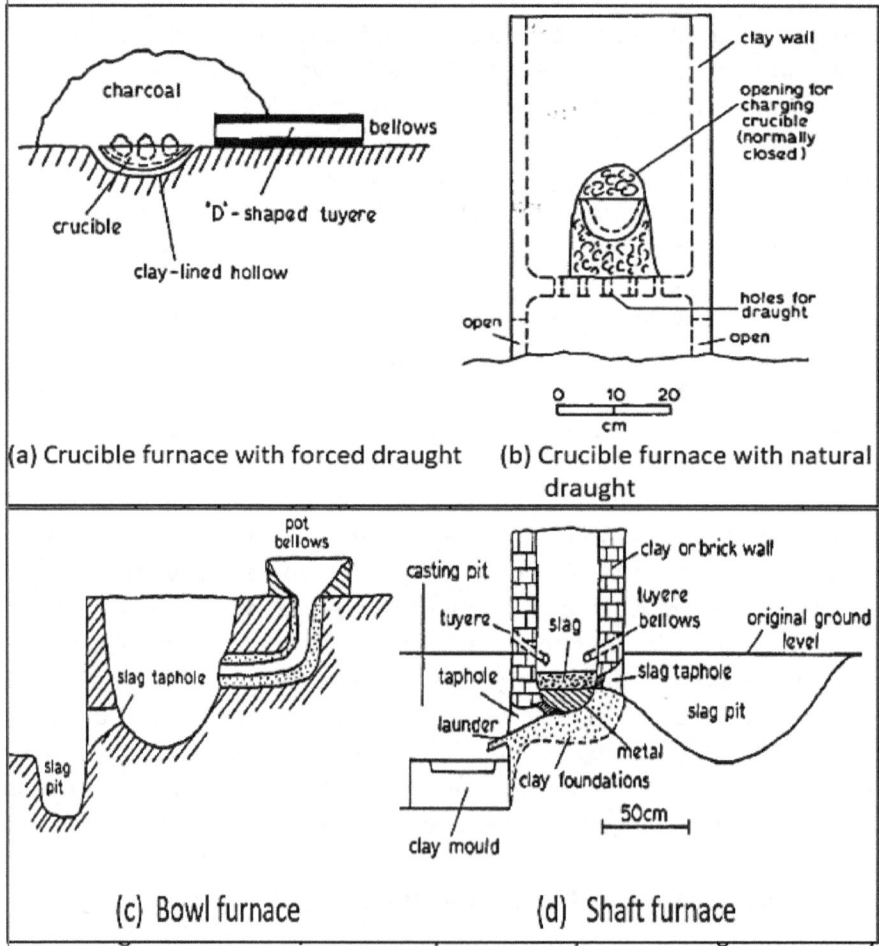

Figure 3.5 Early copper smelting furnaces *(Tylecote, 1975)*.

Some more advanced furnaces were designed to do both smelting copper ores and melting of copper ingots (Figure 3.5c). Metal was first smelted in the furnace and the top slag tapped off, the copper metal at the bottom of the pit would then be remelted with charcoal, with additions of alloying elements such as tin, or scrap copper, and the slag-free molten copper was tapped into sand or stone moulds to produce large ingots or finished objects.

While copper oxide is relatively easy to smelt, sulphides require complex roasting, a technology which may have been mastered in the Copper Age although, as discussed earlier, they may have avoided roasting and the well-known problems by cosmelting mixed oxide and sulphide ores in a single stage. The designs of furnaces and crucibles also show that the early smelters knew how to create oxidizing or reducing atmospheres, and the power of carbon as a reducing agent. While there may be some doubt as to whether alloying elements found in copper and early bronzes were deliberate or incidental, detailed analysis of bronzes dated to 4000-3500 BC show that copper and tin ores were mixed deliberately to obtain the desired alloy properties. It is also clear that the producers knew the positive effect of higher tin content on work-hardening: some objects contained around 7% tin (standard bronze), while the tin content of others was as high as 10%, especially for products like axe heads and spears.

3.3.2.2 *Iron ore smelting*

Pure iron melts at 1538°C and this kind of temperature could not be achieved in any furnace until the 19th century AD. In effect, all early iron (wrought iron) was produced in the solid state by chemically reducing iron ore in the solid state with carbon monoxide produced from hot charcoal at around 1100°C. The reduced iron (sponge iron or bloom) which was a mixture of nearly pure solid iron, slag and pieces of unburnt charcoal was then removed and hot-forged to expel molten slag, weld the iron into a coherent mass, while the retained slag of about 2% formed fibrous inclusions in the product. In some cases, the bloom was broken up by hammering and the small pieces of iron which were visually distinguishable, were separated and welded up into larger pieces by heating them in a smith's fire, followed by hot hammering. Wrought iron contains less than 0.1% carbon, it is tough, malleable, ductile, corrosion-resistant, and easily weldable. Wrought iron began to replace bronze in Asia Minor in the 2nd millennium BC and the technology quickly spread to other regions. As discussed earlier, wrought iron dominated early metallurgy for almost two millennia, but there were some significant innovations, with the development of molten cast iron around 600 BC by the Chinese, *wootz* process for small-scale steelmaking by the Indians around the same time, and the *puddling* process for producing wrought iron from cast iron in 1784 AD. The invention of mass-scale steelmaking processes led to replacement of wrought iron by steel for structural purposes, and, by the 20th century, the use of wrought iron had become principally decorative.

The earliest iron furnaces were probably just holes in the ground filled with charcoal and fitted with a tuyere through which air was blown (Figure 3.6). Mixtures of ore and charcoal were charged in layers into a clay dome above the hot charcoal fire. At the end of the process, the clay superstructure was broken up to recover the bloom and the furnace was cleaned out. over time, a wide range of furnace designs emerged. Most excavated early furnaces were either bowls or shafts or clay cylinders of diameter around one meter, probably up to 2 meters high, enough to create sufficiently reducing atmosphere (Figure 3.6). Most furnaces used in Early Iron Age were non-slag tapping, probably because there were no deliberate additions of slagging ores. However, slag-tapping furnaces became common towards the end of the first millennium BC because the Chinese-type furnaces (blast furnace) with powerful blast now made it possible to produce liquid cast iron. Details of the Chinese cast iron technology are scanty and it is unclear whether pig iron was first

60 *Early metallurgy in Nigeria*

produced, then refined into cast iron, or the ore:fuel ratio was adjusted to produce the required refining in-situ in one process. The blast furnace technology has remained virtually unchanged for almost three thousand years, except in terms of scale and minor innovations such as preheating the blast, introducing supplementary fuels in the blast such as coke breeze, natural gas, coke oven gas. Modern blast furnaces only produce pig iron for further refining since the operating conditions facilitate maximum dissolution of carbon and silicon in the molten iron and typical furnace geometry and size preclude and significant refining to produce cast iron or steel.

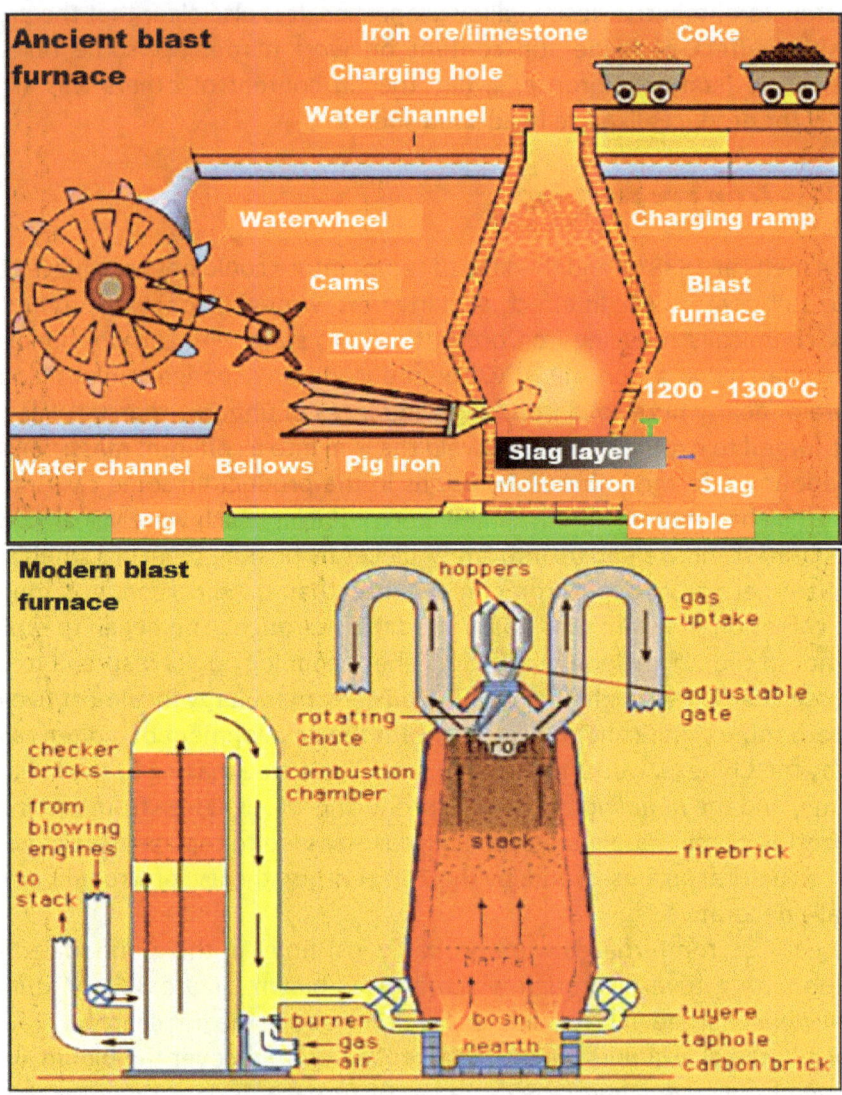

Figure 3.6   Ancient and modern iron blast furnaces *(bbc.co.uk;*

3.3.3 Shaping of metals

The common statement, 'necessity is the mother of invention' typifies the evolution of materials development over time. The early man needed to hunt, hence developed a method of shaping wood into spears, bows and arrows. Soon a stronger tip was needed and a way was found to grinding stone as tips for the wooden weapons. As discussed earlier, there is evidence that native iron obtained from meteorites was also shaped to form tools and weapon tips (see Figures 2.2 & 2.3). With the advent of the Copper Age, native copper became available and was shaped by heating and forging. Perhaps by accident, forest fires melted copper ores, solidified pools were found to be stronger and more malleable than native copper. Soon, copper ores were being smelted in little ceramic furnaces heated with charcoal, and cast into bars and finished objects. The bars were reheated and shaped into a wide range of tools and articles (Figure 3.7).

Figure 3.7   Ancient tools and weapons *(historical.ha.com)*

Again, probably by accident, copper ores containing zinc ore or cassiterite were melted and the products (brass and bronze) were found to have superior properties to native copper. It is not clear how the pre-historic man learnt that quenching hot worked metal or cooling it slowly (heat treatment) can change the properties dramatically. In effect, all the major modern materials shaping technologies - grinding, casting, forging and annealing - date back to pre-historic times. The early man even knew about composites, combining wood and stone; copper and bronze, in implements, tools and weapons and mixing straw with mud (ceramic) to strengthen walls of huts.

3.3.3.1 *Grinding and forging*

In pre-historic times hard stones were used to chip off and shape wood, and grind weaker stones and meteoric iron to make tools and weapons. Available evidence shows that most forging was carried out in cold state but it is possible that hot forging was also practiced by the lithic people. When metals became available, hot forging was introduced and metals heated in coal or husk-fired kilns were shaped into complex tools and implements. Cold and hot forging with intermediate annealing, quenching and tempering were also carried out to obtain desired mechanical properties. The techniques of working and decorating were well developed, including sinking (shaping bowls by blows on the inside of the vessel), or raising (applying blows from the outside) using special hammers and anvils, with the bowl seated in a hard die or mould. Objects were decorated by working patterns on them through hammering and chiseling. There is extensive evidence that the early people had a good working knowledge of localized hardening which they used extensively on arrow and spear tips and on axe and sword blades. Forges also had grinding stones for producing or removing sharp edges. This kind of forge is still in operation in many developing countries today.

3.3.3.2 *Casting Technology*

Casting probably developed in pre-historic times when clay was made into complex shapes by pouring clay slurry into pre-shaped wooden molds, producing intricate human and animal figures, now commonly referred to as *terracotta*. When metals and melting technology became readily available, molten metal was poured into clay molds, producing intricate artifacts and tools. Casting technologies grew in many ways through centuries, and had reached a high degree of technical skill by the Late Bronze Age, including the use of moulds of stone and bronze, and the use of cores for casting socketed objects, as well as the use of multi-piece moulds and multi-stage technologies for the casting of very large objects. Perhaps the greatest milestone of the Bronze Age was the introduction of *lost-wax casting* also known as *cire perdue* or *investment casting* technology in silver, gold and bronze casting. The method of metal casting involves the pouring of a molten metal into a mold that has been created by means of a wax model, thereby producing precision and fine-detailed castings (See Appendix II).The technology is still practiced in the production of fine jewelry, artifacts and complex industrial components. Lost wax casting is complex and requires considerable skill to produce quality products, although modern industrial processes are now largely automated. The origin of the process is unknown but it is believed to have come from Asia or Mesopotamia. There is ample evidence of widespread practice in ancient Indian, Chinese and Egyptian civilizations, and in Mesopotamia by the fourth millennium BC. An object believed to have been produced by the technology and dated around 2000 BC has been found in the Indus valley of South Asia (Thoury *et al*. 2016) and other objects dated 4500-3500 BC have been found in ancient Middle East. However, the technology did not spread to Europe until the 18th century AD. It is a high precision process (of the order of ± 0.05 millimeter per millimeter) capable of reproducing the finest details with exceptional accuracy, often with little or no need for finishing (Figure 3.8).

Despite its origins in antiquity and early restriction to the production of artifacts, the lost-wax casting process has survived and emerged as a modern metallurgical manufacturing technique (now called investment casting) for producing technical components which are usually very difficult or impossible to machine or shape at ordinary temperatures. For such products, lost-wax casting is often the only option. High-technology components being produced by this process include intricate automobile components (for example, the carburetor and aluminium alloy engine cylinder heads of the modern automobile are produced by lost-wax/investment casting). Other products include high-precision aircraft jet engine impellers, gas turbine blades and many aero-space and precision engineering components which would otherwise have required expensive machining. Lost-wax casting is also used to duplicate metal sculptures, and produce precious metal jewelry, dental crowns and inlays. One unique feature of the lost wax process is the tremendous scope for experimentation with and substitution of sub-technologies and materials. These include split mould, single mould, waste/lost mould, use of tallow, resin , textile for wax. In effect, irrespective of the provenance of the technology, early casters needed considerable skill and knack for innovation and improvisation to produce fine castings by this technique.

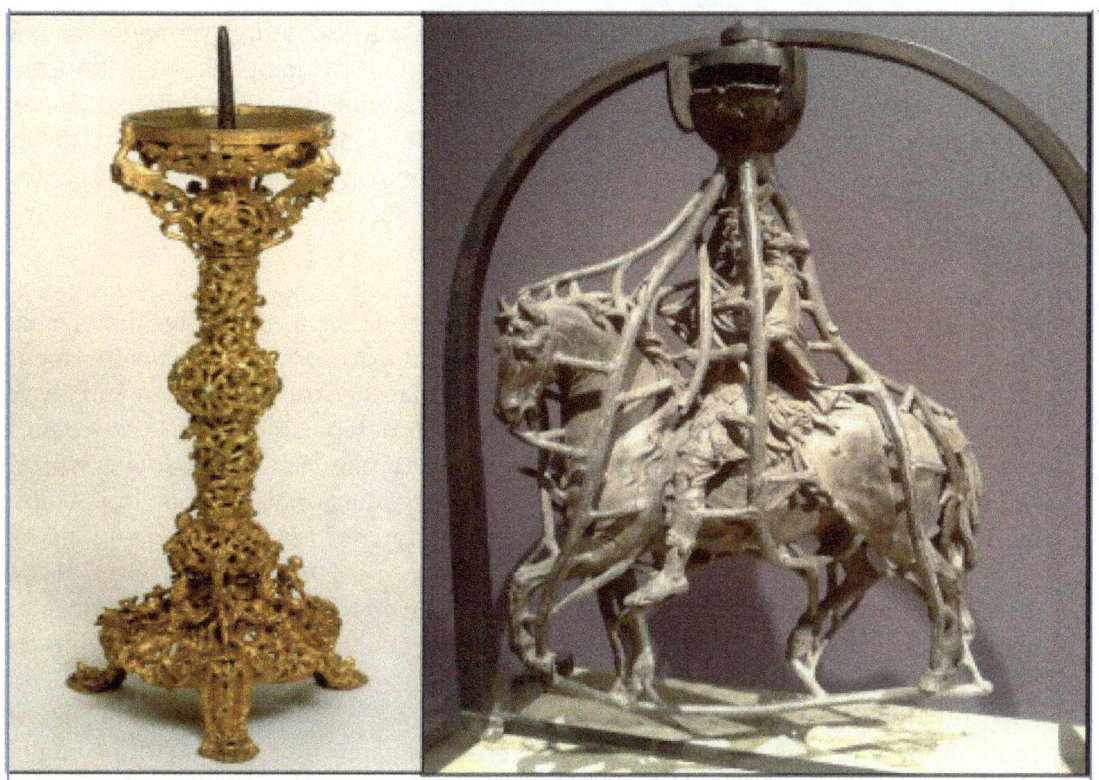

Figure 3.8 Products of ancient lost-wax (*cire perdue*) casting, 11th to 14th century AD. *(V & A Museum//frenchsculpture.org,*

3.3.3.3 *Metal drawing*

Wire was a prominent feature of neolithic artifacts, confirming that the art of drawing bars into wire, was widespread. Many of the designs were very intricate and the wire must have been heat-treated after drawing to have been able to twist them. Since the wires were smooth it is unlikely that they were forged. The wires which were mostly copper were probably cold-drawn through round holes drilled in iron blocks presumably with intermediate heat treatment, and since they were ductile they must have been annealed after drawing. Modern wire drawing is similar, except that dies have become much more complex and are arranged in series, and a wide variety of metals are drawn cold or hot. Furthermore, while the early people worked with copper and brass, modern drawing plants also process a wide range of ferrous and non-ferrous alloys.

3.3.3.4 Joining and Welding

Rope was the main method of joining two pieces of materials together in Pre-historic Period but, by the early Bronze Age, the technique of riveting had become common. Other joining processes which emerged in the Bronze Age were soldering (primarily for jewelry and artifacts) and pressure welding by hammering two lap joints. Early in the Iron Age people were joining pieces of iron by heating and hammering (forge-welding). Soldering, riveting and forge-welding have emerged as modern joining processes but the other modern processes such as gas and arc welding were not invented until the 19th century.

3.3.3.5 Heat treatment of metals

It was well known in the Neolithic Period that heat could be used to alter the mechanical properties of metals significantly. It is probable that hot worked metals were quenched simply to cool them rapidly but it was soon found that the strength and workability of the quenched metal differed from those of the original material. The difference would have been particularly dramatic in the case of arsenical or antimoniacal copper which probably had significant second-phase precipitation and segregation, or high carbon iron which was probably saturated with carbon, one of the most potent hardening elements. In effect, quench-hardening was probably the first established heat treatment process. However, metallurgical analysis of archaeological artifacts showed that the effect of slow cooling on malleability of metals was also well known, hence annealing was also widely practiced. From the early part of the Iron Age, smiths had learnt the techniques of carburizing, quench-hardening, annealing, tempering, spheroidizing, iron to obtain high quality tools. Tools and weapons have been found that were case-carburized on the cutting edges and then quenched and homogenized. These processes are vital tools in modern industrial manufacturing.

Chapter 4

Metals technology provenance theories

4.1 INTRODUCTION

There is a preponderance of intelligent speculations about the origin of various metals technologies, based largely on the earliest dates of archaeological metal objects and artifacts found in different areas. However, it has so far not been possible to identify with certainty any of the sources. Many metals and materials technologies of today have been practiced from very early times and in different cultures at different times, notably melting, ore smelting, forging, shaping, grinding, drawing, casting, welding, heat treatment, and there is no consensus on the provenance of any of them. It is possible and even probable that many archaeological sites which are older than those found so far remain undiscovered. However, there is strong archaeological and archaeometallurgical evidence that the most important technologies - copper, brass, bronze, iron, casting, lost-wax founding, heat treatment technologies - emerged from the ancient Middle East which also hosted the world's earliest civilizations. The evolution of early metallurgy began with the smelting of copper ores to produce pure copper, probably in Anatolia or Iran around 6000 BC or even earlier but did not spread even in the region for around a thousand years. By around the fourth millennium BC, use of copper containing some arsenic or tin had become common across the ancient Middle East. There is no evidence that the alloying was deliberate, arsenic and tin are present in many copper ores and this probably explains their presence in early copper products, although not in sufficient quantities to make much difference to the properties of copper, especially in terms of malleability. Eventually the early metallurgists understood the potential of deliberately alloying copper with arsenic or tin to improve malleability, and ultimately in sufficient proportions to produce bronze which dominated the world for the next three millennia before the use of iron became common. These technologies were apparently confined to the region for millennia before spreading to other regions of Asia, Europe and Africa. There are many theories ranging from local invention to diffusion (spread through wars and trade) about how these technologies were acquired in different places at different times and the most prominent are discussed in this chapter.

4.2 EARLY METALLURGY AND CULTURE

Technology is socially constructed, embedded and mediated, and must be considered in the local context of cultural and scientific attributes, as evident in the regional diversities, that characterized early metallurgy. Many factors: ecological, cultural, environmental, dominant occupations largely determine the capacity of a society to acquire and nurture metals technologies, or indeed any technology. Trade is a particularly strong medium for acquiring and spreading technologies and linking resource-poor and resource-rich societies. Socio-cultural dynamics vary across communities and influence the capacity to absorb and utilize technologies. Usually, there is already some degree of social stratification in potentially recipient societies, but arrival of metal technologies in early societies helped to promote further social stratification. Many societies that acquired metal culture were satisfied with the status quo, with little change, and this explains why some societies particularly in Africa are still practicing early metallurgy today. One of the reasons why early iron technology did not spread quickly in some parts of Europe was reluctance to demote bronze which had become a metal of social prestige, used to adorn buildings and for burial rituals (Kristiansen, 2005). Many foreign cultures also treated iron with reverence and the metal was reserved for worship, burial rituals or special gifts to royalty. It is also significant that Near East which is reputed as the source of many metal technologies lost it all for inexplicable reasons. On the contrary, others, particularly in Europe were able to develop a conducive environment that promoted an early disappearance of ancient metallurgy and moved the region to the Industrial Revolution period that changed the world. In effect, archaeometallurgy of a society or community should be evaluated in the context of anthropological and ethnoarchaeological dimensions which had a great influence on domestic innovation and unique stylistic features of products.

Metals occupied a prime position in most societies of the early world, associated mostly with royalty, the rich, and rituals. Copper alloys, in particular, bronze were very expensive to produce and only the prosperous could afford them. Many of the archaeological ceremonial and ornamental metal objects have been found in graves of prominent members of the early societies - emperors, rulers, etc. When Iron technologies arrived in Africa, they spread very quickly and the metal was being produced on a large scale in many ancient locations. It did not take long for them to appreciate the transformational powers of iron in warfare, agriculture, and rituals. In fact, in many African societies, iron was elevated to the status of a god to be worshipped and iron workers occupied prime positions often of similar ranks as kings. They were believed to have supernatural powers and could kill or heal spiritually. Although iron products dated around 3000 years have been found in some African locations, it is unclear whether they were produced locally or imported since no significant evidence of smelting has been found in some of the locations. The prime importance of metals in African cultures became prominent from about 1400 AD. Ethno-archaeological reconstructions of many early metal cultures in the region show very strong conceptual associations. Bronze became a valuable metal for modeling important symbols of faith and authority, leading to strong bronze cultures in places like the Yoruba and Benin kingdoms. Iron technology became a strong social asset that facilitated the growth several powerful centralized kingdoms in different parts of the continent. It facilitated the fabrication of tools that greatly enhanced extensive systematized agriculture and efficient hunting. It also provided material for the production of weapons needed to defend and expand kingdoms. Iron also inspired a wide range of spiritual beliefs in many cultures all over Africa. Most Nigerian kingdoms shared spiritual beliefs concerning the attributes of iron and ironworking methods, leading to the emergence of the god of iron (ogun in Yoruba culture) as a powerful deity to be worshipped, revered and feared. Iron forges became centers for rituals such as taking oaths and invoking supernatural powers, and ironworkers were respected, feared and highly valuable members of their societies. Iron metallurgy in many cultures across West Africa and several other sub-regional groups was governed by the procreative paradigm which associated the god of iron with procreation. Forges were considered to be female, and the act of smelting iron was equated to the gestation period. Thus the male smith was often considered the "husband of the forge." Although women were involved in many aspects of the iron smelting process, they were excluded from the forge. This perceived link between the god of iron and procreativity was expressed in many ways including furnace design and decoration, and taboos such as rules against the presence of menstruating women or engagement of iron smelters and smiths in sexual relations during the smelt (Ross, 2002).

Iron still occupies a special place in most Nigerian, and indeed African cultures: it is a powerful deity to be worshipped; it can be invoked to rectify problems or settle scores, and iron smiths had high and powerful societal status, many becoming rulers. Most indigenous societies had (and many still have) special festivals for the celebration of 'god of iron.' For these reasons, there are many rules and taboos, for example, women are not allowed anywhere near the rituals which are carried out at night, and iron works are seldom located near residential areas, in some early cultures, they were cited well away from settlements like farms. Iron working was highly ritualized and shrouded in mystique, and supernatural forces were often solicited to participate in and supervise the production process (see Njoku, 1991). Also, some communities remained dedicated to their established methods in spite of the emergence of better procedures for fear of arousing the anger of their ancestral spirits. There is historical and ethnoarchaeological evidence that in some African societies the smelting of iron was perceived as equivalent to the human reproductive system. The furnace was perceived as a woman, and furnaces have been found that were shaped as a woman or adorned with the image of a woman complete with breasts, and the bellows were modeled as male genitalia; the iron forming in the furnace was the fetus, and its male attendants were simultaneously husbands and midwives (Childs, 1991; Herbert, 1994; Schmidt 1997, 2009). In many cultures, men who worked in iron production were prohibited from sexual intercourse for the duration of the smelt and were frequently isolated in smelting camps to ensure compliance. One long-standing issue in African iron metallurgy has been the strict separation of living quarters and smelting sites, the latter being associated with witchcraft, or requiring special protection from uninitiated people; a separation reinforced by rituals and taboos. However, recent research has uncovered a much closer association of living and smelting spaces in some parts of Southern Africa, indicating that such taboos were not universally valid Chirikure *et al.* 2014).

4.3 METALS TECHNOLOGY PROVENANCE THEORIES

Provenance of a metal technology in an early culture means identification of the source from which the ancient craftsmen acquired their skills and possibly relating ancient sites and objects to potential ore sources and regions. This has become one of the most contentious issues among archaeologists who rely on scanty information often derived from archaeological objects or sites. Invariably, there are many more unknowns than known in archaeology and this explains why hypotheses on provenance are always largely speculative and subject to continuous revision in the light of new evidence. Archaeologists rely heavily on comparative dates of early objects or metal smelting sites found in different locations and regions, but this implies that all possible sites in all regions have been located. For example, the Copper/Bronze Culture is widely believed to have originated from Anatolia region in the Near East but, for over a hundred years, many archaeologists have disputed this hypothesis on the basis of the fact that no copper or tin deposits had been found in the region. However, recent excavations have located several local deposits that could have supplied tin-rich copper ores to the Anatolia craftsmen. The reality is that determination of provenance is a lot more complex than is often assumed.

Archaeologists, archaeohistorians, archaeoethnographers, and archaeometallurgists, all have theories and hypotheses on the probable source of metals technology found in any location. Perhaps the oldest provenance theory is the *diffusionist theory* which assumes the emergence of metals technologies from a single ancient source and subsequently spread to other regions by diffusion. The theory suggests a prime role for metals technologies in the cultural development of regions, and competence was indeed a central factor in the development of the earliest civilizations. Metal tools were developed which improved agriculture, led to a rapid population increase and social complexity considered the earliest stage in the development of civilization, and promoted the emergence of elites who controlled production and trade. At the same time, the increasing demand for metallurgical products was a driving force that encouraged the inventiveness and innovations among the craftsmen. The Near East has been the prime focus as the cradle of early metallurgy for centuries, due largely to excavations in Anatolia, Mesopotamia and Egypt where the oldest copper artifacts were found, dated to the earliest stages of the development of complex societies. Diffusion from the region radiated both metallurgy and civilizing impetus to other regions of the early world. However, this theory is being contested in view of discovery in the last few decades of evidences of copper smelting in areas isolated from one another and the practice of metallurgy in the areas did not appear to have had any significant social and cultural impact in the areas (Amzallag, 2009).

The *localizationist theory* postulates a polyphyletic origin of metallurgical technologies in view of the fact that pre-historic societies already had competence in melting native copper in crucibles and casting into objects, and the emergence of copper smelting from ore could have been a logical progression which could have occurred independently in many areas and regions. Furthermore, many smelting sites have been discovered in many regions in the last five decades or so which had significant features of autonomous development (Wenke, 1991; Rothman, 2004). The numerous theories on the provenance of metallurgical technologies appear to have crystallized into two: *diffusion* and *local invention*. While there is ample evidence to support either theory, both appear to ignore the critical potential of innovation, and extensive literature reviewed for this work suggests a feasible third theory: *diffusion-innovation* which is what really propels the proliferation of metal culture.

4.3.1 Techniques for determination of provenance

Rapid developments in archaeometallurgy have provided new tools for detailed evaluation of ancient artifacts and sites. It is now possible to identify and interpret scientific data on metal objects, metalworking structures and waste products such as slags, crucibles and moulds; it is possible to determine the nature and scale of mining, smelting and metalworking, the economy of a site, the nature of occupation, the technological capabilities of its occupants, and their cultural affinities. Archeometallurgy also facilitates the reconstruction of the nature of technologies used in the past as well as their social and economic impact. However, although many new techniques have now emerged that can help clarify provenance issues such as smelting-ore source linkages, similarities in practices across regions, there is still no way of precisely identifying the source of an early metals technology in any region, or indeed the source of the ores smelted. For example, elemental analysis of an object can help identify potential ore sources but this is usually carried out by non-destructive surface analysis using X-ray fluorescence (XRF) techniques. The result does not necessarily represent the whole object due to the effects of segregation, patination and corrosion. Also, lead isotope analysis (LI) which uses the unique properties of lead to characterize ores by comparing isotope abundance ratios is more useful in determining that an ore could *not* have been the source of a metal object, since ore deposits that formed at the same geological time in different locations might have similar ranges of lead abundance ratios. However, consideration of the geography and geochemistry of a specific area can help to positively match the LI ratios of a metal artifact with the LI ratio of a potentially relevant ore deposit (Radivojevic *et al.*, 2019) .

Two tools are particularly important in archaeometallurgical studies of innovation: the types and unique features of furnaces, crucibles and other containers found, all of which give useful information on whether a metal was being melted or smelted from ore; and the nature and chemistry of the slags and other residues found locally. Slags are used as flushing media in the smelting of metal ores, by mixing relatively low melting, low-density, high-fluidity compounds with the ore. The choice of the slagging material also depends on the nature of the associated gangue to be removed from the ore. For example, gangue that is acidic in nature would require a basic slag and vice versa. The gangue dissolves in the flux on melting and floats on top of the heavier molten metal, it is either decanted, leaving the molten metal in the pot or the molten metal tapped from underneath. The latter method of removal is more popular because the molten slag serves as a protection layer against atmospheric oxidation during tapping. The molten metal is cast into objects which are removed from site while the slag is left behind at the working site. This flushing process called *slagging* became common in the Roman Empire times from about 30 BC and has emerged as a prominent component of the modern metallurgical smelting process. The type of smelting unit, the prevailing operating conditions (whether the atmosphere in the unit is oxidizing or reducing), and the method of slag removal greatly influence the morphology and chemical composition of the residual slag. Slagging is also used in refining processes such as conversion of pig iron into steel in open-hearth, converter or electric furnaces. Different furnace types, working conditions and processes result in different types of slag, different composition patterns, and different chemistry and morphologies. Archaeometallurgical slag is usually weather-resistant and well-preserved, and analysis of residual slags has been a powerful tool in determining the types of ores smelted, furnaces and processes used in early metals technologies. It also gives a wealth of information on the technological process adopted. However, while the presence of slag on an archaeological site strongly indicates local metal production, it says little about the source of technology, but it can give a wealth of information about local innovations when local practice is compared with findings in other regions.

4.3.2 Diffusion theory

Diffusion theory simply implies the importation of metals technology as opposed to local invention, and there is little doubt that diffusion played a key role in spreading early metallurgy technologies all over the world but it seemed to have taken a very long time for several reasons. If indeed copper technology had been invented in Anatolia in sixth to fifth millennium BC, it did not seem to have reached Egypt close by for over a thousand years. As will be explained later, the discovery may have been accidental, arising from the melting of oxidized native copper in small, externally-heated crucibles to produce hammer heads, daggers, axes, arrow heads, etc. The same types of crucibles were used for over a thousand years in smelting copper ore. They were small crucibles often no more than 15-20 cm

72 Early metallurgy in Nigeria

diameter and 5-15 cm deep, packed with ore and charcoal. Such a setup would have produced only a few grams of copper per batch and this probably explains why the metal was considered very valuable and reserved for very special applications such as the earliest copper artifacts found in the area which comprised small items of jewelry and artifacts. It is possible or even probable that the technology was a closely guarded secret and, considering that around a hundred kilograms of ore would have needed to be processed in several hundred small batches to obtain one kilogram of copper (copper ores typically contain 0.2-2% copper). Even when the technology eventually reached Egypt, use seemed to have been very restricted and most of the earliest copper objects were found in connection with royalty or in ritualistic or funerary context. As discussed in the last chapter, many copper ore deposits are stratified, with oxides and the upper layers and arsenic-rich sulphides in the middle layers. It would have been relatively easy to smelt the copper oxide ores but the sulphide ores would have needed to be roasted at around 800°C before smelting. It is doubtful if the early smelters were aware of and practiced this complex technology as has been suggested by some archaeometallurgists (see Tylecote, 1980; Zwicker *et al.*, 1985; Rapp, 1989). More recent studies and laboratory experiments have shown that it is possible to cosmelt copper oxide mixed copper oxide-sulpharsenide or iron sulpharsenide ores in crucibles or furnaces (Lechtman *et al.*, 1999). The cosmelting experiments yielded coherent copper–arsenic alloy ingots over a wide range of oxide: sulpharsenide ore mixtures. Crucible/furnace charges containing ratios of between 2:1 and 4:1 oxide:sulpharsenide mineral produced clean metal, fully separated from slag or matte byproducts (see Appendix III). The sulphide ores were not roasted prior to smelting and no flux was added to the charges. As the early smelters exhausted the upper layers of a stratified copper ore deposit, they were likely left with no option but to smelt the middle layers which were rich in sulpharsenide ores, and this probably explains why the Late Copper/Early Bronze Ages were dominated by arsenical copper alloys. All the above developments are believed to have originated in the Ancient Middle East and diffused to other regions (Figure 4.1).

Figure 4.1 Probable origin of copper and iron technologies

A technological invention always starts from somewhere but then gets transferred and proliferated by diffusion as a result of wars, trade, migrations, all of which were prominent features of early civilizations. This theory is supported by the fact that many early metal technologies which were widespread in a particular area and in a particular time were probably not local inventions because they were being practiced earlier in many other areas of the early world. For example the origin of the *lost wax process* which was very widely practiced in many areas of the world at periods separated by thousands of years is unknown and the process technology was probably spread across all regions of the world by diffusion. The diffusion theory is also supported by the fact that the sequential progression from pure copper through pure copper-arsenal copper-bronze-iron was repeated in many different places at times sometimes separated by over 2000 years (Tylecote, 1997). Diffusion requires a transport medium which could have been trade or through wars and conquests, and they were all prominent features of early civilizations.

Diffusion of invention from a source requires a fairly well-established and proliferated local practice as well as a vehicle or medium to spread, and it is usually through cultural ties, trade, or conquests. Diffusion through cultural contacts can be slow and restricted but trade can quickly spread inventions across regions. It is generally agreed that trade was the major vehicle of proliferation of metals technologies across the early world. Although different technologies were probably incubating in different parts of the old world, some possibly simultaneously in several different locations, it was the emergence of intra- and inter-regional trade that propelled the growth of early metallurgy. From about 4000 BC trade among Eurasian communities flourished and silk, horses, weapons, precious stones and many other commodities were traded along connecting routes about 10,000 kilometers long. This route network also known as the Steppe Route is believed to have developed into the famous Silk Road (Route) around 2000 years later (Figure 4.2).

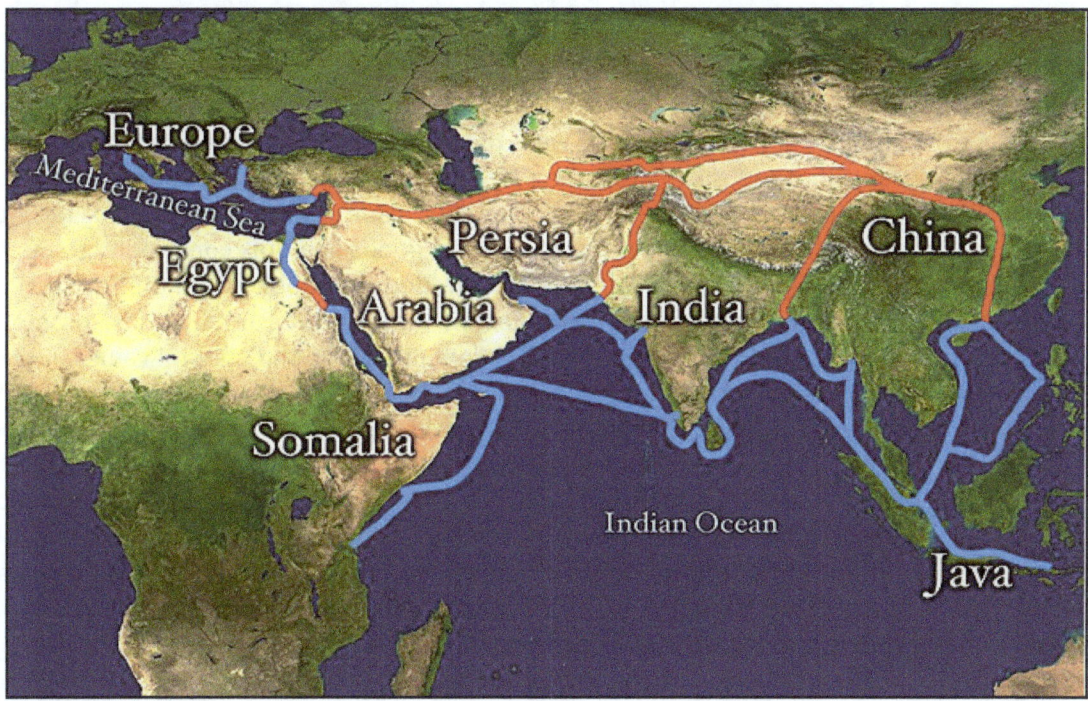

Figure 4.2a The Silk Route *(google.com)*

74   Early metallurgy in Nigeria

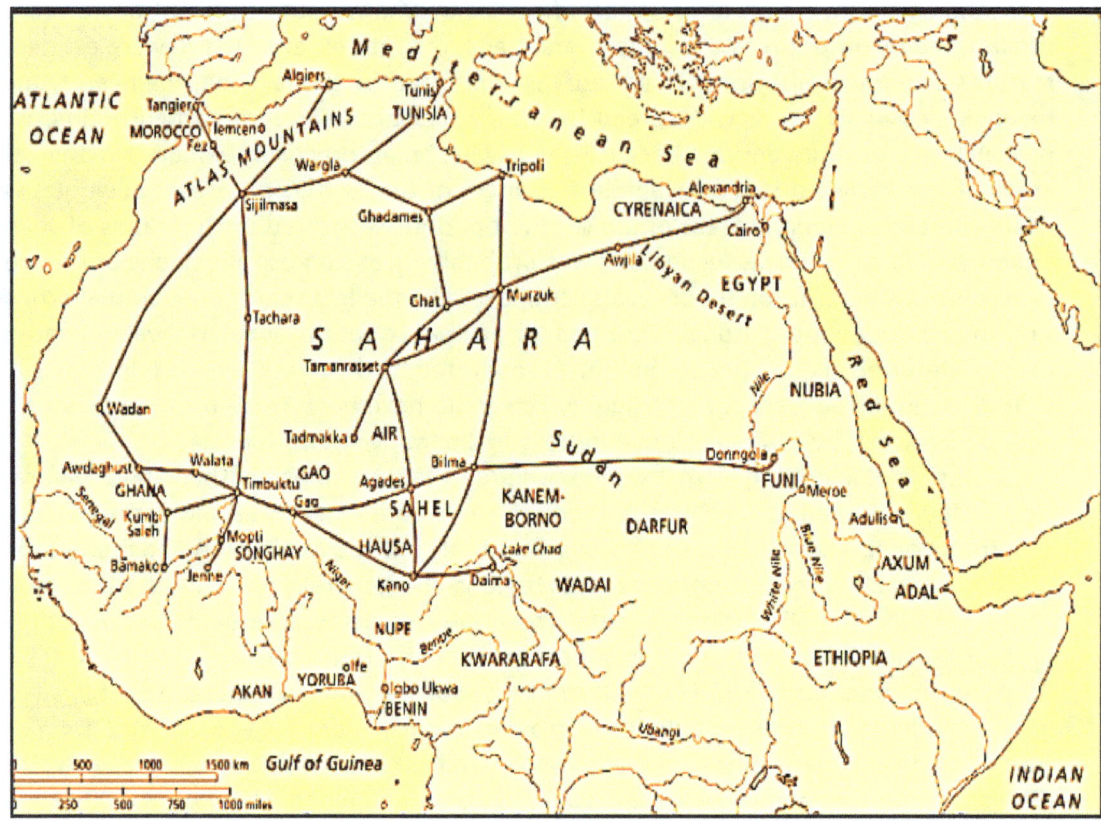

Figure 4.2b Medieval Trans-Saharan Trade Route *(google.com)*

The Silk Road extended beyond Eurasia, connecting societies across regions from the East to the West, in Asia, Mediterranean, Europe, Africa, and South America, exchanging goods and disseminating technologies and innovations, especially in iron and bronze technologies. Camels and horse-driven caravans were the major terrestrial transportation systems, but marine transportation is known to have been practiced in Asia, the Arabian Peninsula, and North Africa between 4000-3000 BC. Maritime trade connected many coastal cities across regions and facilitated bulk transportation of goods and bulk commodity trade. The Silk Road (which derived its name from the most traded commodity from the Far East) was one of the first trade routes to join the Eastern and the Western worlds, promoting cross-cultural interaction and exposure to different life-styles and cultural values. It was a network of terrestrial and maritime routes which developed in the second millennium BC, connecting Asia with most other regions of the world. Apart from promoting interregional trade, the Silk Road played a significant role in the development of civilizations across the old world, opening up long-distance economic, political, cultural and religious relations between the civilizations. Although silk was the major commodity traded between China and the rest of the world, other goods such as spices, jewelry, artifacts, metal ingots and finished products, were traded as well. The trade route network in the Middle East was particularly strong, connecting the major early metallurgy centers: Mesopotamia, Anatolia, Egypt, with Asia and the rest of the world and several other routes connected different parts of the world. including South America. A transportation network of concrete-paved highways was built by the Roman Empire around 300 BC, connecting the Mediterranean world and Europe.

The Sahara Desert was once a fertile region: evidence dating to 7000 BC and as late as 3500-2500 BC shows that farming and animal breeding flourished in several areas of Northern Africa, and this must have been an attraction to foreign traders, in particular, from the Mediterranean, possibly from prehistoric times (Shillington, 1989). It is possible also that the trade route came down through Africa until the hostile Sahara Desert emerged. Even then, strong trade with communities in the sub-Saharan region flourished again from about 300 AD, with the use of caravans of camels (Figure 4.2b). The average size per caravan was 1000 camels and some caravans were as large as 12,000 (Rouge, 2007) Because of the danger of crossing the Sahara, trade was restricted to precious goods, but the route now known as the Trans-Saharan Trade Route remained active, facilitated the spread of Islamic culture and religion to the rest of Africa. Initially trade was mainly in sub-Saharan African gold from places like Ghana in exchange for salt but it soon expanded to slave trade from about the 10th century AD.

Copper and tin ingots featured very prominently in early intra- and inter-regional trade largely because ore deposits were relatively scarce. While iron ore deposits are found in many locations in all regions of the world, only a few copper ore deposits occur in a region, and significant deposits of tin ores (cassiterite) have been found in less than ten locations in the world. In spite of the well-known superiority of bronze over copper, the rarity of tin, a vital component restricted proliferation for more than two millennia, and the True Bronze Age only took off in communities that had no ore deposits when they gained access to tin and copper ingots through trade. Tin deposits are usually associated with certain types of granite mainly as cassiterite (SnO_2) and occur in a few well known locations in the world such as Britain, Malaya, China, Bolivia, Saxony-Bohemia and Nigeria, and these were believed to have been the main sources of tin in the early world. However, it is possible that there were many more alluvial or mined tin deposits that had been worked at early times and closed. For example, contrary to the earlier belief that Near East was devoid of tin ores, small tin deposits have recently been found in Egypt, Turkey, although they are of comparatively low grade. One of the deposits also contains copper ore in the deeper layers, and many similar deposits may have been exploited in Iran, Iraq or Turkey in view of archaeological evidence found in the Turkish mine at Kestel and dated at fourth to third millennium BC.

Most copper ores have low copper content, often as low as a few percent and hardly ever higher than about 30%. Tin ores are even poorer, usually as low as 0.2%. Even in modern times, ores this poor are considered workable if there are sufficient quantities in a location, and tin ores containing more than 1% Sn before dressing are considered high grade. In modern practice, the ores are upgraded by beneficiation before transportation to customers but in early times, the ores would have been smelted on site and cast into ingots with over 90% metal content. This explains why several ship wrecks carrying hundreds of copper and tin ingots dated to the second millennium BC have been found off the coast of Turkey (ancient Anatolia) and elsewhere (Bass *et al.* 1961, 1967, 1984). It may also explain why evidence of extensive smelting activities have been found in places like Niger, Sudan and Nok, Nigeria without proliferation of local use. The True Bronze Age in which high-tin bronze alloys contained the standard 7-10% tin is believed to have arrived in Sumer, Persia after 3000 BC, based on the earliest archaeological discoveries. This period coincides with the ability of the region to trade with other regions over considerable distances. It is possible, even probable that the Sumerians were already smelting local low-tin/low-copper ores and making small items wherever they came from before settling in the Mediterranean area around 3500 BC, which also coincided with the emergence of strong intra- and intra-regional trade links believed to have been promoted by the Phoenicians. There is substantial evidence that trade was certainly coming through the straights of Hormuz up the Persian Golf to supply the needs of the cities of Mesopotamia and Anatolia by around 2500 BC. The rise of empires, caliphates, intra and inter-regional conflicts disrupted the Silk Route many times over three thousand years before it finally collapsed in early 18th century AD.

4.3.3 Polyphyletic/Local invention theory

Some archaeologists believe that many technological innovations and developments in materials and metallurgy were local inventions in view of the unique styles and characteristics attributable to their products. This is feasible or even probable when the inputs were locally available. The main problem with this theory is that technologies have been found to flourish in areas where the input ingredients were not available. For example, bronze culture flourished in many areas which had no known deposits of copper or tin or both. However, it is possible that many early mining sites have not yet been discovered or semi-finished ingots were imported and re-melted for local use. Iron technologies may have been local inventions in many places considering that iron ore deposits were widespread, in particular the sulphide types which are relatively easy to smelt. Once people mastered copper/bronze technologies (although this is not a prerequisite), it would not have been difficult to experiment with iron ores: it would have been only a matter of raising temperatures by another hundred degrees centigrade or so to effect solid-state reduction of iron ore by charcoal. In any case, iron oxides were commonly used as fluxes in copper and bronze smelting and, as has been discussed earlier, iron may have been produced accidentally from the process. There are two possible circumstances in which metals technologies may have been local inventions and these are discussed briefly below.

4.3.3.1 *Accidental discovery hypothesis*

The accidental discovery hypothesis arises from the possibility of producing nearly pure copper accidentally in the process of hot forging or melting native copper. There is substantial evidence that Neolithic people were working native copper and iron to make small tools and implements. No evidence of hot forging has been found but it is likely that they would have tried it since they had access to fire. If small pieces of native copper (which can be heavily oxidized) were heated under a heap of charcoal, with air supplied from powerful hand bellows, it is possible that a sufficiently high temperature may have been achieved in a moderately reducing atmosphere to cause release of carbon monoxide that would have reduced the oxidized copper and produced nearly pure copper. Evidence of melting of native copper around this period has also been found in several regions of the early world, probably carried out in externally heated closed crucibles, considering the large number of crucibles found in the vicinity of smelting sites. The reducing atmosphere would have been much better in such situations and more of nearly pure copper than expected could have been produced. Communities that had access to copper ore deposits being exploited already for cosmetic use and which were probably also the sources of native copper pieces would have been encouraged to try melting copper oxide ore as well. As discussed in the last chapter, copper deposits are usually stratified, with oxide in the uppermost layers and rich sulphide in the lower layers. The upper layers are usually very low in copper content, associated with ferrous oxide and silica, which will react to form complex ferrosilicate slag that floats on top of almost pure copper. Sulphide ores which are usually found in the lower layers of copper ore deposits would have needed pre-roasting at about 600°C prior to smelting which may have been discovered through experimentation or, as discussed earlier, they cosmelted mixtures of copper oxide and copper sulphide ores without prior roasting.

Bronze could also have been discovered by accident, and this could have happened independently in many areas. Many copper ores contain some tin which could account for tin content as high as 2-3% in the finished product, enough to make a significant improvement in the workability and strength of copper, but too low for bronze. This explains why many copper artifacts found were erroneously classified as bronzes. A minimum of 7-8% tin in copper is required to be classified as bronze. However, a few well-known tin deposits, like those in Cornwall, Britain and Saxony contain tin as well. A copper ore containing around 12% copper and 0.92% tin, when smelted will give a copper:tin ratio of 93:7, high enough to be classified as bronze and any attempt to work the product would have quickly revealed the superiority of bronze over copper in terms of workability and mechanical properties. Similar low-tin/low-copper ore deposits may have been exploited elsewhere, including Ancient Middle East. The earliest bronzes have been found in the early city-states of Mesopotamia dated 3000-2500 BC, probably made from imports of copper from Anatolia and tin from elsewhere. Interestingly, Anatolia itself appeared to have arrived at the Bronze Age much later in 2200-1900 BC.

It is well known that most early people who had access to any native metal or mineral ore usually experimented and found some use for the ore. Knowledge on global mineral ore deposits is still severely limited because vast areas of the world remain unexplored. Furthermore, many deposits considered too poor or uneconomical today would probably have been exploited in early times. Evidence is emerging that widely held views about locations of copper and tin deposits in the early civilization may require an upward review in view of the fact that some areas that were thought to be devoid of deposits may in fact have had access to small deposits which were exploited and are now unknown. This is supported by recent discoveries in Asia Minor and elsewhere of small copper and tin ore mines that had evidently been worked from the fourth millennium BC and closed. Maybe there are several other similar copper deposits rich in tin elsewhere in the world that could have led to accidental, independent invention of bronze in places other than Anatolia, especially as evidence is emerging of deposits of lean tin ores and copper ores containing tin in several locations in Ancient Middle East (Yener, 1989). The fact that evidence of use of low-tin copper alloys has been found in nearly all early civilizations of the world also suggests that deposits of these types of ores may have been much more common than previously thought. Furthermore, many copper ores contain both tin and arsenic and, since the effect of both elements on the mechanical properties of arsenical bronzes is more or less additive, a copper ore that contains 1-2% tin and 1-4% arsenic would have mechanical strength and working characteristics that are close to those of standard 7% tin bronzes.

78 Early metallurgy in Nigeria

A similar accidental discovery could have happened in the case of iron, especially as iron ore deposits are much more common all over the world. As mentioned above, copper ores are usually mixed with iron oxides and silica (silicon dioxide). While most of the gangue will inter-react to form molten ferrosilicate slag, if the coal:ore ratio is high, it is possible that some of the iron oxide will be reduced to iron in the solid state by carbon monoxide and would be found as solid pieces in the molten copper. It is conceivable that the pieces or iron were gathered and consolidated into larger pieces by hot forging, and this experience would have motivated further experiments that eventually led to the invention of wrought iron. In effect, while it is generally accepted that iron technology originated from Anatolia, it could have developed independently in many other locations that had access to iron ores, before or after Anatolia, especially if they already had experience in copper ore smelting.

The arrival or iron quickly displaced bronze, not because it has superior mechanical strength and working properties but because of the relative scarcity of tin for making bronze which severely limited the scope of applications. Furthermore, working bronzes containing 8-10% tin requires a good knowledge of the complex heat treatment of bronzes, although high-tin bronzes (7-15% tin) were in common use mostly in the 'as-cast' condition in the late stages of the Bronze Age, except for localized heat treatment to improve hardness. On the other hand, iron ores are available all over the world and this made possible iron production in many areas in relatively large quantities. Furthermore, wrought iron is malleable and can be made stronger by carburization and heat treatment, hence the arrival of iron marked the beginning of the demise of the Bronze Age in many places.

4.3.3.2 Autochthonous discovery hypothesis

It is possible that Neolithic people who had access to copper deposits and were already producing glazes and paints from ores could have deliberately experimented with copper or iron ores. Copper oxide ores mixed with charcoal would have been much easier to smelt because of the relatively low temperature of copper (1085°C), possibly in an enclosed crucible or buried in a bed of hot charcoal to create a reducing atmosphere. This could have happened first in Anatolia but there is no reason to preclude its occurrence in other locations or regions around the same time or even earlier. Iron would have been more difficult because of its higher melting point (1538°C), and there is no record of achievement of this high temperature in any furnace anywhere in the world before the 15th century AD. This explains why most of the iron produced in early times was in solid state (wrought iron) which could be produced at around 1150-1200°C. Natural draught or bellows-blown forced-draught furnaces simply could not achieve the required temperature to melt iron: the earliest evidence of molten iron probably occurred in China around 600-500 BC and it was only possible because the reducing conditions in the furnace were sufficient to cause maximum dissolution of carbon in the iron, thus reducing its melting point to around 1200°C, which was achievable with the use of powerful mechanized bellows. The cast iron produced was useful for many applications but was too hard and brittle for many others. However, China was able to produce malleable wrought iron on a relatively large scale by heating molten cast iron in air for long periods to remove most of the dissolved carbon. On the other hand, India was able to increase the carbon content of wrought iron and improve its strength by carburizing in closed crucibles, thus producing the famous *wootz* (or Damascus) steel that was used for making swords and other objects exported to many parts of the world for centuries. It is possible that China acquired the technology from Asia Minor considering the strong trade links by the Silk Route, but is it also possible that it was an independent invention, especially because China appeared to have produced molten cast iron before wrought iron and evidence of a similar development of comparable dating has not been found elsewhere in the early world. The mechanized forced-draught blast furnace developed has changed very little till today, except for size and the replacement of charcoal with coke.

Experience in copper smelting would certainly have been useful in the process of invention of iron smelting but it is not a prerequisite. In fact, the only major difference between the two technologies is the significantly higher melting temperature of iron. While a 2-meter high cylindrical furnace with manual forced-draught or natural draught through several tuyeres would have sufficed for copper smelting, simulated laboratory experiments indicate that a temperature as high as 1220°C needed to melt iron would have been very difficult if not impossible to achieve. China did it by developing water-driven powerful blowers and modern blast furnaces use electric blowers and coke to achieve the typical temperatures of around 1250 °C. It is possible however that temperatures of early copper smelting furnaces were boosted to around 1150°C, high enough to induce solid-state reduction of iron oxide and produce wrought iron, by manually blowing through several tuyeres, and evidence of furnaces with multiple manual bellows have been found in excavations. In effect, people with no experience in copper metallurgy but with access to iron ore deposits could have invented the technology inadvertently especially if they were already building ovens for firing clay and terracotta works and smelting ores for decorative use. It should be noted that only a relatively small part of the ancient civilization has been fully investigated and there may be many sites yet to be discovered. This explains why theories and hypotheses in archaeology are being reviewed regularly as a result of new evidence.

4.3.4 Diffusion-Innovation theory

A third theory is a combination of the above two theories and appears the most probable in many situations. The fact that artifacts are found in a location is no evidence of local production because they could have been imported. Many processes were learnt through diffusion but there needs to be a sustainable critical mass of local interest, evidence of domestication of the technology, and infusion of local innovations to the extent that the development becomes largely indigenized. Also, the socio-cultural setting has to be appropriate to stimulate invention or acquisition, hosting, domestication and proliferation of metal technologies. For example, the Romans were known to have invented very little but they were experts in acquisition, adaptation management, domestication of existing technological developments acquired through wars and trade, and infusion of innovations to the extent that history often credits them with the invention. Iron technology did not emerge in China and India until around 600 BC, probably from Asia Minor, yet the region is credited with the first production of liquid cast iron, invention of the iron blast furnace, as well as low-carbon steel. Europe did not invent iron technology, in fact, it only became widespread in the region between 800 and 500 BC, many hundred years after the Asia Minor, yet Europe is largely responsible for the enormous infusion of innovations that propelled iron and steel to its prime role today as the metal of choice for structural applications. Henry Ford did not invent the automobile, but he succeeded in moving it from an exclusive preserve of the wealthy to an everyday utility. In effect, the source of a metals technology, or indeed any technology is largely irrelevant and inconsequential: *it is the extent of domestic infusion of innovations that really matters.*

4.4 EARLY METALLURGY: BETWEEN INVENTIONS AND INNOVATIONS

Humans are believed to have inhabited the Earth for at least 3.5 million years, based on dating of archaeological findings, and the use of materials (stone, flint) dates back to the same period. The evolution of metallurgy has been an extremely slow process, probably starting from the Neolithic Period some 12000 to 10000 years ago. The stone-copper-bronze-iron technology transformation process has been so slow (around 8000 years) that any attempt to trace the origin of any of the technologies would be largely speculative. A lot of useful energy is expended on efforts to determine who invented what and when, and this has been a source of controversy in the archaeological world. Most of the early inventions in metallurgy probably evolved from a combination of intuition, observation and experimentation. Even in modern history of technology, few inventions can be considered original: most of the initial ideas came from somewhere else. For example, the invention of electricity by Thomas Edison in the late 19th century was inspired by the work of physicists and earlier inventors dating back several hundred years. Nikola Tesla invented the alternating current but he never succeeded in exploiting this life-changing invention, it was the infusion of innovations by Edison that propelled the invention to its current status as global standard for household and industrial electric power. Laslo Biro invented the ball point pen in 1938 but he failed to commercialize the invention; it was Milton Reynolds who developed the invention to the point that it changed the world of writing. The Wright Brothers did not invent the aircraft, (in fact they drew from the work of around a dozen scientists and inventors) but their innovative and monumental contribution made possible the first manned, powered flight in 1903, the humble beginning of the modern aircraft industry. In essence, invention is relatively unimportant compared with the ability to innovate. The impact of an invention tends to be minimal and localized unless innovation takes it to a level of development that attracts mass interest, and this is why inventions of metal technologies incubated for thousands of years before spreading, and why thousands of patented inventions remain undeveloped. The same applies in historical metallurgy: virtually all major inventions - copper, bronze, iron technologies - have been attributed to the early Middle East, based on dating of the earliest objects. The people of this region had advanced civilizations and were prolific traders from very early times and it is not unlikely that some of the ideas may have originated from observations of inconsequential practices elsewhere. However, they were also prolific innovators in terms of development and diffusion. They succeeded in infusing technologies with innovations, irrespective of the original sources and diffusing the products over long distances.

Current techniques for dating archaeological objects are very imprecise and subject to substantial errors: radiocarbon dating of charcoal has been found to be capable of giving erroneous results, especially charcoals (old wood) found in a site may be much older than the objects being dated, and therefore generate a chronology that is considerably older than the actual metalworking objects and operations. Also, radiocarbon C_{14} dating has been found to be more precise than C_{12}. and earlier dates are being revised. Furthermore, thermoluminescence dating can be erroneous when the ceramic object is vitrified. It is not surprising therefore that earlier dates determined for the Nok culture have recently been back-dated by about 500 years. In effect, dates quoted for any archaeological site or object should be regarded as tentative and treated with caution. In any case, while anthropologists, archaeologists, archaeohistorians place a lot of emphasis on dates, they are of little importance in archaeometallurgy compared with the technical and innovative features.

Recent findings in archaeometallurgy are providing new material evidence showing that metallurgical technologies may have been practiced earlier elsewhere but on small scale, possibly just for local use. On the contrary, the trade culture of the early Middle East must have provided a major motivation for innovation and scale-up. Asia has also played a major role in early development of metallurgical technologies, but all material evidences indicate that the ideas came through trade with the early Asia Minor around 600 BC, but this does not detract from the monumental innovative achievements of the region: China was the first to design and operate a blast furnace successfully to produce molten cast iron, India pioneered production of steel by carburizing ductile wrought iron, and, between them, they evolved a technology for making steel by de-carburizing cast iron. For the next two thousand years, Asia sold iron weaponry and other products to the rest of the world, and these technologies that had flourished in the region from around 500 BC did not reach Europe until the late 15th century AD. Early wrought iron technology appeared in the advanced and wealthy Etruscan civilization in Italy around 750 BC. It is unclear whether it was a local invention considering the proximity to the highly mineralized Tuscan area, or it was diffusion through trade with Anatolia which is believed to have had the technology around seven centuries earlier. In any case, the technology quickly spread to other parts of Europe in view of widespread access to iron ore. However, charcoal supply remained a major limitation and the industry remained small-scale for over a millennium until coking technology emerged and charcoal was replaced by coke, an innovation which moved ferrous metallurgy from the small scale technology that persisted for two millennia to its current dominance in the world of engineering materials today. Henceforth, Europe pioneered the development of iron and steel to its current status as a prime source of primary metal to the global economy. In effect, Europe did not invent any of the three major metals technologies that currently dominate the modern engineering world: iron and steel, copper and aluminium, but the region is credited with the development of these technologies to the extent that they currently account for over 90% of the world demand for primary metals.

4.5 REVISITING DATING PRINCIPLES IN ARCHAEOMETALLURGY

Archaeometallurgists determine the arrival of a metals technology in an area or region, based on two factors: evidence of local smelting from ore; and widespread use. This hypothesis ignores the possibility that there could be substantial evidence of early local smelting activities in an area but with scanty or no evidence of local use. It is also possible that a particular metal was used widely in an area but no evidence of local smelting could be found. Archaeology is a permanently evolving subject and many new discoveries are emerging constantly that were not thought to have existed a few decades ago. In effect, there could be evidences of metal smelting or use waiting to be discovered. Furthermore, the hypothesis ignores the possibility that a metals technology could flourish in an area producing primarily for export using local skills, and such areas have been found in several regions of the early world. Perhaps it would be more appropriate to base the dating of arrival of a metal technology in an area on significant domestication of skill rather than evidence of use.

Chapter 5
Early metallurgy in Africa

5.1 INTRODUCTION

Africa is believed to be the birthplace of humankind and the region has the longest record of human habitation in the world. It is believed that the first hominins emerged 6-7 million years ago and many of the earliest anatomically modern human skulls and fossils have been found in Southern Ethiopia. The earliest stone tools and stone artifacts were found in Kenya, and Ethiopia, dated to 3.3 million years. The history of metals dates back less than ten thousand years and, unlike the well-documented evolution of metals technologies in other regions of the early world, relatively little is known about the history of metals on the continent of Africa. Another problem arises from the fact that the evolution of metallurgy in Africa did not follow the typical pattern of Copper-Bronze-Iron Age. On the contrary, most of Africa moved from the Neolithic Age of stone, flint, wood and pottery straight to the Iron Age, with the Bronze Age arriving nearly two thousand years after the Iron Age (North Africa was an exception due probably to its proximity to Anatolia). Furthermore, the metallurgical heritage of the continent has received relatively poor attention compared with the ancestral history of the world which is generally believed to have originated from the continent. While there is some documented archaeological evidence of early metals technology practice in several parts of Africa, the archaeometallurgist prefers to focus on more reliable material evidence such as comprehensive analysis of metal objects, ores, slags found on sites, furnace design, etc., all of which give vital clues to the technologies and local innovations behind the products, and this chapter will focus on such evidence. This is not to diminish the importance of substantial evidence from other sources, rather, it is an attempt to complement available information from the metallurgical viewpoint. A simple example is the confusion between the Copper and Bronze Ages which arose because the historical archaeologist is not equipped to visually recognize the difference between copper and bronze, especially when the objects are badly weathered. However, the archaeo-metallurgist has the tools to easily identify metals and this has led to the reclassification of many copper objects which were previously classified as bronze until the last century. Most were found to be arsenical coppers, and, contrary to earlier hypothesis of a Bronze Age from about 5000-4000 BC, the True/Full Bronze age arrived when the use of pure and arsenical copper began to decline around 3000 BC, and did not spread until about a thousand years later because tin was rare and expensive. The earliest widespread use of bronze was mostly in areas that had access to tin deposits, for example, Cornwall, England. Emergence in most other regions depended on access to tin, probably through import, and this probably explains the considerable overlap between Copper Age and Bronze Age in some regions.

5.2 EARLY COPPER/BRONZE AGE IN AFRICA

Archaeologists consider Africa unique in not following the recognized transition from the Bronze to the Iron Age. It is a common postulation that Africa skipped the Copper/Bronze Age and transited straight from the Stone Age to the Iron Age, ending up in the Copper/Bronze Age but there is an increasing body of evidence that disproves this theory. However, this general hypothesis may have arisen due to lack of information about the African continent, but emerging evidences show clearly that there was an Early Copper/Bronze Age in some parts of northern and sub-Saharan Africa. Furthermore, the logical transition theory is based on the assumption that iron technology is much more complex than copper/bronze technologies and societies needed to progress to iron technologies by building on the experience gained in smelting copper and bronze. However, from the metallurgical point of view, although experience in copper smelting would have been useful in transiting to iron metallurgy, it would not have been a precondition. There is little doubt that the early copper smelters would have tried smelting iron ores which were used as fluxes in copper smelting but it would have been extremely difficult to achieve the temperature needed for solid-state reduction of iron oxide in the various types of crucibles which dominated the first three millennia of the Early Copper Age (about 1150°C compared with 1085°C for copper). The transition from crucible copper smelting to bowl furnaces, crucible furnaces and, eventually to blow furnaces and induced- and forced-draught furnaces was very gradual in most regions of the early world and this would have been a major constraint to iron smelting. However, a well-designed induced- or forced-draught copper smelting furnace with the right physical dimensions could easily have achieved the desired temperature for solid-state wrought iron production. This type of furnace technology had become fairly well-established in Egypt and Buhen by the third millennium BC, and in Cyprus by the middle of the second millennium BC. Many of them featured advanced tuyere designs and multi-bellows blowing, both of which would have raised furnace temperatures significantly. Furthermore, as discussed earlier, invention of iron technology could have been accidental, occurring in the process of smelting copper ores containing iron oxide as flux, and this could have happened in Buhen or Cyprus. Since many communities in Africa had access to iron but not copper ores, they would have tried to smelt iron ores in these types of furnaces. In effect, a location like Buhen could have been the source of iron furnace technology in sub-Saharan Africa. However, this does not rule out the possibility that iron technology came to Africa by diffusion but, as will be shown later, these was substantial local innovation.

5.2.1 Copper Age in North Africa

As discussed earlier, a period in history is named after a material in a region when evidence of substantial, sustained, and widespread use of the material has been found. In archaeometallurgy, evidence of melting and smelting is the main criterion. The prevalent opinion in historical metallurgy is that Africa skipped the Copper/Bronze Age and transformed straight into the Iron Age. This is in fact not applicable to Northern Africa where there is substantial evidence of early copper smelting and use. Egypt had acquired copper technology by 2600 BC, with extensive use of arsenical copper and copper-tin alloys for tools, statures and figurines (Tylecote, 1965), and by 2000 BC, the true Bronze Age had arrived in the region. Sites of extensive exploitation of copper ore deposits have been found in Sinai. The combined arsenic and tin contents of early copper objects found in the region were no more than about 1% and must have come with the copper ore as impurities. However, true bronzes containing 7-10% tin soon began to appear. The provenance of tin is unclear but it may have come through trade from any of the well-known tin deposits in Italy, Bohemia, Saxony, Malaya, Asia or Nigeria.

Some of the earliest evidences of copper and bronze cultures have been found in Egypt. The earliest copper objects found in Egypt and dated 5000-4000 BC were evidently made from native copper, but axes made from impure smelted copper dated 3000 BC have also been found, while bronzes did not seem to have appeared and spread before 2600-2000 BC. Detailed examination of the axes showed that they had been made from copper castings hot-worked or cold-worked and annealed. Sites have also been found that showed extensive exploitation of copper-base minerals, some of them containing arsenic. Bronze objects dated to around 1800 BC have been found and the statue of Pepi I dated 2200 BC was made from sheet copper (Figure 5.1).

Figure 5.1 Statute of Pepi I made from sheet copper dated 2200 BC. *(ancient-egypt.org).*

Bronze figurines made by investment or lost-wax casting dated to around the same period have also been found (Tylecote, 1975). There is substantial evidence that Egypt set up an outpost in Buhen in 3000-2000 BC to smelt copper ores from Nubia, Sudan, which explains why crucibles and slags were also found in nearby Kerma, Sudan. Some of the objects found in the area and dated around 4000 BC were probably imported from Egypt but evidence of local smelting is dated around 2600 BC. It is probable that the copper ingots produced were traded or used in Egypt since no significant evidence of local use has been found. The proximity of Egypt to Anatolia sub-region and probable trade links with the Asia Minor may have greatly facilitated copper technology diffusion to Africa (Figure 5.2).

5.2.2 Copper Age in sub-Saharan Africa

The main reason for the widely assumed no-copper-Age Africa is that no significant evidences of copper smelting and widespread use have been found. However, it is inconceivable that Anatolia, Persian Gulf, Syria, Palestine, Egypt all had Copper Age dated 5000-2000 BC, and the technology did not reach the rest of Africa for over two thousand years in spite of the strong trade links. For over three hundred years archaeologists and archaeohistorians had made passing comments on the early existence of metals technologies in Africa,

88 *Early metallurgy in Nigeria*

based largely on speculations. It was not until the looting of Benin artifacts in 1897 that the outside world became aware of the rich metal culture of West Africa. It took the accidental discoveries of the Nok Iron Culture, Igbo-Ukwu Copper Culture and Ife Bronze Culture some four decades later to trigger systematic investigations of some archaeological sites in the region. Even then, most of the early work was by french ethnographers and anthropologists who focused on the socio-cultural aspects, based on the conviction that social forces often determine which technologies are selected and how they are applied. Perhaps the first set of systematic studies began in the late 1950s, with the work of Fagg on the Nok Culture (1959); Willet on Igbo-Ukwu and Ife Bronze Cultures (1967, 1972); Tylecote on Meroe and Nok Culture (1970, 1975); Shaw on Igbo-Ukwu Bronzes (1970). Subsequent investigations have found evidence of early metal smelting in several parts of Africa.

Although Egypt is believed to have been smelting copper ores from at least 4000-3000 BC and producing bronze from around 2600 BC, the earliest reported evidence of metal smelting in sub-Saharan Africa is from Nubia where small numbers of copper artifacts dated around 4000 BC have been found, believed to have been imported from Egypt (Childs and Killick, 1993). The Egyptian outpost in Buhen established in 2600 BC has provided extensive evidence of copper smelting (Figure 5.2b). Buhen sourced copper ores from Nubia, Sudan where early copper smelting sites dated second millennium BC have also been found. A crucible furnace for casting bronze, dated 2300-1900 BC has been found in Kerma and, although the source of the tin is still unknown, ingots may have been imported through the trade routes, or possibly from Plateau Area in North Central Nigeria. Apparently the rich gold deposits in the desert of upper Nubia had been discovered by 2700-2200 BC and were being mined and traded by the Egyptian dynasties for centuries. It is probable that copper was also being smelted in Meroe, northern Sudan from around the middle of the first millennium BC and a fully developed bronze and ironworking industry had developed in Ethiopia by the fifth century BC, believed to have diffused from Southern Arabia because of the strong stylistic affinities.

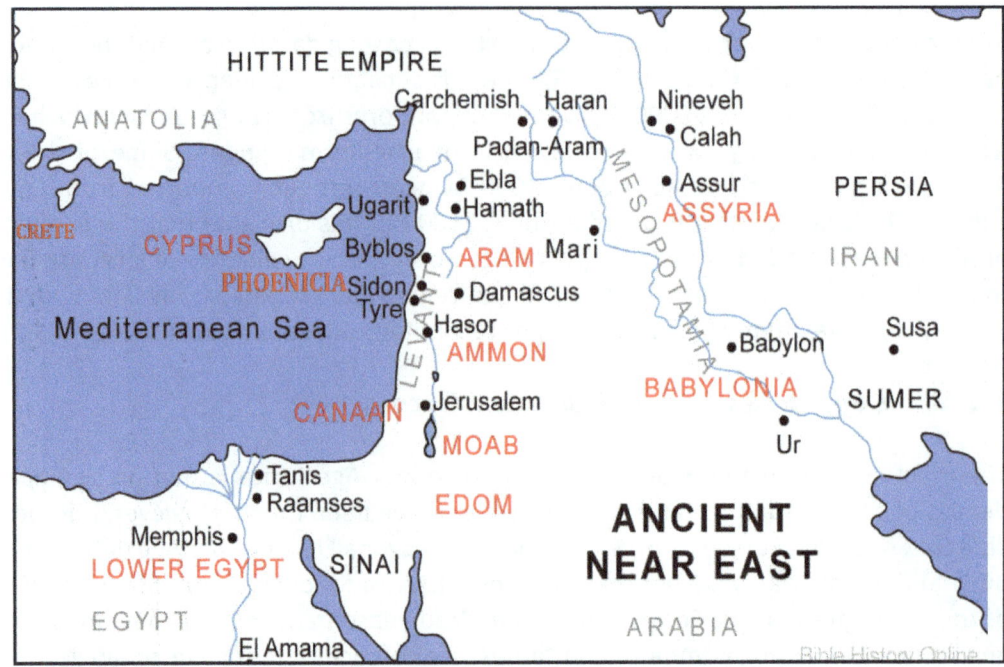

Figure 5.2a   Early Asia Minor *(bible-history.com)*.

Figure 5.2b   Nubia and Buhen in ancient Egypt
(bible-history.com; google maps)

Niger was working native copper from neolithic times and substantial evidences of copper smelting dated between 2600 BC and 100 BC have been found in several areas of the country, including heavily weathered native copper, copper slags and copper smelting shaft furnaces: in Agadez, Eghazzer Basin, and Afunfun regions of Niger (Herbert, 1973, 1984; Tylecote, 1982, 1983; Grebenart 1985, 1987, 1988; Killick et al. 1988; Childs and Killick, 1988, 1993). Niger has copper ore deposits and a link with Buhen, a copper smelting center further north would not have been difficult. It is in fact possible that the Buhen smelters also exploited the Niger ores. Several small copper mines and a smelting site have been excavated at Akjoujt, Mauritania, dated from ninth through the third centuries BC. It is difficult to imagine that copper metallurgy existed in Egypt, Buhen, Nubia, Niger, Mauritania and did not diffuse to other parts of Africa for over a thousand years in spite of the strong trade ties. The simple explanation may be that Africa's archaeological history is largely unexplored. Moving from each stage of the metallurgy evolution process was a steep learning curve in areas that did not skip any step, sometimes spanning hundreds or possibly thousands of years and archaeologists consider it inconceivable that any region especially Africa could have skipped a major step. However, evolution steps in metals technologies do not necessarily reflect increasing complexities and need not be systematic. Such factors as socio-cultural settings, availability of inputs, and timing of arrival can largely determine the speed of acquisition and domestication, and this is happening with modern technological innovations.

90 Early metallurgy in Nigeria

The rich copper deposits in Niger and tin deposits of northern Nigeria would have been an attraction to the early traders who probably introduced metals technologies to the areas (Figure 5.3). Most of early Africa was occupied by small rural farming communities which would normally not be associated with metal cultures but local people would probably have been trained to smelt ores. Most copper and tin ores have very low metal contents, (0.5-1% Sn for tin ores, as low as 2% Cu for copper ores), and it is probable that ores were smelted in the vicinity of deposits and cast into ingots with metal contents as high as 95% which were traded across regions, and substantial evidence has been found in sunken ships in most regions of the early world. This may have accounted for the fact that substantial evidence of copper smelting was found in Niger, Nubia, Mauritania but there was no evidence of widespread use. The same may be true for most other early metal sites of Africa, including the Nok Iron Culture. Also, local experimentation may have translated to local invention of metal technologies in areas which had access to ores.

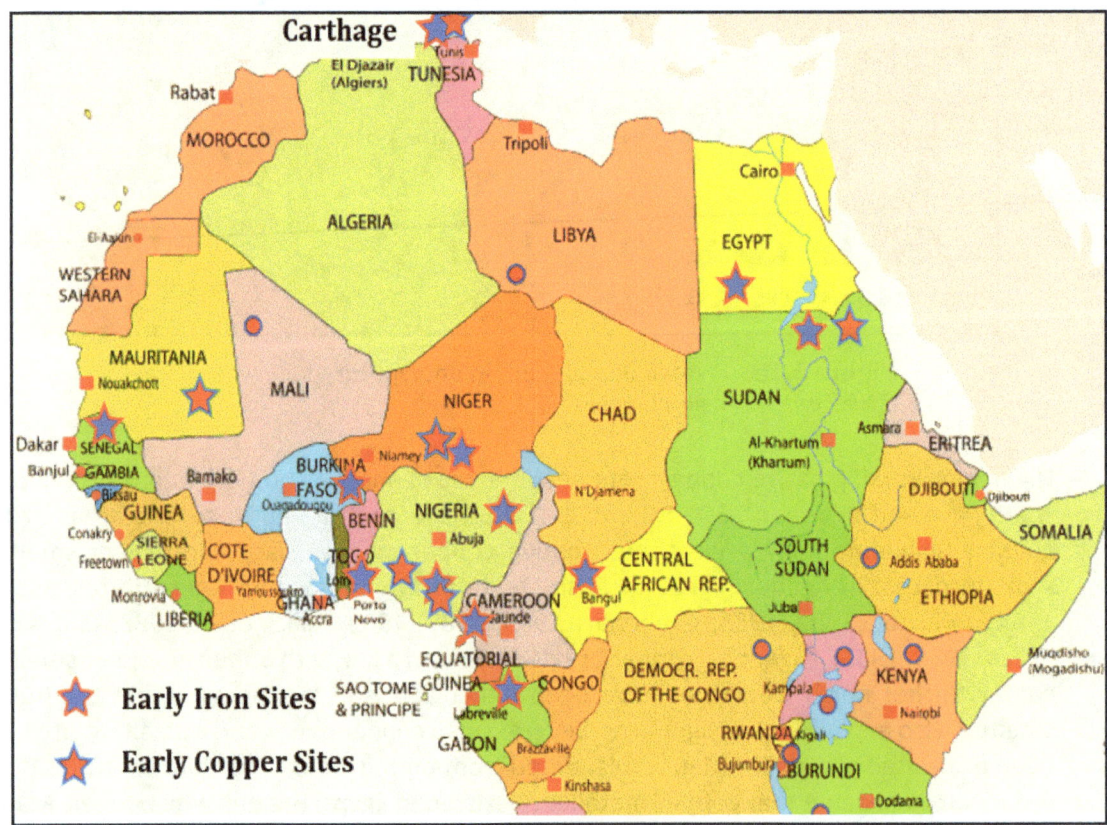

Figure 5.3   Some early African copper and iron sites

The most probable reason for the absence of Copper Culture in Africa may have been due to the slow emergence of large settlements which were prerequisites for the domestication of metals technologies, in particular, use of the products. In the early Copper Age Period (4000-2000 BC) most of Africa was occupied by small, isolated, rural farming communities that would not have been receptive to copper technologies. Even if foreign traders used their skills and labour to smelt metals, it is unlikely that the local people were aware of the potential value of their products, and were satisfied with the attractive foreign gifts they received. Also, as discussed earlier, metal technologies are expensive and, from early times, only the wealthy such as kings and rulers in socially stratified societies could afford to sponsor and promote local metal artifact or weapon production.

5.3 EARLY IRON AGE IN AFRICA

There is a lot of confusion about the sequence of arrival of the Iron Age in Africa, arising apparently from the poor access of local archaeologists to expensive dating technologies, but also because most of the previous studies have been carried out by archaeologists who rely a lot on descriptive characterization. Their findings have been complemented by the work of Tylecote (1974) which relied primarily on metallurgical analysis of early sites: furnace design, analysis of furnace linings and slags, all of which gave a lot of insight into metallurgical activities at the time, in particular, local infusion of innovations. The presentation in this section is based on reliable archaeometallurgical evidence and may not necessarily agree with some of the opinions expressed by archaeologists in recent literature about early metallurgy in Africa. Many early iron production sites have been identified in different parts of Africa, based largely on objects found. However, the discovery of an object is not a reliable indication of local production in view of the strong trade links that connected the early world. In effect, the sites discussed here are those in which substantial material evidence of iron smelting has been found and documented. Furthermore, compared with copper/bronze objects, relatively few early iron objects have been found anywhere in the world in a well-preserved state, especially when they are in plate form. The environment (soil physics/chemistry, aeration, humidity, acidity, etc.) in which the object is found largely determines the rate of degradation. In view of the fact that agriculture was the primary occupation in sub-Saharan Africa, iron would have been used mostly for farming implements which are mostly flat products (hoes and cutlasses). Such objects would probably have been discarded above ground and, even if eventually buried, would have corroded fast in the largely acidic and humid soil of the region.

The first early iron site was found accidentally at Nok, North-Central Nigeria in 1928. A terracotta figurine had been found during opencast tin mining and this led to further excavations which found many more figurines, around thirty iron furnaces, smelting slag residues and some iron objects dated around 800-400 BC in Taruga near the state capital of Abuja. Since then, many more furnaces have been found in the area and many more sites have been located in different parts of Africa (Figure 5.4). Several sites in West, East and Central Africa have also been assigned similar dates as Nok but most of the others are dated from early first millennium AD. Evidence of extensive wrought iron and bronze smelting from around the beginning of the first millennium BC to the second century BC has been found in several locations in Carthage, North Africa (Kaufman, 2016). Carthage, a trading hub of the Phoenicians also specialized in centrally organized ferrous metallurgy in centers located at the fringes of settlements such as Bir Massouda and the Byrsa Hill. Niger is known to have been smelting copper ores from the third millennium BC. If the smelters of Carthage or Niger were using iron-rich copper ores or ferruginous fluxes during copper smelting as was the practice in most other regions of the early world, it is possible that the furnace conditions were such that some of the iron oxide in the flux was reduced in the solid state, with pieces embedded in the molten copper at the bottom of the furnace. The smelters would probably have removed the iron pieces and tried to work them, and the quality of the wrought iron produced would have encouraged them to try smelting iron ores which were also abundant. This accidental invention could have occurred anywhere in the early world where copper ores were being smelted and gives credence to speculations that invention of iron technology may have occurred independently in many parts of the early world including Africa.

Evidences of iron smelting in many other African locations all dating back to around the middle of the first millennium BC or much earlier have been published in recent times: Burkina Faso, Cameroon, Central African Republic, Gabon, Togo, Senegal (Holl, 2009) (Table 5.1). However, these dates have become subjects of intensive dispute because of probable sampling errors or inadequate statistical analysis of radiocarbon dating. Around a hundred more late iron sites spread all over the region and dated post BC have also been identified (Figure 5.4). The major Early/Late Iron sites of Africa have been comprehensively reviewed recently by Chirikure (2015). Irrespective of whether iron technology came to Africa by diffusion or was a local invention, it quickly proliferated to all sub-regions of the continent. It is unknown why the technology disappeared from Nok almost without trace, but it persisted in most other sites until early 20th century. Although AD 1900 is the cut-off date of ancient metallurgy in Africa, some iron sites are still operating till today. Perhaps the most important innovations in Early Iron metallurgy that came from Africa were in the design of furnaces. The very wide varieties that have emerged have not been found anywhere else. Early iron furnaces up to around 1000 BC were non-slag tapping, cylindrical and mostly forced-draft. Very little slag was produced because most of the ores used were self-fluxing, and the amount of slag produced depended on the ore chemistry. Virtually all iron ores contain silica which reacts with iron oxide to form ferro-silicate slag but if the ore contains some limestone ($CaCO_3$), slag production could be substantial. It was only in the late Medieval period that the practice of adding limestone (calcium carbonate) as a fluxing agent emerged and if the smelters in the Late Iron Age adopted this practice, slag production may be sufficiently copious to warrant slag tapping as clearly occurred in Lejja, eastern Nigeria where large heaps of slag have been found.

Table 5.1 Early iron smelting sites in Africa.
(Extracted from Holl 2009 Early African Metallurgy; Chirikure, 2015)

COUNTRY	SITE	DATE
Niger (7 sites)		1254-577 BC
Nigeria	Taruga Nsukka-Lejja Nsukka-Opi	846 – 98 BC 545 BC-398 AD 596 BC-70 AD
Cameroon		1096BC-324 AD
Gabon		883BC-212 BC
Senegal		800-550 BC
Central African Republic		836-430 BC
Togo		800-400 BC
Burkina Faso		400 BC-AD 100
South Africa		137-569 AD
Zimbabwe		386-886 AD

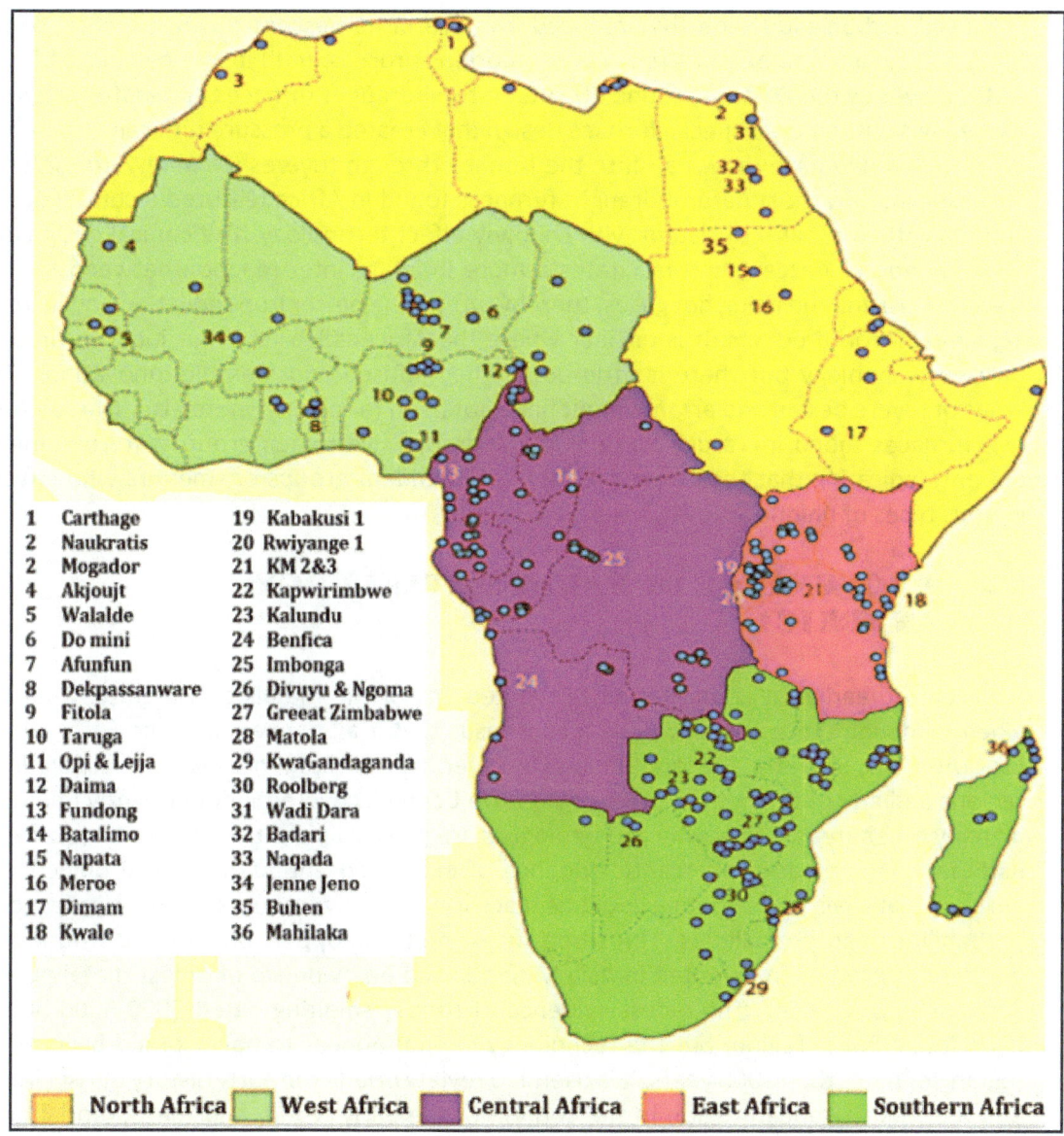

Figure 5.4 Early/Late African iron sites *(Chirikure, 2015).*

The furnaces found in Nok-Taruga were all cylindrical, non-slag tapping, and forced-draught, a strong indication that they were of the Early Iron Age, but they were in groups featuring different designs, especially in terms of tuyere size and arrangement. Most of the other furnaces found in the area which were also in groups clearly belonged to the Late Iron Age and many were of natural draught design. Even though natural draught metal furnaces associated with early metal period, in particular, Copper Age have been found elsewhere in the early world, it was Africa that quickly appreciated the relative advantages and adapted the technology to iron smelting. Most of the furnaces found in most areas of Africa, dated post AD 1000 were natural draught furnaces, some with as many as a hundred tuyeres (Tylecote, 1976). Induced-draught furnaces required manual wooden bellows to supply air (oxygen) through a tuyere or tuyeres for charcoal combustion which in turn produced carbon monoxide that reduced iron ore in its descent down the shaft of the furnace. Working the bellows was a very laborious process, until it was mechanized with water power by the Chinese around 600 BC. Natural-draught furnaces eliminated the need for bellows but required special furnace design that created a pressure difference, a driving force that would have drawn air into the furnace through tuyeres (*chimney/stack effect*). This explains why most natural-draught furnaces found in Africa featured a conical design and many tuyeres, all consistent with chimney effect technology. The conical design also slows down ore descent and facilitates a more intimate inter-reaction between the descending ore and the rising hot gases, thereby promoting better iron reduction and increasing yield of iron products. It is unclear where the Africans learnt about induced draught furnace technology but there is little doubt they infused considerable innovations. The types of tuyere design and arrangement have not been found anywhere else. The Late Iron Age furnaces found in Taruga were in many groups, with each group featuring unique designs, indicating that they were probably independent groups of smelters who infused various types of unique innovations.

5.4 PROVENANCE OF EARLY METALLURGY IN AFRICA

As discussed earlier, it is unclear who invented any of the metals of antiquity, where or when, although there appears to be a consensus that it all happened in the Early Middle East (Anatolia, Sumeria, Mesopotamia). However, all the metal ores were available in all regions and any of the technologies could have been discovered independently and used in many other areas. This is why archaeologists are careful in identifying specific sources of early metallurgy, based on scanty evidence of excavated antiquated metal objects and auxiliary materials whose dating could be inaccurate, and hypotheses are usually based on probabilities and possibilities. The three major metals: copper, bronze and iron are all believed to have been invented in Asia Minor, based on evidence of oldest metal objects and smelting activities. The oldest evidence of copper smelting dated 6000-5000 BC has been found in the region, but the technology did not appear to have spread beyond the region for more than 2000 years. It is useful to review briefly the early history of Asia Minor and the Mediterranean region in the context of the early world, and the potential of its close proximity to Africa as a source of metals technology diffusion. Examining the probable relationship between the two regions in the context of metallurgical theory may facilitate appreciation of the possibilities and probabilities of provenance of metals technologies in Africa (Figure 5.2a).

5.4.1 Anatolia (Asia Minor)

Anatolia was a pre-historic part of the current Middle East (most of which is currently occupied by Turkey) which is believed to have been occupied by some of the earliest people. A stone tool found in the region was dated to 1.2 million years ago, and homosapiens footprints believed to be about 27,000 years old found in the region proved human existence in Anatolia in this period, but it is clear that several other civilizations have occupied the region since prehistoric times. One of the world's oldest towns, Catal Huyuk emerged in the region in about 6500 BC, and recent excavations found extensive mud houses, evidence of clothes woven from wool, use of jewelry, farming, and animal husbandry. The inhabitants of Catal Huyuk wore clothes woven from wool, and jewelry made from stone, bone and shell. Also, the earliest evidence of copper smelting dated 7000–6000 BC was found in Catal Huyuk. The city was abandoned about 5000 BC for unknown reasons, possibly as a result of conflicts or due to climate change, and little was known about its existence until its discovery by Lames Mellaart in the late 1950s. However, evidence suggests that the region may have remained occupied by different people, new cities flourished, and metals culture was sustained. Evidence of copper smelting and bronze production dated about 3000-2200 BC has also been found in Troy, Crete and several other parts of Anatolia. Ancient Mesopotamia sandwiched between two rivers (Tigris and Euphrates) was very fertile land and would have attracted extensive agriculture, a fortuitous recipe for the considerable wealth and civilization that flourished in the area in the early times, both prominent drivers of metals technologies. It is unclear why Anatolia civilization, perhaps the earliest in the ancient world, collapsed but conflicts and wars may have been the primary causes. This is feasible considering that the metals technologies incubated in the region for several millennia without spreading and eventual diffusion may have been the result of migration from conflict areas.

5.4.2 Persia (Greater Iran)

Persia (modern Iran) is one of the world's oldest, continuous major civilizations, with agricultural communities in the south-western part dated 10000 BC and urban settlements dating back to 7000 BC (Xinhua, 2007). Evidences of advanced civilization include excavated 7,000-year old jars of wine, and the earliest-known clay vessels and modeled human and animal terracotta figurines. Evidence has also emerged of cultural linkage with Anatolia and Egypt, and of extensive copper smelting dated 3800 BC. Persia became a unified nation and empire in 625 BC and, over the next three centuries or so, expanded to the Balkans and North Africa. The Empire is estimated to have hosted nearly 45% of the world's population around the middle of the first millennium BC. Evidence of copper smelting (crucibles, dross, metal objects) dated 4083-3800 BC has been found in Tal I Iblis, Tepe Giyan, and Tepe Yahya, Iran, and many low tin bronze objects dated 2100-1800 BC have also been found in different parts of Persia. However, none of these bronzes contained more than about 2% tin. It was not until 1500-700 BC that true bronze with 7% or more tin content became common in Persia, apparently as a result of access to tin supply from other regions. Magan south of Iran (present day Oman) was apparently the main source of copper to the Mesopolitan civilizations. The rich copper ore deposits (around 30% Cu) had been worked from the third millennium and extensive evidence of smelting in the area has been found. Also, bronze objects containing tin as high as 13% dated around 2000 BC have been found in Tepe Giyan in North-West Persia.

5.4.3 The Egyptian Empire

The River Nile valley was home to many neolithic cultures, mostly nomadic hunters and gatherers collectively known as Egyptians and evidence of small settlements and lifestyles dated 12th to 8th millennium BC have been found along the river and around oases. However, climate changes from around the 8th millennium began to desiccate the extensive pastoral lands of North Africa, eventually forming the Sahara desert by the 25th century BC and forcing inhabitants to migrate to the Nile valley areas and form settlements, but little archaeological evidence has been found about these settlements before the 6th millennium BC when agriculture flourished and construction of large buildings began. Different cultures, starting with Amratian culture began to emerge from about the 4th millennium BC and settlements grew into villages which eventually coalesced into two blocks: Upper and Lower Egypt, eventually merging to become Egypt in about 3100 BC. Egypt grew to become perhaps the most powerful and influential civilization of the ancient world, in fact, it is widely acknowledged as the earliest major civilization in the world. Its political structure, language, religious traditions, and philosophy dominated the ancient world from the third millennium BC and, in spite of many civil wars and dynasty changes, Egypt remained a powerful and influential kingdom until it became a province of the Roman Empire in 30 BC. The earliest metal objects found in Egypt dated 5000-4000 BC were probably made by forging native copper, but evidence of metal smelting dates back to around 4000 BC when axes were being made of impure smelted copper. By 3000 BC objects made of arsenical coppers began to appear, but the full Bronze Age arrived around four centuries later (2600 BC). Bronze was used for statutes, doors, furniture components. Egypt had an outpost in Buhen which smelted copper ores from Nubia, Sudan in the third millennium BC, but ores may also have been obtained from other sources, probably from other parts of Africa.

5.4.4 The Hittite Empire

It is not clear where the Hittites came from, but it is believed they were an Indo-European group that occupied Anatolia (modern Turkey) about 2000 BC, conquering Hattusa the powerful city of the Hatti that had existed since 2500 BC. They formed several separate states before being united in 1650 BC. They were warriors and were in constant conflict with neighbouring communities: they occupied Babylon, and, by the middle of the second millennium BC, had conquered most of Anatolia and parts of Syria and Palestine, and established an empire. They challenged the supremacy of Egypt which was already an established and powerful empire; they had very formidable war arsenal which included chariots, iron armor, bronze-tipped arrows; and they are believed to be the first to weaponize iron. The Hittite empire collapsed around 1200 BC and broke into powerful Neo-Hittite city-states that were eventually absorbed into the Assyrian empire.

5.4.5 The Phoenicians

Phoenicia was an ancient civilization and part of Canaan which spread along the fertile western coastline of the Mediterranean sea. The Phoenicians who were enterprising maritime traders built several cities and developed strong trade links across the Mediterranean from 1550-300 BC, starting with Greece and spreading to most of North Africa. They traded in a very wide range of products: timber, animals, precious stones, wine, gold, silver, copper and tin ingots, etc. They were probably responsible for the eventual establishment of the Bronze Age in the region because they traded copper ingots from Cyprus, and iron ingots probably from Anatolia, Nubia and elsewhere, and tin ingots from Britain and possibly Nigeria. Apart from being excellent craftsmen, the Phoenicians were also famous for many inventions including an alphabet which the Greeks developed to the alphabet in use today. The decline of Phoenicia began with conquest by Persia in 539 BC and, over the next two hundred years or so, most of the Phoenicians migrated to their colonies, including Carthage in North Africa. It is widely believed that they could have been one of the major diffusion sources of metals technologies in Africa.

5.4.6 The Sumerians

Sumer (current southern Iraq) is the earliest known civilization in ancient southern Mesopotamia. The earliest known permanent settlements in the area are dated between 5500 and 4000 BC and archaeological evidence indicates that there were around a dozen city-states by the fourth millennium. The homes were built of mud and the cities had temples and defensive walls. The largest of them, Ukuk had around ten kilometers of defensive walls and the population around 3000 BC is believed to have been between 40,000 and 80,000. Other evidences include extensive farming and irrigation practices. In spite of the language and cultural symbiosis between the city-states, they were constantly at war with each other, and this led to many military technology innovations in the region, including bronze or iron-tipped spears, copper helmets and shields, lances, battle axes, swords, daggers metal tools, military chariots. The Sumerians are credited with the invention of bronze, wheeled vehicles, cuneiform writing, core agricultural techniques such as large-scale intensive cultivation, irrigation and mechanized agriculture, and many arithmetic and geometric principles and measurement systems that are still in use today. The Sumerians were ardent traders who built one of history's earliest trade networks over both land and sea, to access vital supplies of timber, mineral ores, precious stones which the region lacked. Trade networks were developed with Anatolia, and places as far as Afghanistan, Egypt and Ethiopia. Since the area was devoid of minerals and fuel, it is probable that the copper and bronze objects found in the area were made from imported copper and tin ingots.

5.4.7 Chad

Chad has been identified by archaeologists as one of several potential sites in Africa where humankind originated, in view of the discovery of a 6 to 7 million-year old hominid-like skull in the area (Wood, 2002). The area is believed to have been occupied on and off over the years by different people but the most recent continuous settlement in the area is estimated to have happened in the last ten thousand years or so. Pastoral farmers lived and farmed around the shores of lakes from about 5000 BC and by 3000 BC Chad had been connected by the first trans-Saharan trade route (Kuper and Kropelin, 2006) (See Figure 4.2). From around this time several prominent ethnic groups emerged and built fortified walled cities. Change in climate forced migrations to the fertile areas around the lakes in the northern central basin of the Sahara and around Lake Chad. Evidence of advanced civilization has been found on both the Chadian side and Nigerian side of the lake. Daima is perhaps the most prominent on the Nigerian side and recent archaeological excavations in the area indicate that the area has been occupied since prehistoric times but concrete evidence of settlement and advanced civilization dates to the last quarter of the second millennium BC (Graham Connah, 1976, Breunig and Rupp, 2016).

5.4.8 Nubia

Nubia is one of the earliest civilizations of ancient Africa, occupying areas along the Nile river and spreading from Aswan in Upper Egypt to Khartoum in northern Sudan. Historical records indicate that the civilization had flourished by around 2500 BC with an advanced culture known as Kerma Culture. By about 1700 BC, Kerma had emerged as a populous, formidable empire which began to challenge the supremacy of Egypt. The empire was eventually subdued and absorbed by Egypt around 1500 BC. It is believed that the Kerma people re-emerged from Egypt as an independent Kingdom of Kush located at the Sudanese and southern Egyptian Nile Valley, with the capital at Meroe around the eleventh century BC. The Kush Empire became very powerful and invaded and occupied Egypt from the 8th century BC until they were expelled about a century later. The kingdom remained powerful until the fourth century AD when it was weakened by internal strife and eventually disintegrated (Torok, 1997; Edwards, 2004).

5.5 THEORIES OF PROVENANCE OF EARLY METALLURGY IN AFRICA

It is always difficult to determine the source of early metallurgical inventions and innovations because conclusions are based on findings in a particular location. However, this does not prelude the possibility of the same event occurring independently in other places at the same time or even earlier. However, as discussed in the last chapter, the source of an invention is of little importance compared with the extent of local infusion of creativity and innovation. Global debate is extensive, intensive and sometimes acrimonious on how Africa acquired metals technologies. In most regions of the world, the Iron Age was preceded by a pyrometallurgical tradition with copper and bronze. The fact that this was absent in most of the African region has fueled an intensive debate on the competence of the region to invent iron technology without prior experience in pyrometallurgy. Ferrous metallurgy is more complicated than copper metallurgy and prior experience in the latter would definitely be beneficial to the process of acquiring iron technology, but it is not a prerequisite. The most difficult part would have been the achievement of an additional fifty to a hundred degrees centigrade or so in a copper furnace to smelt iron and, by the time the African Iron Culture was emerging, copper smelting furnaces operating within Africa had already reached such a degree of sophistication that it would not have been too difficult for African iron smelters to achieve the desired temperatures, for example, by increasing fuel:ore ratio, or by adding tuyeres, or both. Therefore it should not have been difficult for an African a society to transit straight from Neolithic to Iron Age if the socio-cultural setting was right and there were strong trade connections with other societies and cultures.

There is significant uncertainty about when or how iron technologies emerged in Africa, in particular the sub-Saharan region. Contemporary archaeologists believe that knowledge of ironmaking had arrived in northern Africa by the first millennium BC, subsequently disseminated to the south through migrations and trade. However, more recent research suggests much earlier dates, possibly as early as 15th to 13th century BC. A burial site found (probably the grave of a dignitary) in the DR Congo recently was dated 8th to 10th century BC. Objects found included iron tools and artifacts, a forged iron anvil, a pierced and richly engraved iron axe blade, iron pins that may have been components of wooden carvings, pottery, iron tools, iron and copper jewelry. Iron objects dated to a similar period have been found in Zimbabwe which included a substantial number of farming implements (hoe blades, etc.) which must have sustained prosperous agriculture in the city-state believed to have flourished in the area in the 13th to 14th century BC. Iron excavations in Compo, Cameroon have been dated 4th to 2nd century BC. It should be noted however that no significant evidence of local smelting from ore has been found in these locations and the objects could have been imported.

There are two main theories about provenance of iron technology in Africa: diffusion and local invention, and both are feasible and credible. Both autochthonous and diffusionist models arise from speculations which have equal chances of being right or wrong. A key factor in the growth and spread of metal culture is the existence of appropriate cultural setting. Throughout early world metals history, incubation and spread have been embedded in advanced, dynamic cultural settings that could have provided the capability and resources for the invention or acquisition, domestication and diffusion of early metal technologies. Access to raw materials, in particular, mineral ores from local sources or through trade would also have been crucial. There is ample evidence that copper metallurgy was widely practiced in northern Africa, possibly as early as 2500 BC and Iron Culture had appeared in northern Nigeria anywhere between 1500 and 800 BC (Figure 5.5).

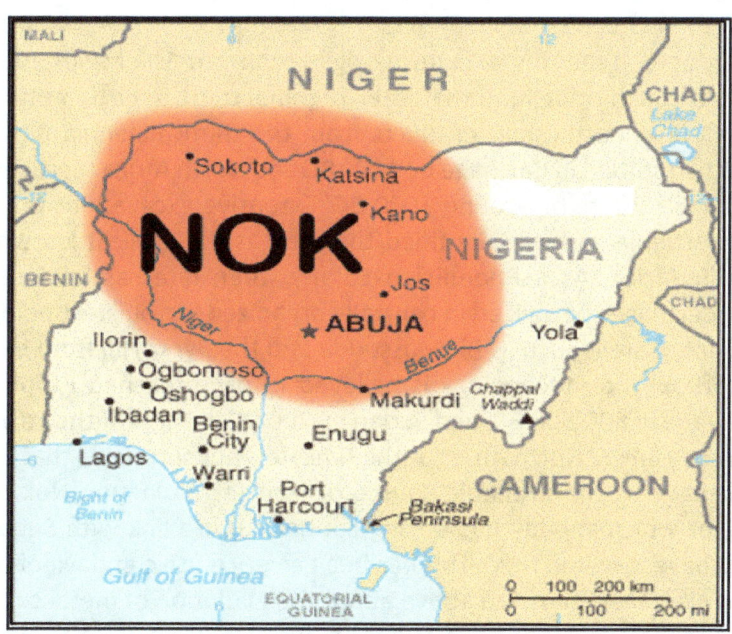

Figure 5.5 Nok Iron Culture, Nigeria *(wikipedia.org)*

One major issue with the Nok Iron Culture which makes the determination of provenance difficult is the uncertainty about the time of its appearance and disappearance. Dating of the objects found on sites in the area has been revised several times and currently places the start of the Nok Culture at around 800 BC. However, the results of a recent study suggest it could have been much earlier, around 1500 BC and may have lasted for a long as 2000 years (Breunig 2014). The circumstances and time of disappearance are just as mysterious: published dates range from 90 BC to 500 AD.

The archaeology of African continent is largely unexplored and undocumented, and it is premature to make definite conclusions about its metal culture or the provenance. Virtually all the discoveries that have been made so far were incidental. For example, Nok Iron Culture would probably be unknown today but for accidental discovery of a terracotta figurine in an opencast tin mine in the area. It is possible or even probable that many more rich sites like Nok are yet to be discovered. The peculiar socio-cultural values and practices of many African societies could also be important in locating archaeological sites. For example, iron quickly emerged as a 'god' to be worshiped in many societies and women were usually excluded from the rituals, or even moving near iron smelting and working sites. For this reason, they were often located well away from residential areas in early times. Since there has been no systematic, comprehensive archaeological study of most identified early iron cultures on the continent, many sites are probably yet to be discovered. Furthermore, ethnographic and anthropological studies are of little use when sites are 2000 years old or more, and site occupancy has probably changed many times over time. For example, the current people of Nok were totally unaware of any early metal culture until the discovery of the ancient terracotta figurines which led to further excavation that located the iron smelting sites.

5.5.1 Diffusion from Asia Minor through Carthage

It is generally agreed that metal culture originated from Asia Minor and spread to the rest of the world through trade, and that inter-regional trade in both metal ores (in particular, tin) and semi-finished/finished products from the third millennia BC was extensive. The Phoenicians had settled in Carthage by 1100 BC and North Africa (Carthage, Egypt) had been linked by the Silk Route by around 1000 BC. Extensive excavations in Carthage and other Phoenician settlements have identified the area as the earliest known center of ferrous metallurgy in Africa. As a Phoenician colony, then later as an independent imperial metropolis, Carthage specialized in centrally organized ferrous technology at the fringes of the settlement in areas such as Bir Massouda and the Byrsa Hill from before 700 to 146 BC (Niemeyer, 1999). Iron technology is believed to have reached Egypt by 700 BC, Nok in northern Nigeria in 800-500 BC, and Sudan by 200 BC. In view of the strong Silk Route trade that had already linked North Africa at the time, it is not surprising that most archaeologists identify Carthage as the probable source of iron technology in Nok, Nigeria and Sudan through Egypt which already had strong copper culture link with Sudan. Why would the Phoenicians have targeted Nok? This has been a very elusive and widely debated dilemma. However, in view the discussion above about the evolution of metal culture in North Africa and the strong regional trade links, the probable attraction was the extensive, rich alluvial tin deposit in the Plateau region which includes Nok, and, although there are no archaeological finds, there are strong reasons in support of this theory. The Bronze Age had started in Asia Minor by around 2000 BC but could not properly take off because of scarcity of tin, which quickly became a traded commodity in the Silk Route trade. As discussed earlier, copper and tin ores can be very lean and would have been smelted to nearly pure metals in the vicinity of the deposits before they were traded, and t in and bronze ingots have been recovered from ships which were sunk in the Mediterranean during the early Bronze Age. It is not unlikely that the Phoenicians established a trade link with Nok (located at the center of Nigeria's rich tin deposits), and were trading in tin ingots in exchange for salt which was very scarce in sub-Saharan Africa at the time. Some archaeologists have disputed the origin and date of emergence of iron technology in the world, claiming earlier arrival dates in North-Central Africa of between 2000 and 2500 BC, which in effect means that iron technology emerged in Africa before the rest of the world (Pringle, 2009; Zangato and Holl, 2010). Another recent publication claims that iron technology arrived in Lejja, eastern Nigeria between 2000 and 1450 BC (Eze-Uzomaka, 2009, 2010). There are many other claims about different early Iron Age locations in Africa, some dating back to third to second millennium BC (Holl, 2009). A critical appraisal of the new dates has been published recently and raises considerable doubt on the credibility of these dates (Chirikure et al., 2010). One major problem may be with radiocarbon dating which can give very spurious results without diligent sampling and proper statistical analysis. However, as discussed earlier, while who discovered what and when may be of interest in archaeology, it is inconsequential in archaeometallurgy, what is more important is what was done, how it was done, and the extent of domestication and innovations. The quality and diversity of innovations found in early African iron smelting sites have been very impressive.

The most popular diffusion theory postulates that the early iron industry penetrated into sub-Saharan Africa through North Africa to Nigeria, and through Egypt to Sudan. Iron metallurgy had been well established in Anatolian-Iranian region for more than one thousand years prior to its arrival in sub-Saharan Africa. By 1000-100 BC the technology had spread across parts of Europe, Asia and North Africa. The Phoenicians who lived in present day Lebanon and parts of Syria had acquired iron technology by around 1000 BC and spread it across the Mediterranean through their extensive trading networks that reached Carthage in North Africa. Greece was practicing iron smelting by 900 BC and probably spread it to Egypt by about 700 BC. In view of the strong Silk Route that had already linked West Africa with the north, it is highly likely that the technology spread quickly, either from Carthage or Egypt, reaching Nigeria around 400 BC. However, this hypothesis breaks down if in fact Nok Iron Culture had been in existence since around 1500 BC, which means than none of the above could have been the source.

The diffusional route of iron technology to Egypt is believed to have been along the coast of Palestine. There is ample evidence that the Philistines had mastered iron technology very early, probably by the 11th century BC, due probably to contacts with the north or migration due to the breakup of the Hittite empire. In the meantime Egypt and Galilee were still in the Bronze Age. Although various iron artifacts, tools, weapons, furnaces found in the region are dated between 1350 and 870 BC, there is no concrete archaeological evidence that the Egyptians were smelting iron before 700 BC, or were responsible for the spread of the technology to the rest of Africa. The more probable source was Carthage which had been occupied by the Phoenicians from the beginning of the first millennium BC, and who were known to have had expertise in iron technology. Sudan may have acquired iron technology around 200 BC through the Greeks, Egyptians or through Mesopotamia, Ethiopia or even Nok. Central and East Africa probably received the technology from Nigeria from around 500 AD through the migration of the Bantu tribes who also took it eventually to Southern Africa around 1000 AD.

If in fact Early Iron metallurgy originated from Anatolia, occupation by the Hittites who were warriors from about 2000 BC would have provided the propulsion needed to proliferate the technology. They established a vast empire covering most of early Near East; they would have taken over the iron technology and developed it to feed their war arsenal, and spread the technology to all the corners of their vast empire. In the meantime, the Phoenicians who were ardent traders had established a strong trade link over a wide area, from Greece to most of North Africa, with a major hub in Carthage. There is no strong evidence that they came as far as Nubia, Niger or Nigeria, but they traded extensively in copper and tin ingots, and the deposits of both ores in Niger and Nubia and tin ore in Nigeria would have been major attractions. Since both countries also have iron ores, it is possible that they trained locals to upgrade the ores near mine sites before exporting the nearly pure ingots to their widely spread customers. One potential issue with the diffusion through Carthage theory is that evidence is emerging which shows that the Nok Iron Culture may in fact predate the emergence of iron technology in Carthage. However, it is possible that the Phoenicians had already established trade links with sub-Saharan Africa while Carthage was still a trading outpost and metals technologies had not flourished.

One argument that is often used in support of diffusion is the fact that Africa could not have progressed to iron metallurgy without prior experience in copper/bronze technology. This is erroneous: as explained earlier, the only major difference between copper and bronze technologies is the temperature difference and, considering the extensive ingenuities and innovations that have been identified in many early African furnaces: like multiple tuyeres and simultaneous operation of multiple blowers, it would not have been difficult to achieve the 1150°C or so that is required for producing wrought iron especially if they had access to copper smelting shaft furnaces which had been well established since the Full Bronze Age. Furthermore, Egypt, Sudan, Niger all had long copper smelting experience dating back to second millennium BC or earlier and any of them could have moved seamlessly to iron production. Furthermore, Africa has a very long history of terracotta artworks which involved baking in ovens and furnaces, any of which could have been adapted to smelt iron ores.

It is also claimed that the type of advanced culture that could have facilitated invention of iron technology was absent in Africa. Again, this is erroneous: Egypt had perhaps the most advanced and powerful empire in the early world, and Niger has been inhabited from neolithic times. Substantial evidence indicates that the Sahara was fertile pastoral grassland (Green Sahara) that sustained extensive large settlements, animal rearing and pottery from about 7500-7000 BC. There is also evidence that northeast Niger was inhabited by a succession of Holocene societies from about the middle of the tenth millennium BC until about 3500-3000 BC, punctuated by long periods of draught. Evidence of rock paintings have been found and several archaeological sites dated to the Green Sahara period.

The Sahara desert emerged from about 2500-2000 BC and forced migration of settlements to areas around Lake Chad and oases around Air mountains in the north and Koumar north-south cliffs of north-east Niger. Koumar was particularly famous for salt and date, and featured prominently in the trade route between Carthage and Egypt which were both terminals for West African gold, ivory, salt, metal goods, beads, cloth and slaves by at least the 5th century BC. Also, large areas of Africa remain unexplored and most of what is known today emanated from the work of foreign archaeologists and many potentially interesting archaeological sites remain undiscovered. Unfortunately, African archaeologists appear to be too ill-equipped in terms of funding and analytical facilities to make a difference. Also, the intense controversy surrounding debate on the provenance of early metallurgy appears to cloud the real need for diligent, in-depth investigation of potential early metallurgy sites by local archaeologists, focusing on unique features and innovations rather than dates. It is interesting to note that, eight decades after the accidental discovery of Nok, most of what is known today about the site emanated from the work of foreign archaeologists, and the same applies to many archaeological sites in Africa.

5.5.2 Autochthonous African invention

As discussed earlier, the neolithic people were working native copper and meteoric iron to make tools and implements, and there is also some evidence that they were melting the metal, probably in closed crucibles, and casting into objects before they progressed to smelting copper ores. Native copper can be highly oxidized and attempts to melt could have led to accidental discovery of copper smelting. The melting temperature of native copper and the closed crucible could have provided a sufficiently reducing atmosphere for the oxide component and the result would have been a higher yield of almost pure copper than normally expected from native copper. Also, native copper is often found as small pebbles in copper ore deposits and, if this was the source, they would have tried copper oxide ore as well. In effect, copper technology could be a local invention in areas that were already melting and casting native copper, and there are several potential sites in Africa, Niger being perhaps the most likely because highly oxidized native copper has been found in the area.

The thermodynamics and complexity of producing pure liquid iron from its ores are formidable, much more difficult than copper ores largely because of the higher melting temperature of iron. However, all early iron technologies produced wrought iron from ores in the solid state at around 1150°C, or cast iron at about 1200°C because the temperature necessary to produce pure molten iron could not be achieved (1538°C compared with 1085°C for copper), and this persisted for around three thousand years before pure molten iron could be produced. As discussed earlier, iron metallurgy could have been discovered accidentally in the process of smelting copper ore because the ores nearly always contain iron oxide and silica. It is possible that the charcoal:ore ratio of a particular run was unusually high or blowing was powerful, which could have resulted in the extra 50-100°C or so needed to reduce iron ore in the solid state. The result would have been small pebbles of iron mixed with molten copper at the bottom of the crucible which they would probably have picked out and tried to work. They would have found the very low-carbon wrought iron much more malleable and easier to work than copper. Most copper oxide ores also contain iron oxide and silica which would inter-react to form ferrosilicate slag and the early smelters also deliberately mixed iron ores with copper ores as fluxes. In effect, both copper and iron technologies could have been accidental discoveries and could have happened independently in many locations of the early world where either or both of the ores were available.

There are many places with copper deposits in Africa where autochthonous invention of copper technology could have happened, notably Egypt, Nubia/Sudan, Carthage, Niger, Zimbabwe. Niger is the most probable because of the very long experience in working and melting native copper, some of which is found in copper ore deposits which Niger also had and were smelting from around the third millennium BC. Accidental discovery of iron technology could also have occurred in the area and the early local culture of the people was sufficiently advanced to have hosted the accidental (or deliberate) invention of both metal technologies. The same could also have happened in Nubia. The fact that evidence of wide local use of metals has not been found in either location could be because most of the areas remain unexplored, or they were producing ingots mainly for export. Iron ore is the fourth most abundant element in the Earth's crust and occurs as complex oxides, carbonates or sulphides, mixed with other minerals such as silicates and carbonates. Most communities that had deposits would have experimented with the ore especially red iron ore - haematite) in many ways, just like copper ores which were being processed and used as cosmetics from Neolithic times. Many communities in Africa have outcrops within reach and had used products for cosmetic and ritualistic purposes. Furthermore, production of oven-baked terracotta flourished in many areas from around the third millennium BC, which means they were familiar with oven technologies. It is quite possible that any of them could have tried heating iron oxides in such ovens and may have succeeded after many failures. This could have happened in Niger, Buhen or Nubia all of which were advanced cultures and already had a long experience in copper metallurgy .

5.5.3 Does provenance really matter?

Debate on whether Africa invented iron technology or acquired it by difusion has been intensive, controversial, futile and counter-productive. As discussed above, who invented what is nearly always inconsequential: it is the degree of domestication and infusion of innovations that should matter, and Africa performed excellently well. It is incontrovertible that the region introduced extensive innovations, based on the very wide varieties and unique features of furnaces, tuyeres, blowing systems, slag residues that have been found in different locations. Even furnaces found in locations a few hundred kilometers apart had very different and unique features, from small bowl furnaces of Kordofan in the Sudan and Central Africa to the large induced-draught furnace of Togoland (see Figure 6.4). Some of the induced-draught furnaces had more than a hundred tuyeres and similar technologies have not been found anywhere else in the early world. One type of furnace found in the Mandara Hills in the Nigerian Plateau had a unique feature that had not been seen anywhere else: it had a single, long tuyere which was positioned down the center of the shaft, terminating just above the hearth. Most furnaces found in Africa were non slag-tapping, rather, they had slag pits beneath the hearth. Experienced archaeologists who had worked in Africa agree that many furnaces found had unique and advanced features, and some products were of relatively high quality. Some objects found in Taruga, North-Central Nigeria showed an extraordinary degree of purity and freedom from slag. Apparently, the iron had not been produced in the usual manner by hammering iron and residual slag together at high temperature to produce wrought iron. It is probable that the raw bloom was cooled and broken by hammering. It would then have been possible to pick out the iron pieces without the slag, reheat in the bloomery and consolidate into larger pieces by hammering. The product contained about 0.1%C compared with around 0.08% for wrought iron, hard enough for a hoe blade or cutlass (Tylecote, 1976). Blooms of iron produced in Oyo, Western State of Nigeria around the beginning of the 20th century AD had 1.67%C, typical of modern high-carbon steels which could be hot-forged, quenched and annealed to produce very strong tools and implements. It is likely they were produced by carburizing wrought iron in a deep, hot bed of charcoal, or embedded in charcoal in a closed crucible buried in a heap of burning charcoal, similar to the Indian method of producing *wootz* steel.

The Iron Age arrived at a time when farming settlements in sub-Saharan Africa had become fairly large, and the region had been linked to the Silk Route. Diffusion of iron technology to the region would have been easy considering that it provided iron for making farming implements which could not have been made from copper or bronze. The most reliable published works suggest that the technology spread from southern West Africa with the migration of the Bantu tribes out of Nigeria starting from the middle of the second millennium BC and finally ending before 1500 AD. They spread across sub-Saharan Africa to Central and East Africa around AD 500, eventually reaching Southern Africa about five hundred years later (Tylecote 1970). With them, the Bantu brought new technologies and skills such as cultivating high-yield crops and iron-working which produced more efficient tools and weapons. It is generally assumed that the technology spread from Nok area in Nigeria to other parts of the country (Lejja in the East, Ilorin and Oyo in the west), and to all the other identified sites in Central and Southern Africa, notably Gabon, Togo, Niger, Cameroon, Sudan, the Urewe archaeological sites that extend from Zaire to Tanzania through Uganda, Rwanda, Burundi and Kenya, and many more (Figure 5.4). However, it could also have arrived independently in places like Niger, Sudan, Gabon, or even East Africa (Kenya, Zaire) through direct trade with North Africa in particular, Ethiopia which was a link in the Silk Route. Unfortunately, most of the sites have not been investigated in depth and objects from some of the sites have not been accurately and comprehensively dated, with the possible exception of Nok Iron Culture, which has been well investigated and the latest published date of arrival is around 850 BC. How and when it disappeared is unclear and published dates range from 200 BC to AD 650.

Chapter 6

Early iron and copper metallurgy in Nigeria

6.1 INTRODUCTION

Metal cultures are conferred on regions, communities, societies when evidences of substantial, widespread, sustained production and use of a particular metal are found in the area. Two metal cultures have been identified in Nigeria: the Early Nok Iron Culture which emerged in the northern part of what is now Nigeria around 800 BC, and is believed to have spread to other parts of Nigeria and the rest of sub-Saharan Africa; Late Copper Culture which has also been found in three locations in Southern Nigeria, dated from about the 9th to 17th century AD. Most of what is known about Nigeria's archaeo-history came from work by foreign archaeologists in the 1950s and 1960s, and lately by the work of German archaeologists between 2005 and 2010. Nigeria is a very difficult terrain for archaeological studies: the country is very large, with extensive vegetational zones, swampy areas, thick rain forests in the south, extensive desert areas of the north, all of which pose formidable obstacles for field investigations. Furthermore high humidity, acidic soil and extensive erosion issues mean poor survival of archaeological objects. Local archaeologists are severely handicapped: they are too few and poorly funded to embark on any extensive, systematic site investigations; and access to analytical and dating facilities are very limited. In effect, much of the archaeological history of the country remains unknown, and this has led to considerable, unsubstantiated speculations in archaeo-literature about early metal history of communities and provenance of metal cultures. There are conflicting views about where iron, copper and bronze technologies came from, when they arrived, or the possibility of local inventions. However, the main focus in this discourse will be on the extent to which the technologies were domesticated and infused with local innovations. A fair understanding of the basic metallurgy of copper and iron will be useful in the subsequent discourse and is presented in Appendix III.

6.2 NOK IRON CULTURE

The story of Nok Iron Culture began in the late 1920s with the accidental discovery of a fragmented terracotta figurine during opencast mining of tin near Jos in North Central Region of modern Nigeria. The work of the British archaeologist, Bernard Fagg helped to reconstruct the object and excavations unearthed many more fragments in the vicinity. Over the next three decades Fagg, his daughter Angela, and several local archaeologists, notably Nigerian archaeologist, Jemkur unearthed many more figurine fragments most of which were badly weathered and had to be reconstructed. Since then many more exotic figurines have been found in the area and other areas of northern Nigeria (Figure 6.1) Comprehensive details about the terracotta figurines have been presented in many publications (Fagg 1977; Fagg 1972, 2014; Jemkur 1992, 2014). The terracotta culture of the area has been investigated extensively by many archaeologists and archaeohistorians (see Manuel and Breunig, 2016). A lot has been published on the stylistics of the artworks, the purpose for which they may have been made, ethnography and the socio-cultural characteristis of the societies that made them. It appeared that terracotta artwork predated Iron Culture and was widespread in the northern parts of Nigeria in view of similar figurines found earlier in Sokoto and Katsina areas. Some terracotta objects found in Nok area were dated around 1500-1200 BC and many more of similar dating have also been found in other parts of Nigeria.

110 *Early metallurgy in Nigeria*

Figure 6.1 Nok Culture terracotta figurines *(Frank Willet, Jos Museum)*

Systematic excavations in the Nok area stretching 500 km east to west and 300 km north to south in the 1960s unearthed many more figurines, pottery, stone axes, tools, iron furnaces, objects and slags in Taruga, near the state capital, Abuja, which provided the first evidence of an iron culture in sub-Saharan Africa (Fagg, B. 1968; Tylecote 1975; Fagg, 1972, 2014; Jemkur, J. 1992, 2014). The objects were originally dated 500 BC to 200 AD, but more recent radiocarbon dating of charcoal found in some of the figurines and thermoluminescence dating methods suggest an earlier period : 800 BC (*Boulier et al*. 2003; Breunig and Rupp, 2016). Further excavations in the area in the 1960s unearthed extensive evidence of iron culture in Taruga, near Abuja. Thirteen large furnaces were recovered in groups, and the most recent work found many more, again in groups. The furnaces were all of the same design, large (around one meter diameter and possibly two meters high), with only one tuyere with its tip at the center of the furnace. Tylecote (Fagg 1968; Tylecote 1975). Dating of the first set of furnaces places them in the Early Iron Age. Over the years, many more excavations have been carried out by different teams, extending the area to around 80,000 kilometers, and many more furnaces and figurines have been found (Fagg, 1969; Shaw 1969; Tylecote 1975; Rustad 1980; Alpern 2005; Breunig and Rupp, 2016) (Figure 6.2). The first group of furnaces was found in Taruga, south of Abuja in the 1970s but extensive excavations in the last decade have generated a wealth of new information about the Nok Early Iron Culture. In some cases, the new furnace excavations were similar to those from the Taruga valley but the two groups differ significantly in terms of variety of designs and number of furnaces, although some have been dated to the first millennium BC. Most of the newly excavated furnaces are of different design: they are around one meter diameter and apparently sat on partially-filled slag pits. Only some of the furnaces found in Taruga exhibit these characteristics (Junius, 2016). The furnace variability at Taruga may be due to the fact that the site was used continuously or intermittently over a long period, considering some features of objects which are attributable to different periods in the evolution of early metallurgy. Modern era finds like a clay smoking tuyere, the variability of furnace design, the high number of furnaces per site, and the wide dispersion of dates all suggest that the new sites were operating for very long periods, probably overlapping the Late Iron Age.

Published literature on the Nok Iron Culture is extensive, but each new publication appears to raise more questions than answers to unresolved puzzles about the site. There is little doubt that Nok area was inhabited from about 800 BC to around 200 AD, but, contrary to the widely held belief that occupation was continuous, possibly by the same people, new information has emerged from a recent comprehensive site investigation, indicating that sites within the Nok area were recurrently occupied during different periods of the Nok Culture or in subsequent times which left no clear occupational layers or stratigraphic separation. Most sites investigated had brief occupation episodes and only small excavated materials were found (Breunig and Rupp, 2016). This latest study has also identified three possible phases of the Nok Culture: the Early, Middle and Late Nok phases. The Early Nok phase refers to a pre-iron culture which probably started around the middle of the second millennium BC based on remains of human occupation found. It is unclear where the occupants came from, they were probably migrant farmers from the Sahel region in view of the types of crops they planted, in particular, millet, based on charred grains that were found and dated to the middle of the second millennium BC (Neumann, 2016).

Figure 6.2a   Locations of Early/Late metal cultures in Nigeria

112 *Early metallurgy in Nigeria*

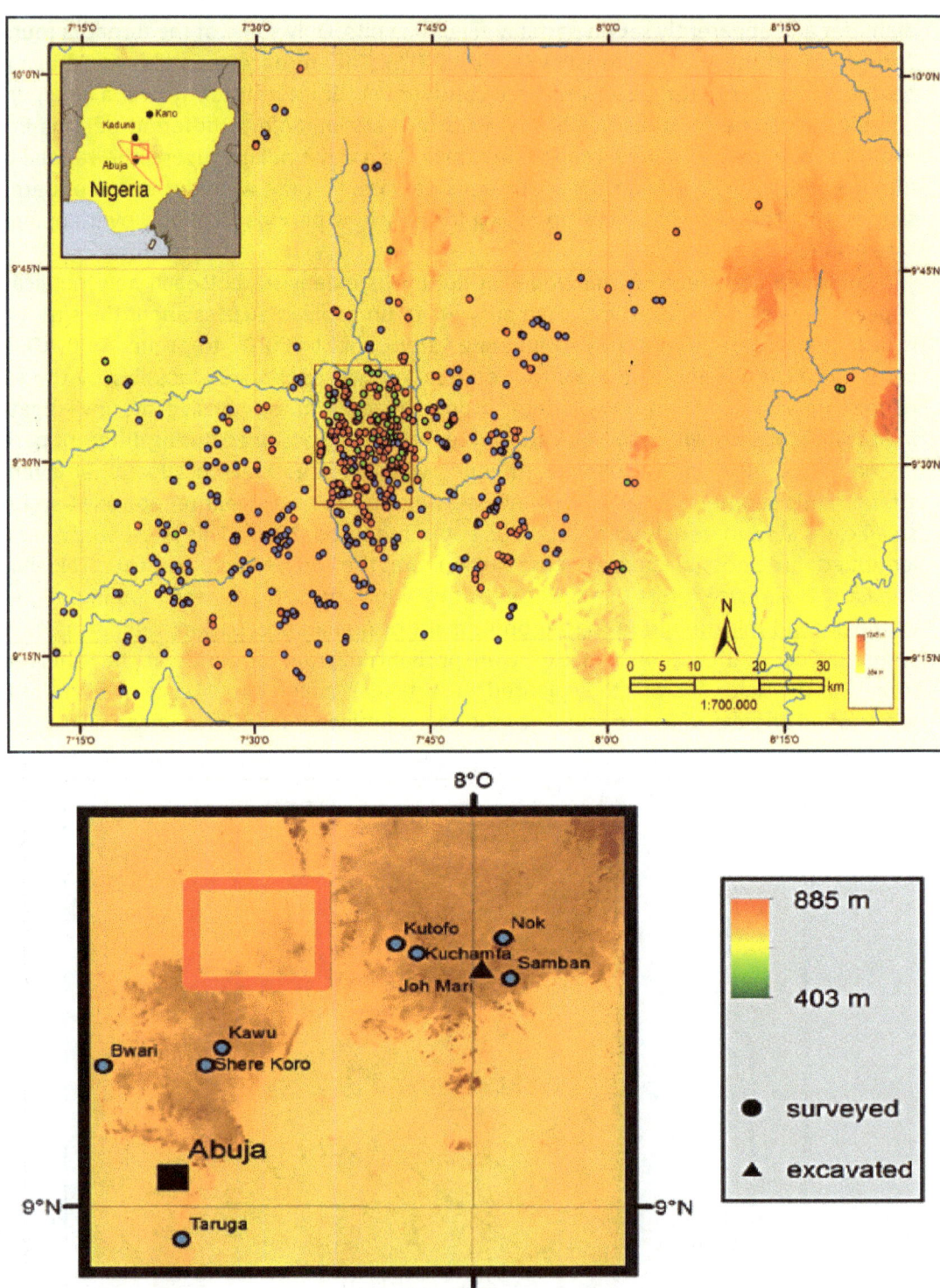

Figure 6.2b Locations of furnace groups excavated in Nok area. The outlined rectangle denotes the key study area with recorded (red dots) and excavated sites (green dots). *Breunig and Rupp, 2016; Junius, 2016).*

There is substantial evidence in support of the theory that Sahel migrant farmers were most probably the predecessors of the terracotta and iron producing people of the middle Nok phase. Prosperity appeared to have grown over the next few centuries, leading to a flourishing period from around the beginning of the first millennium BC. The beginning of the terracotta production in the area has been dated fairly accurately at the 9th century BC but dating the beginning of the Iron Culture has proved more difficult, with published dates ranging from second millennium to mid-first millennium BC. However, the most recent dates place the site between 800 and 400 BC. (Figure 6.3).

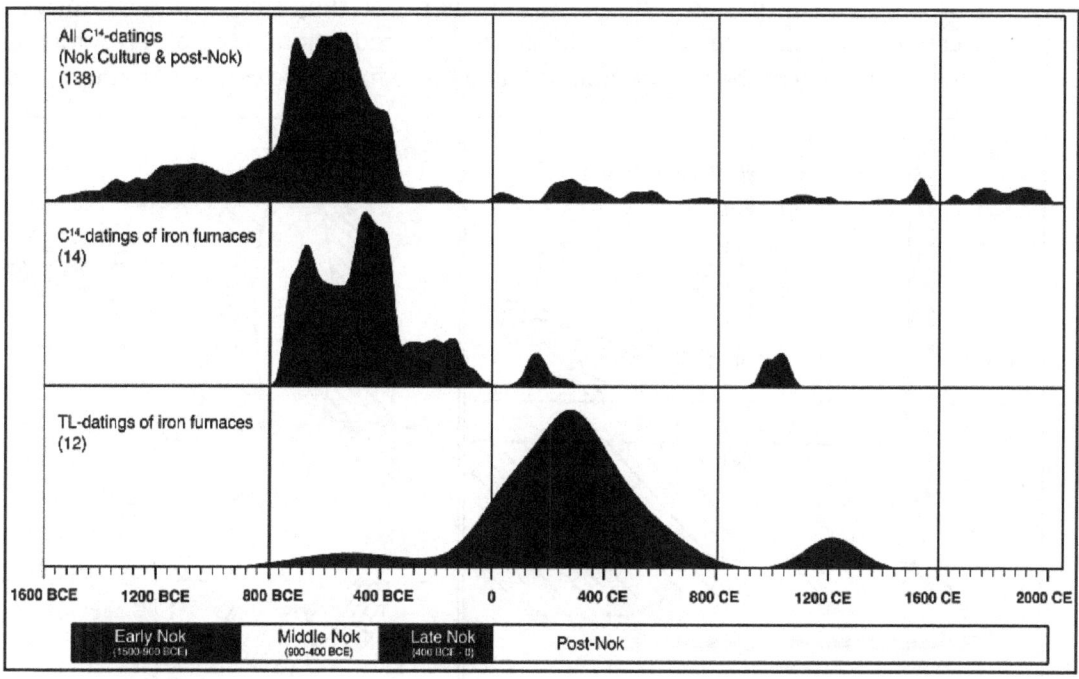

Figure 6.3 Dating of the latest Nok excavations *(Breunig and Rupp, 2016)*.

The Middle Nok is believed to have started around 900 BC, marked by sudden increase of settlement density as well as distinctive activities such as pottery and iron metallurgy. Evidence from pottery analysis indicates that iron production did not start much earlier than the 7th century BC (Franke, 2015, 2016). Archaeological evidence indicates a flourishing, socially complex period with an abundance of sites and a large production of terracotta sculptures. It is unclear why this period ended around 400 BC, in view of the significant drop in archaeological evidence in form of sites and finds. However, production of Nok well-defined and distinctive terracotta sculptures and Nok pottery appeared to have continued until about the turn of the eras, hence the period from 400 BC to the end of the first millennium has been named Late Nok.

It is unclear when or why the Nok Culture disappeared at the turn of the eras but it could have been as a result of migration due to war or unfavourable environmental changes. Subsequently, the site appears to have been occupied on and off up to modern times in view of younger sites which have been found, probably still operating iron smelting until the early part of the 20th century, hence a fourth period named Post-Nok phase, marked by complete absence of Nok sculptures and a marked difference in pottery stylistics and decoration techniques Beck 2015; Franke 2015).

114 *Early metallurgy in Nigeria*

Hundreds of iron furnaces and smelting remnants have been found in groups over a wide area of the Nok site, other areas of Nigeria and the rest of Africa, and there are strong indications that there could be many more yet undiscovered, although, clearly they span many generations (Figures 6.4 and 6.5). However, those that belonged to the Middle Nok Culture had distinctive characteristics which have made it easy to differentiate them from more recent furnaces. They were about one meter in diameter at the base, with a preserved height of about one meter, but probably around 2 meters high. With the tuyere system used, they would have needed a height:diameter ratio of 2:1 to achieve the appropriate reduction zone that promoted sufficient contact between the rising carbon monoxide and the descending iron oxide to achieve solid-state direct reduction of the ore. Not much slag has been found in any of the Middle Nok sites and those found are currently being analyzed.

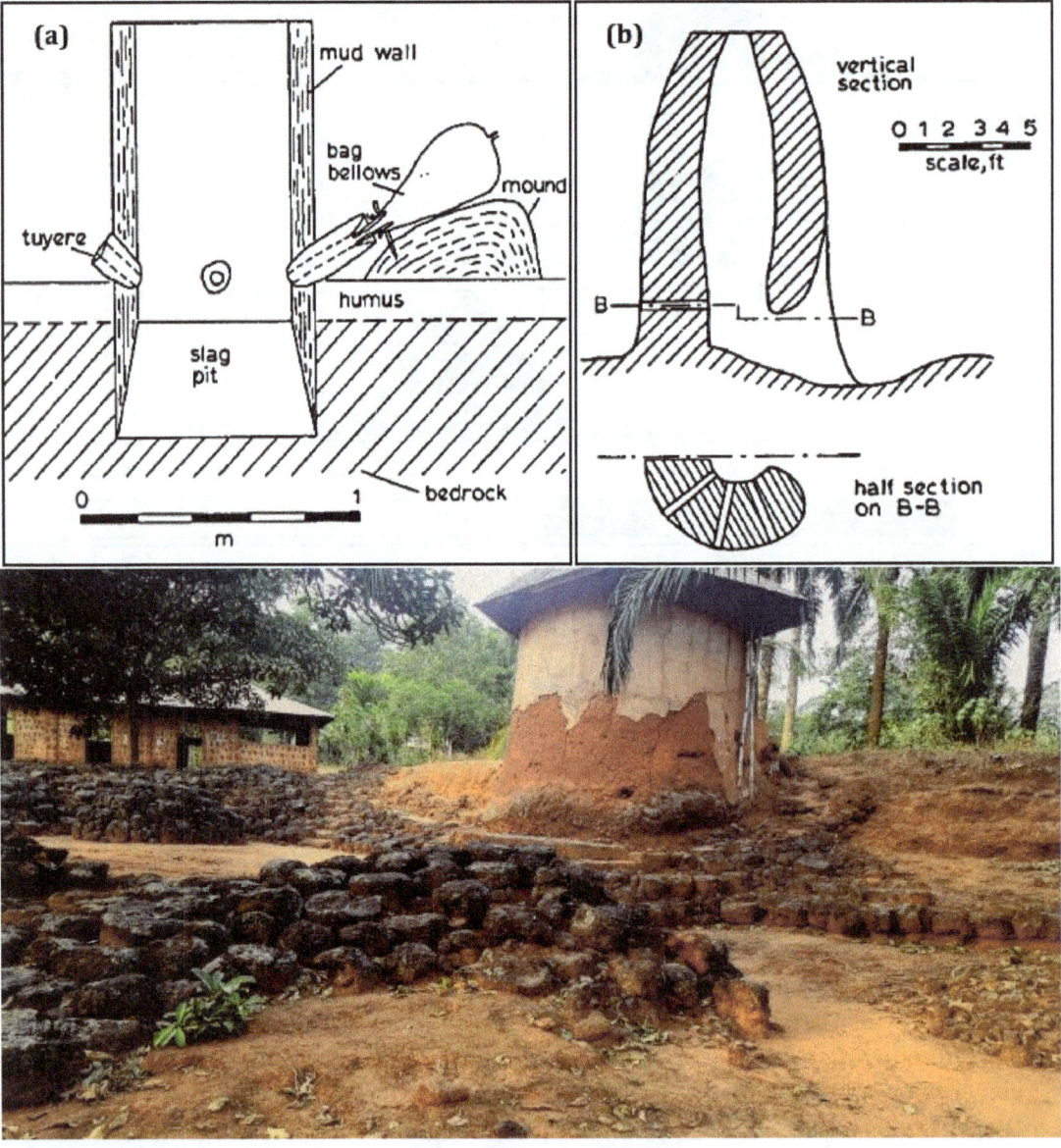

Figure 6.4 (a) Early iron furnace from Taruga, Nok, Nigeria (b) Early iron furnace from Togoland (c) Late iron furnace and slag deposit from Lejja, eastern Nigeria *(Tylecote, 1995; google images).*

Early iron and copper metallurgy in Nigeria 115

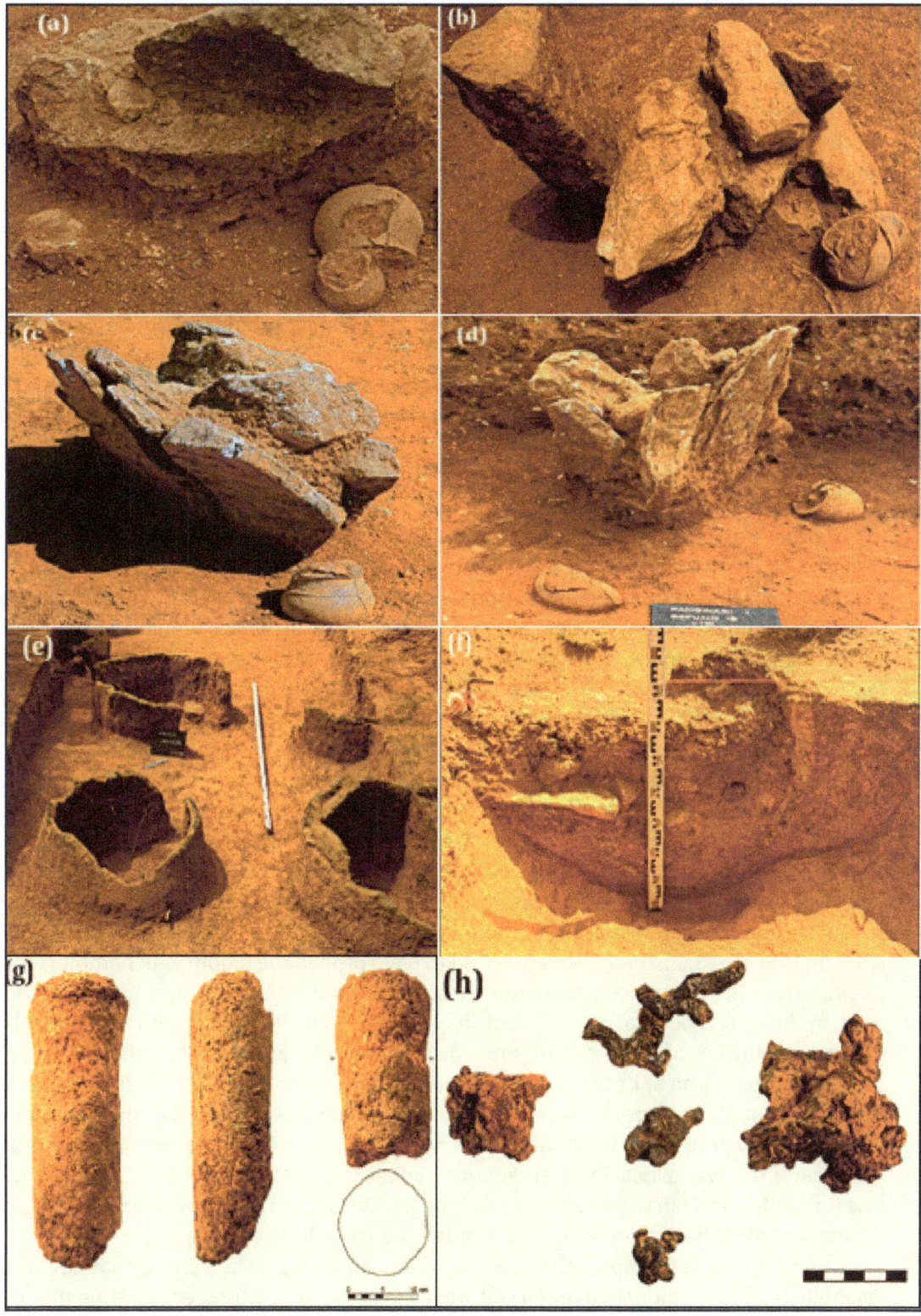

Figure 6.5 Recent excavations from Nok early iron site, Nigeria
(a)-(d) Breunig & Rupp, 2016; (e)-(h) Junius, 2016.

The paucity of slag at the sites has been a puzzle but the source or type of iron ore used (which is currently unknown) may yield some explanation. Evidence of deliberate slagging has not been found on iron sites anywhere in the early world, probably because most iron ores are self-fluxing, and this may explain the paucity of slag finds in the Taruga excavations which are evidently older than the latest ones, Apparently the little slag formed from the natural flux components of the iron ore would have been hammered along with the smelted iron blooms to produce wrought iron. The development of deliberate slagging came later in the Iron Culture, appearing in Europe only in the Roman Iron Age towards the end of the first millennium BC. The Early Iron Culture furnace had no slag outlet and the slag ran down forming a cake at the bottom of the furnace, in some cases, just small rounded particles also known as *prills*. In fact, the ability to tap slag is a distinguishing feature between earlier Iron Age furnaces and the later Roman furnaces that started to appear from around the beginning of the first millennium AD. Most iron ores are self-fluxing to some extent: silica in the ore will react with iron to form ferro-silicate slag, while the presence of calcium carbonate (limestone) will promote slagging. In effect, the amount of slag produced in any smelting process would depend on the chemical composition of the iron ore unless there is deliberate slagging.

Another puzzle about Nok is the paucity of iron artifacts at the smelting sites or in the surrounding areas that probably hosted communities. This is typical of many early iron sites all over the world due probably to the relative susceptibility of iron to corrosion and oxidation compared with copper and bronze, the rate of which would depend on the surrounding environment, in particular, acidity, aeration, temperature. It also depends on the relative dimensions of the product. While a cast iron axe-head may survive for several thousand years in favourable, poorly aerated environment such as in a buried coffin, a flat product like a hoe, matchette, sword, abandoned on ground will likely not survive this long under any environmental conditions.

All available evidence shows that the Nok Culture people were farmers and if they had access to iron metallurgy, would probably have been making mostly flat farming implements such as hoe and cutlass. However, it is probable also that they may have been making blooms as well for export. This theory is supported by the exceptionally high quality of the few iron products found so far. Apparently, they did not simply hammer slag-laden blooms into wrought iron ingots, instead, they appeared to have broken the bloom with hammer, sorted the iron from the slag pieces, and then consolidated the iron pieces into a relatively large solid by heating under a mass of burning charcoal and hammering. This would have enhanced diffusion of more carbon into the iron, raising carbon content from the typical 0.8% for wrought iron to between 1-1.6% and yielding a heat-treatable product. By working the product at high temperatures and quenching, followed by annealing, they would have produced a much stronger implement than would have been possible with wrought iron. It is unclear if this was a local innovation but a similar technology had proliferated in ancient Asia (in particular, China and India) around the middle of the second millennium BC and the technology could have been acquired through the trade links.

A third puzzle is the apparent absence of any advanced local culture that could have invented, hosted or nourished metal culture, especially Iron Culture, considering that there was no earlier Copper Culture experience that could have served as training ground. However, as explained in the last chapter, the only major difference between iron and copper metallurgy is the melting temperature, and the extra 100°C or so needed to cause solid-state reduction of iron oxide by carbon at around 1150°C could have been achieved without prior experience with copper metallurgy, perhaps by using higher fuel:ore ratio, more powerful bellows, or deploying several bellows simultaneously as has been found in many of the Nok furnaces. Furthermore, copper smelting technology was already established in places like Buhen and Nubia in North Africa. Both areas were already linked to the early Trade Routes, and either could have been the source of furnace technology which was then adapted to iron ore smelting at Nok. A feasible explanation of the mystery of incompatible socio-cultural setting of Nok will be discussed in some depth in a subsequent section.

A fourth puzzle is the prominent thesis that Nok Iron Culture disappeared almost without trace around the fourth century BC. However, evidence is emerging suggesting occupation possibly by different groups of iron smelters from early first century AD, and the technology may have been sustained for more than two thousand years up to around 1900 AD which marked the beginning of New Iron Age. It is believed that many African countries received the iron culture late, possibly from Nok and were still practicing the technology as late as 1940s (in fact, the technology is still alive in some African countries). However, many moved away from ore smelting when scrap iron became widely available. For example, the debut of railway in Nigeria in the first two decades of the last century made available large quantities of malleable rail steel (about 0.6%C), which effectively put an end to ore smelting, although smithing is still widely practiced.

6.3 PROVENANCE OF THE NOK IRON CULTURE

Archaeology is an important yet imprecise science which seeks to determine what may have happened in as far back as prehistoric times (8000-6000 BC) from very scanty concrete evidence, which explains why virtually every statement is qualified with 'possibility' or 'probability.' Most metals would have reverted to the natural state as a result of oxidation or corrosion unless they were buried in benign environment. Currently Available dating techniques are imprecise and are continuously subject to upgrading (see Appendix II). This makes dating of archaeological objects largely tenuous and tentative and it is normal to keep revising hypotheses and dates in the light of new evidence. It is unproductive therefore, especially in archaeometallurgy to try and determine with any precision the origin of an invention or technology. As discussed earlier, any of the early metal technologies could have been a local invention considering the ingenuity of pre-historic and early people in shaping and adapting their environment to meet their many needs, probably through experimentation. From pre-historic times, developments in materials technology have been inspired primarily by need: shelter, remote hunting, farming, territorial defense, etc. Shaping of stone to tools (the humble beginning of materials technology) was practiced in Africa more than a million years ago; using composite clay-straw materials in shelter construction and processing metal ores for many applications (cosmetics, decorations, etc.) were in common practice in many cultures from Neolithic times.

Some inventions may have been accidental, such as the possible discovery of copper smelting technology in the process of preparing red oxide iron or copper-base minerals for neolithic pottery glazes, or melting of highly oxidized native copper. It is also possible that the discovery of iron technology emerged in the process of smelting iron-rich copper ores or adding iron oxide ores as flux. Iron ore deposits are very widely distributed all over the world and many had been worked by local communities for purposes other than metals production from Neolithic times. Many of these processes involved the use of ovens and furnaces. Any indigenous community anywhere in the world could have experimented with local ores in many ways and stumbled on an invention which may remain localized for centuries. For example, there is significant evidence that iron technology was being practiced somewhere in Anatolia or Iran from the beginning of the second millennium BC but it remained localized for around a thousand years and did not reach other regions until the beginning of the first millennium BC when trade links with other regions emerged.

China is believed to have invented cast iron around the sixth century BC but the technology did not appear to have reached Europe for nearly two thousand years (around 1400 AD). The same could have happened to any invention anywhere in the world. As discussed in some depth in the last chapter, invention makes little impact unless there is a vehicle for proliferation and it is infused with local innovations. Furthermore, proliferation of local practice and use depends largely on availability of a sufficiently socially-stratified and hierarchical culture that can domesticate and fund the expensive technologies. It is interesting to note that no invention of any metal technology has been attributed to Europe, yet, bronze could have been invented independently in England which had copper deposit with high tin content as well as tin deposit. Furthermore, it is indisputable that Europe was responsible for most of the innovations that propelled both ferrous and non-ferrous metal technologies to the current dominant global statuses. Debate has been intensive since the 1950s on whether iron technology emerged autochthonously in Africa or was imported from the Mediterranean North. This issue has been discussed in some depth in Chapter 5. There are credible reasons to believe that iron technology at Nok could have been a local invention, or could have diffused from somewhere else including locations in Africa, and both hypotheses deserve some in-depth analysis.

6. 3.1 Local invention hypothesis

As explained earlier, the common hypothesis that Africa did not have a copper culture is incorrect: Egypt, Niger, Nubia had copper smelting culture dating back to possibly the middle of the second millennium BC, probably earlier in Egypt. It is also not true that experience in copper smelting would have been a prerequisite for the invention or acquisition of iron culture. A third fallacious hypothesis is the absence of advanced culture in Africa that could have nurtured the invention of iron metallurgy: Egypt had the early world's most advanced civilization and culture; Niger, Togo, Nubia in Sudan, Daima in the Lake Chad area of Northern Nigeria all had advanced cultures dating back to third to second millennium BC; and recent findings indicate that a prosperous culture probably flourished in Nok from at least the middle of the second millennium BC, prior to the Iron Era (Breunig and Rupp, 2016). All these nation states were in close proximity of each other and were already connected by trade, hence an invention in any of the locations would have spread easily across the region (Figure 6.6, see also Chapter 5).

Niger and Nubia had both copper and iron ore deposits and there is substantial evidence that copper was being smelted at both locations and the Buhen outpost of Egypt from the middle of the second millennium BC. Iron metallurgy could have been invented in any of the locations, especially if they were smelting iron-rich, highly oxidized copper ores. Furthermore, iron ore deposits are very widespread in Africa and it is premature to exclude the possibility that independent invention somewhere else on the continent could have happened independently, considering that much of the continent remains archaeological virgin land. Many early metal cultures have also been identified in central and southern Africa, some of which may have similar dating as those of the northern and western sub-regions (see Chapter 5).

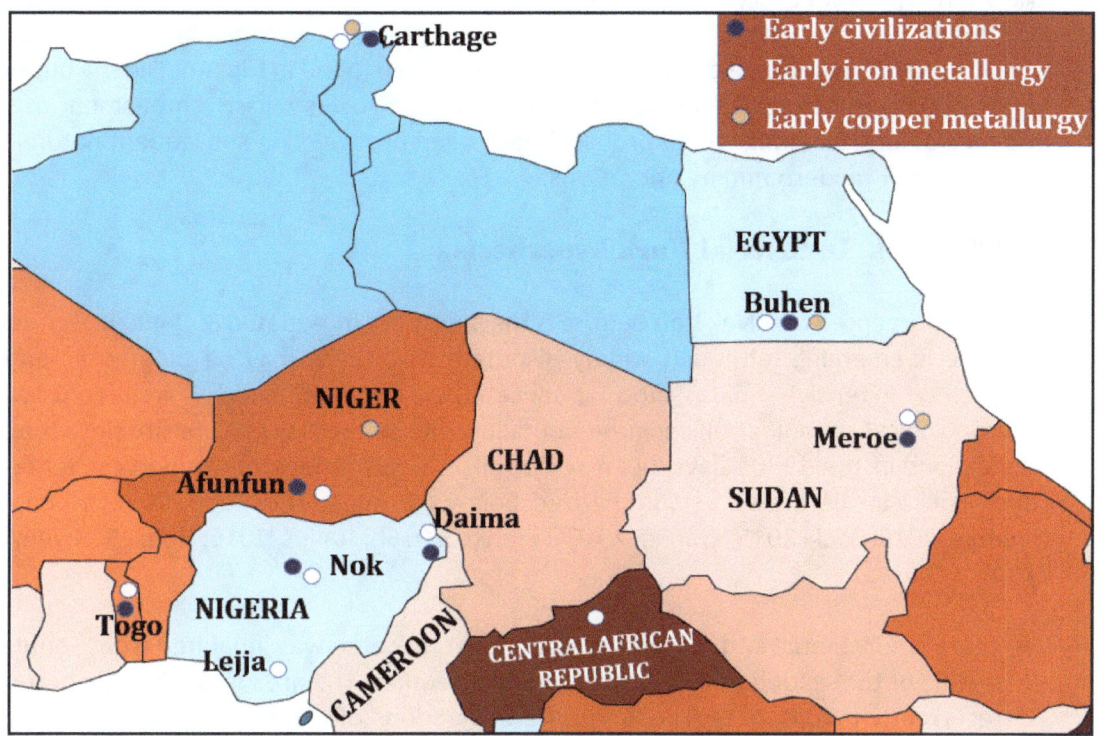

Figure 6.6   Early copper and iron metal cultures in Africa

6.3.2   Diffusion hypothesis

As discussed earlier, assuming that both copper and iron cultures originated from Anatolia, the impact remained local, spread possibly by cultural interaction within the region for centuries, until the establishment of the Silk Route starting from around the middle of the third millennium BC and developing into a major trade link between most regions of the early world by the second millennium BC. The Phoenicians who were ardent traders on both land and sea are believed to have been the main vehicle of proliferation of metal technologies. They traded in ores, in particular, copper and tin ingots: some shipwrecks containing both and dated to the second millennium BC have been found (see Chapter 5). There is little doubt that they had extended strong trade routes to Egypt, Nubia, Carthage, Ethiopia, and possibly Niger by the beginning of the first century BC. Furthermore, Niger probably had been linked to the Silk/Trans Saharan Trade Routes by around 3000 BC. One major attraction to Niger or Jos in the Nok area Nok of Nigeria would have been the rich tin deposit which was extremely scarce in early times. Considering that tin ores are usually very lean, often containing less that 1% tin, it is quite likely that they would have established smelting facilities near the mines, producing ingots as rich as over 90-95% tin (leaving most of the gangue behind) which they traded widely. They may have done the same with copper ores which could also be very lean, often less than 5% copper content. In such circumstances, they would probably have trained local smelters who would prepare ingots ready for them. This does not rule out the possibility that the Niger smelters received the technology from elsewhere and traded ingots on the trade routes. This may explain why ancient copper smelting facilities for copper have been found in Niger, Buhen, Nubia but no evidence of wide local use. No evidence of early tin smelting has been found in Niger or Nigeria but since tin is normally mined by opencast technology which involves massive movement of soil, evidence of local smelting would probably have been destroyed in subsequent natural soil movements or modern mining operations.

6.3.3 Nok Industrial Park hypothesis

It is widely accepted that Nok Iron Culture is the oldest in Africa, dated 800-400 BC but some evidence is emerging (although widely disputed) that there may be older sites on the continent. Extensive data and publications (archaeological, archaeohistorical anthropological, ethnological, and arheometallurgical) on the Nok Culture site since the first publications in the 1930s have been reviewed in depth and some important tentative conclusions can be drawn as summarized below (Breunig and Rupp, 2016; Honn and Neuman, 2016; Beck, 2015; Franke, 2016a; Franke, 2016b; Junius, 2016; Holl, 2009; Jemkur, 2014).

- There is substantial and credible evidence that Nok area was inhabited from about the middle of the second millennium BC, possibly earlier. The area was probably occupied recurrently by different groups in different periods of the Nok Culture. The earliest occupants were probably migrant farmers (Early Nok phase). Middle Nok phase appears to have begun from in early first millennium BC with distinctive features, notably a sudden increased settlement density, flourishing prosperity, the beginning of elaborate terracotta artwork from the 9th century, as well as iron production from around the 8th century BC. Although no evidence of social complexity has been found, it may have emerged and flourished during this phase. Late Nok phase apparently began around 400 BC, marked by a significant decline in both terracotta work and iron technology, vanishing almost entirely around the turn of the eras, possibly due to unfavourable environmental changes. A Post Nok phase has also been identified in which the Nok area remained occupied in the early millennium AD but with complete absence of Nok sculptures and a marked difference in pottery stylistics.

- Nok area which spreads over around 80,000 square kilometers was a major center of iron smelting for around four hundred years (maybe much longer) in the first millennium BC, possibly by several different generations or different societies.

- While over a hundred iron smelting sites have been identified within the area, all of them containing groups of iron furnaces with a wide range of features identifiable with both the Early and Late Iron Cultures, there is no evidence of continuous occupation by the same group, and some were probably operating until the early part of the twentieth century AD.

- No significant ancient slags or iron objects have been found in the area and the local iron deposits that have been found have not been positively identified as the source of supply to the early iron producers.

- No evidence of advanced culture, complex social stratification or hierarchical political structures that were typical of other early metal cultures and could have hosted the invention or acquisition of iron technology has been found in the area and no visible impact of iron technology on the culture of host communities has also been found. There has been no indication of agglomerations of people above village level, and no evidence of social stratification which is always associated with social complexity has been found. No evidence has been found of towns or any kind of urban environment, and the small quantities of cultural remains found rule out village communities. There is no evidence of high population density and, in spite of the very large body of evidence collected, no attributes of social complexity like signs of inequality, hierarchy, nucleation of settlement systems, communal and public monuments, or alternative African versions of complexity has been found. On the contrary, the area was probably occupied at different times by pastoral groups (Holl, 2009.

There is little doubt that iron metallurgy was practiced extensively in the Nok area, possibly at different times, probably from early in the first millennium BC to the beginning of the 20th century. The fact that no evidence of advanced culture has been found in the Nok area may suggest that Nok was some sort of 'industrial park' where people came to smelt iron from neighbouring advanced cultures such as are believed to have existed in nearby Niger, Daima at the border of Nigeria, Chad Republic, Nubia (Sudan), Egypt and Carthage (Figure 6.6). This suggestion is feasible for several reasons:

- Iron was (and still is) ritualistic in many African cultures and iron smelting or smithing (a predominantly male occupation) was surrounded by many taboos, including the exclusion of women and strict rules about the conduct of people involved in either craft, all of who were revered in their communities. Perhaps to preserve secrecy, smelting was always carried out far away from living areas.

- At least three iron ore deposits have been identified in Nok area and there are probably several more undiscovered. Since the iron content of the ore would have been between 5% and 30% or so, it would have been preferable to smelt at or near the site rather than carry large quantities of ore to far away locations to smelt. Furthermore charcoal was (and still is) always produced away from living areas and the right types of hard wood were probably found in the relatively fertile Nok area.

- The tin deposit in Jos was one of only five or so known deposits in the early world, its exploitation may have been the primary attraction for foreign traders in the first place and tin smelting in the area may have predated iron smelting. Since tin is mined by opencast technology, signs or mining or smelting may have been obliterated by natural or mining-related land movements.

- Another attraction to Nok could have been the many streams around the area which would have provided the much needed water for ore beneficiation, cooling and bathing after work (one of the rules that early African iron smelters were expected to keep). It is possible also that early iron smelters were doing preliminary concentration of the ores by panning or primitive jigging, both of which would have required a lot of water.

- Since metals became common inter-regional trading commodities perhaps in the latter part of the third millennium BC, it is logical to assume that upgraded ores and refined ingots were being traded as well (as discussed earlier, metal ingots dated to the first millennium BC have been found in sunken ships). It would have been unlikely that lean ores of copper or tin (around 0.5-5% of metal) would have been transported over long distances. This may explain why many early metal smelting sites with no evidence of metal use have been found all over the early world.

- Nok area was surrounded by advanced cultures, all only a few hundred kilometers away (Figure 6.6) any or all of who could have set up operation posts in Nok area and carried away the products. Since no evidence of major metal use has been found in any of the advanced cultures, it is probable that they were trading the products with foreigners like the Phoenicians.

- Hundreds of furnaces found in the Nok area were in discrete groups, featuring different designs and innovations, and with datings spanning a period of around two thousand years, suggesting that different groups practiced iron technology concurrently or recurrently over a very wide area around Nok, possibly until the beginning of the 20th century AD.

In view of the above deductions from the extensive literature on the Nok Iron Culture over the last ninety years or so, the following hypothesis is proposed:

> *Nok was an industrial park in which people from different local areas (or even from other regions) set up smelting facilities and took away their refined products, either for working in their domains or for export to other regions.*

This may explain why little slag deposits have been found in the area: most of the early furnaces were non-slagging and the smelters would have carried away the crude iron castings with most of the small quantities of slag entrapped and worked them elsewhere. There are several features of the area that could have made it an attractive industrial park: the rich tin deposit in the area may have been the primary attraction and exploitation may have predated iron technology, considering the extreme rarity of tin in the early world and its vital role in the production of broze; there were several iron deposits in the area, and there were also many streams that would have provided vital water supply. Furthermore, there was good vegetation in the area that would have supplied charcoal. People could have come from Niger, Daima, Chad or even Lejja (all of them a few hundred kilometers away), working their smelting furnaces and carrying the products back to their domains for working.

The possibility that the Phoenicians may have been involved cannot be ruled out, considering the attraction of valuable tin deposits in the area. It is also possible that they introduced the iron technology which they had been practicing in Carthage from around the beginning of the first century BC, probably much earlier in their base in the Early Middle East. The Philistines were smelting iron in Gerar where smithing furnaces and iron objects dated to between 1200-870 BC have been found (Tylecote, 1972), although Egypt did not appear to have adopted the technology until about 700-600 BC, possibly around the same period as Nok. It is unlikely that the Egyptians did not have the knowledge of iron technology well before this time considering their proximity to Anatolia. The Philistines may have acquired the technology through migration from Anatolia after the breakup of the Hittite Empire, and the Phoenicians who were already active in the region in the second millennium BC could have brought it directly to Niger or Nok, not necessarily through Carthage. Diffusion through Nubia was also unlikely because iron technology appeared to have arrived there after Nok, either from Egypt, in fact diffusion to the area could have been from Nok.

6.4 NSUKKA IRON CULTURE

Early iron smelting sites have been found in many locations around Nsukka, South-Eastern Nigeria. The three oldest sites: Opi, Lejja and Aku have been dated to 765 BC to AD 75. It is difficult to relate the early iron metallurgy in the area to the history of the current Igbo occupants whose antecedents or origin remain a mystery and a subject of much speculation and controversy, unlike the Yorubas who are widely believed to have descended from Oduduwa and the Hausas who have traced their origin to Bayajidda in Daura. Speculations are based on scanty and fragmentary oral traditions and correlation of cultural traits. Communities in Owerri, Orlu and Okigwi believe that they were the original occupants of the area which ultimately expanded due to migration from all directions around AD 1400-1500. In effect it is unclear whether the early metallurgy area has been occupied by the same people from as early as 800 BC. In any case, the area has several iron deposits and there is little doubt that iron was being smelted probably as early as the first quarter of the first millennium BC (see Okafor 1993, 2004). The rigorous sampling and dating processes adopted by Okafor have conferred a considerable degree of confidence in the dates. This dating implies that the Nsukka Iron Culture emerged around the same time as the Nok Iron culture and could have been initiated by the same diffusion process (or local invention). However, more recent studies have revised the date to the middle of the second millennium BC or even earlier, with claims that the Iron Culture of the area predates most other centers found anywhere in the world (Eze-Uzomaka 2010, 2013), but this has raised considerable controversy in the world of archaeology, especially the reliability of the dating process.

The major issue with Nsukka early iron metallurgy is the lack of any evidence of human existence or civilization earlier than AD 900 or so. It is possible however that more extensive and detailed study of the area may yield some credible evidence in support of these early dates. However, it is possible that occupancy of the area had changed many times prior to 900 AD and probable that the people of the area were experimenting with the relatively rich local hematite iron deposits like many other early people in other regions. As explained earlier, invention of iron technology could have occurred accidentally. If this happened, the possibility that Lejja was the source of diffusion of the Nok Iron Culture cannot be ruled out. Nsukka early iron site is only a few hundred kilometers from Taruga in Nok area and there are several iron deposits in both areas. The widely accepted dates of both sites fall in the same range in the first millennium BC, and either site could have been the source of diffusion to the other. If indeed enough archaeological and socio-cultural evidences can be found to support the hypothesis of autochthonous invention at Nsukka, it may have diffused to Nok area. On the other hand, the rich hematite ore deposits of the Nsukka area may have been an attraction for the Nok industrial park to have spread to the area.

6.5   AFRICAN LATE IRON CULTURE

The Early Iron Culture in the world ended officially in 1900. Most smelting sites in Nigeria are dated from around AD 200 and probably folded up when scrap iron became widely available at the beginning of the nineteenth century AD, but smelting and smithing continued in other parts of Africa for many decades, as late as the 1970s in some areas, and smithing is still widely practiced in most countries of the region/ Smelting from ore is also still being practiced in some countries in central and southern Africa. Evidence of Early/Late Iron Culture has been found in the three main regions of Nigeria: Nok, Daima, Benin, Jebba, Ilorin, Old Oyo, Ile-Ife, etc. Ilmenite-rich iron ores were being smelted in Yorubaland in the eighteenth and nineteenth centuries AD (Ige and Rehren, 2003; Chirikwure, 2015). Ilmenite, a titanium-iron oxide mineral also known as menaccanite accounts for the production of around half of the world's annual output of titanium dioxide used extensively in paints and for the production of titanium, an exceptionally hard metal. Titanium is also an important alloying element in heat-treatable steels because it forms a complete solid solution in iron above about 950°C, and confers exceptional hardness. Most modern blast furnaces prefer not to smelt ores containing more than about 2%wt titanium oxide, not because it cannot be done but because of its undesirably high melting point (1668°C compared with 1538°C for pure iron). Also, sinter mixes containing more than this threshold produce weak sinter which tends to reduce permeability in blast furnaces. Furthermore, smelting such ores increases consumption of coke, the most expensive input in blast furnace smelting, significantly. The fact that the Old Oyo people were able to smelt ilmenite-rich iron ores successfully indicates that they were able to achieve higher temperatures than required for other common iron ores, probably through efficient furnace/tuyere design and increased charcoal:ore rate. It also explains why iron objects found in the area were of unusual hardness. As mentioned earlier, the people were producing wootz-type hardenable grade mild steel (1.6%C) probably by carburizing wrought iron in a heap of hot charcoal, similar to wootz/Damascus steel production in India around 5th century BC and the English cementation process of the 17th century. However, it is more likely that they quench-hardened iron produced from titanium-rich ore. Either option could be verified by metallography but this has not been done.

6.6   IGBO UKWU LATE COPPER/BRONZE CULTURE

Igbo-Ukwu is a small town located about forty kilometers southeast of Onitsha in Anambra State of Nigeria. The town became famous internationally due to discoveries of exotic copper/bronze castings excavated in the 1960s. The story began in 1938 with the discovery of a metal object buried about 2 meters deep, in the process of digging a well in Anozie's family compound. This object was later identified as a bronze casting. Many more castings and other artifacts were excavated in the process of digging the well but the digger was oblivious of the tremendous value of his discovery and simply piled them up with other rubbish from where people picked up items believing that they could have fetish powers. News of the finding eventually reached the British Commissioner who recovered as many of the objects as possible, most of which are now on display in the British Museum. The Federal Department of Antiquities also succeeded in recovering some which are on display in the Nigerian Museum. Not much else happened until 1959 when the British archaeologist Thurstan Shaw who was invited by the Antiquities Department of Nigeria to investigate the site, carried out extensive excavations in the area. He was also employed by University College, Ibadan in 1960 to establish the country's first Department of Archaeology.

6.6.1 Archaeology of Igbo-Ukwu artifacts

Shaw identified a cultural complex comprising three contiguous compounds of three Anozie brothers and carried out excavations between 1959 and 1964. Because of their functionally distinct features, they were named *Igbo Isaiah, Igbo Richard and Igbo Jonah*. A large number of objects, were found: all the sites together produced 685 artifacts of copper and bronze weighing over 75 kilograms of which 110 are major pieces, over 165,000 beads of glass and stone, nearly 22,000 potsherds, the majority consisting of distinctive and characteristic ancient Igbo-Ukwu ware with deep grooving, protuberant bosses and patterns found in basketwork. Other items include iron artifacts, ivory tusks, fragments of textiles, and calabashes. The copper/bronze objects found include a roped pot, altar stand, swords, large variety of bronze pots, ornaments, two ornate scabbards, bells, chains, necklace, pendants, anklets, staff heads, altar and wristlets, hundreds of ritual vessels and regalia castings of bronze or leaded bronze which include masks, pendants, crowns, breastplates, staff ornaments, swords, decorated pottery, ivory tusks, glass beads, animal bones. Others include copper pectoral plate, a copper fan holder, a copper crown, copper anklets, wristlets and beaded armlets, copper pointed rods. Other findings include some iron artifacts and iron slag, ivory tusks, pieces of textiles and calabashes. All the objects found have been described in detail in several Shaw publications (Shaw, 1960, 1965, 1970, 1973, 1977). It subsequently became clear that antiquity items had been found in the other sites apart from *Igbo Isaiah* as far back as 1922 but were never investigated.

The *Igbo Isaiah* site was clearly a storehouse or shrine for the keeping of well-preserved sacred vessels and regalia used for ceremonial or ritual purposes, with the ware meticulously stored in a pit, around 2 meters wide and three meters deep. The inventory of objects found on this site include a richly decorated water pot encased in a bronze rope work of reef knots and set on the top of a pot stand (Igbo-Ukwu-1, Figure 6.7a). This roped pot, perhaps the most outstanding and complicated of all the artifacts, must have been produced by a very complex lost-wax casting technology, probably cast in five separate parts and joined together by burning-in more metals at the joints. Definitive description of the production technology would require an unacceptable process of sectioning the object. However, Shaw (1970) described in detail the likely processes involved, based on extensive experience with the lost-wax technology. Shaw also described in detail some other unusual objects found: *"a bowl resting on an openwork stand which was cast in two sections and joined together also by burning-in strips decorated with insects and openwork spiral forms.*

There is also an openwork stand with a male and a female figure on opposite sides which are separated by openwork motifs of intertwined snakes with eggs in their mouths. Still another is an annular pot-stand with a textured surface of triangles connected by dots. There are also six large single-handed bronze bowls in the form of a calabash fruit cut diametrically in two and elaborately decorated on the outer surface with zones of raised loops, quatrefoils, lozenges, conical bosses, and bands of tiny spirals and dots. Also, there are smaller sickle-shaped bowls; modeled shells with incised and raised patterns, spirals with dots in the center, crickets, flies, frogs and snakes; textured staff heads and mid-sections and ends decorated with insects, frogs, snakes and multi-colored beads; a scabbard in the form of a double-headed snake, each head holding a frog and a pangolin in its mouth; various ornate pendants in the form of a ram head and an elephant head; and a medallion decorated with four intertwined snakes with eggs in their mouths. There are also pots decorated with channel pattern and projecting bosses. Some of the items were clearly part of the regalia of the priest in charge of the shrine". Shaw speculated that the site may have been abandoned in an emergency.

The *Igbo Richard* excavation was clearly a burial chamber of some dignitary, nearly four meters deep. The inventory of the chamber as recorded by Shaw included: *"a decayed human skull and long bones; enamel from the decayed teeth of five individuals; copper wristlets, one of which showed traces of decayed human bones; a bronze skull of a leopard mounted on an iron rod; a pectoral plate; a coronet; a fan holder; a bronze hilt; two mounted brackets; a stylized equestrian figure wearing Igbo facial scarifications and believed to be a fly whisk handle; over one hundred thousand multi-colored beads; and three ivory tusks".* Judging by the rich content of the chamber, the excavator, Shaw, concluded that this was a burial chamber of a person of high status, perhaps an Eze title holder which is the highest title in Igboland. The corpse was buried sitting on a stool studded with brass bosses in a wooden paneled chamber while his hands were propped up by two copper brackets. He wore a coronet and a breast plate; a fly whisk and a fan holder were inserted into each hand. After this arrangement was complete, the chamber was covered over with wooden panels and the corpses of five individuals meant to accompany him were placed above the roof of the chamber and then covered up (Shaw, 1970).

The *Igbo Jonah* was a pit containing animal bones and burnt material. Shaw initially thought it was a dump pit for spent sacrificial objects but a closer study of the site revealed interesting contents which made him conclude that the pit was dug purposely for placing a collection of ritual and ceremonial objects, possibly after a shrine was burnt down and not for the disposal of household refuse. (Shaw, 1978). Inventory of items includes copper wire links, wristlets of different patterns, bells, staff ornaments, and iron blades. It also includes many fragments of pottery and whole pots, the most remarkable of which is forty centimeters high and forty-five centimeters in diameter. It is decorated with deep channeling patterns and projecting bosses. Its five handles are separated by relief models of a ram head, a coiled snake, a chameleon, and a humped object. Remains of both human and antelope bones were found inside one of the pots.

The objects excavated from all the three sites at Igbo-Ukwu did not appear to belong to a commoner or to main stream culture of the producers. Rather, they appeared to be symbols of special wealth or religious ceremonies. Shaw concluded that *"Igbo-Ukwu must have been the center of a social institution which attracted to itself considerable wealth, probably an office which combined the attributes of priest and king and which was recognized over a considerable area, and the excavated sites served as both the shrine and burial site of the paramount head of the community"*. The very large stock of glass and carnelian beads estimated to be over 165,000 were believed to have been imported, probably from Egypt through Lake Chad area both of which were already prominent hubs in the Trans Saharan Trade Route by the 7th to 8th century AD. Most of Igbo-Ukwu castings are outside Nigeria but some of the most metallurgically interesting selections from publications by Shaw, (1970) and others that are on display in the Nigerian and British museums are presented in Figure 6.7.

Figure 6.7a Igbo-Ukwu bronze castings *(Willet 1973; National Commission for Museums, Nigeria; British Museum).*

128 *Early metallurgy in Nigeria*

Figure 6.7b Igbo-Ukwu bronze castings *(Willet 1973; National Commission for Museums, Nigeria; British Museum).*

Early iron and copper metallurgy in Nigeria **129**

Figure 6.7c Igbo-Ukwu bronze castings *(Willet 1973; National Commission for Museums, Nigeria; British Museum).*

130 *Early metallurgy in Nigeria*

Figure 6.7d Igbo-Ukwu bronze castings *(Willet 1973; National Commission for Museums, Nigeria; British Museum)*.

Figure 6.7e Igbo-Ukwu bronze castings *(Willet 1973; National Commission for Museums, Nigeria; British Museum).*

132 *Early metallurgy in Nigeria*

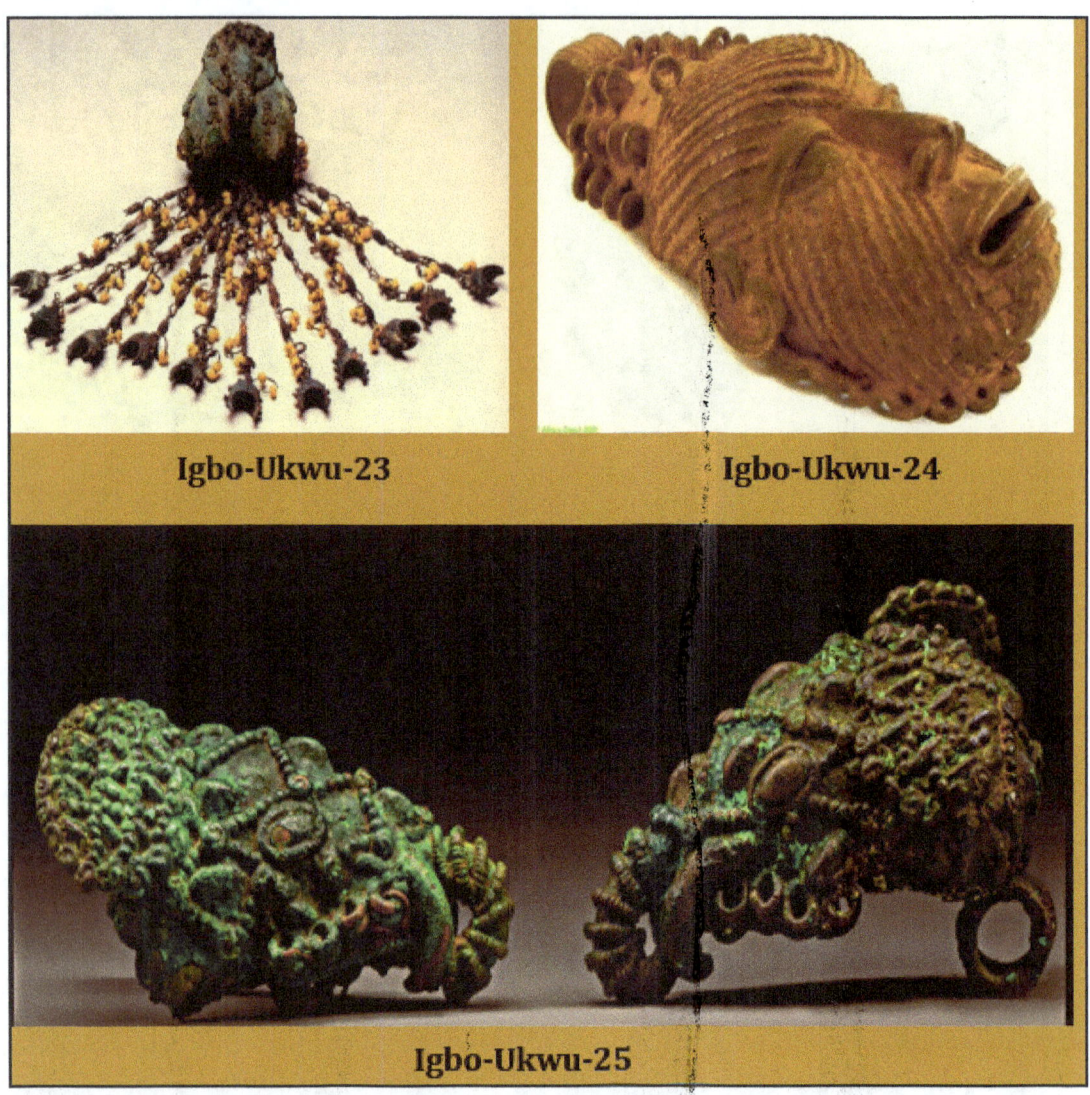

Figure 6.7f Igbo-Ukwu bronze castings *(Willet 1973; National Commission for Museums, Nigeria; British Museum).*

Shaw originally obtained five radiocarbon dates on several materials: wood from some of the objects, charcoal from excavated pits, and determined that four fell in the 9th century AD while the fifth fell in the 15th century, possibly due to sample contamination. Three more dates were later obtained from the British Museum (Table 6.1). Calibrating the results of the two remarkably close dates from two different sources according to the dendrochronological calendar puts seven out of the eight dates in a period between 8th and 11th centuries AD, with a high probability of the 9th century AD considering the likelihood of contamination of one of the samples from Pit IV by younger clay. The stylistics of the ceramic postherds is very much consistent with Igbo art and culture and there is little doubt that they were of local origin. However, the very large number of glass beads and carnelian found did not appear to have been produced locally. In fact the characteristics of many were consistent with Indian or Venetian products, possibly imported through Egypt. Also, evidence has been found confirming that similar beads were being produced in Old Cairo which predates the Muslim conquest of Egypt in the 7th century AD. This indicates with a high degree of certainty that Igbo-Ukwu was in trade contact with some other parts of the world.

Table 6.1 Dates for Igbo-Ukwu artifacts *(Shaw 1983, 1995a, 1995b).*

Dated item	Shaw date (AD)	British Museum date (AD)
Igbo Richard wood stool	850 ± 120	1010 ±370
Igbo Jonah charcoal Pit VI	875 ± 130	
Igbo Jonah charcoal Pit IV	840 ± 110	690 ± 310
Ditto	840 ± 145	850 ± 260
Ditto	1445 ± 70	

The archaeologists who worked on Igbo-Ukwu Copper/Bronze Culture considered the site mysterious and puzzling for several reasons: no evidence of metal smelting was found in the area; no deposits of copper and tin were found; no associated settlement context at all, let alone the usual advanced, complex, stratified social settings associated with metal culture, was found. The occupation of Igbo-Ukwu at the time is believed to have been acephalous or egalitarian, lacking hierarchical or stratified social structures (Garlake, 2002). No evidence has been found that the people had competence in metalworking, wire production, or lost-wax casting; the artifacts have been dated around five centuries before Nigeria's first contact with Europeans. However, the reality is that too little was known about Igbo-Ukwu at the time that could have served as a basis for any reliable conclusions, and evidence is emerging that could help resolve some of the puzzles. There is little doubt that the excavated area served both as ritual site and burial site of an important member of the community, possibly the paramount ruler. Considering African tradition of locating metalworks well away from living areas, it is unlikely that such a venture would have been sited any where near such a holy site. In effect, archaeologists should be looking for evidence of smelting well outside the excavated area. Such sites may still exist or may have been inadvertently destroyed in the course of township expansion. Copper and lead deposits some of which are still being worked have been found in the Abakaliki district of the Benue Rift, about 100 kilometers east of Igbo-Ukwu and tin deposits are available around three hundred kilometers further north-east in the Plateau area of North-Central Nigeria. Small-scale mining of lead and copper ores is still active in the Abakaliki area and products are used as cosmetics and sold at markets across West Africa. A study by Cradock *et al.* (1997) compared lead isotope (LI) ratios of some of the old copper workings with those of a small selection of the castings and concluded that the copper for at least some of the Igbo-Ukwu castings most probably came from the Benue Rift.

Another excavation was carried out by Hartle in the early 1960s at Ifeka Garden, a burial site presumed to belong to a local dignitary in Ezira, around 25 kilometers east of Igbo-Ukwu. The concept was similar to the *Igbo Richard* grave site but the setting was less rich, although the objects were also of exquisite manufacture. Objects interred with his body include bronze anklets, rings, bells, iron gongs, and many ceremonial objects with

134 *Early metallurgy in Nigeria*

decorations similar to Igbo Ukwu decorative patterns, all placed at the feet of the occupant of the grave. (Hartle 1967, 1968). This has led to speculations that many other interesting archaeological sites in the area may be waiting to be discovered. The radiocarbon date for the Ezira site was AD 1495; information about the objects is scanty; and the reliability of the single dating is questionable. However, considering the fact that one of the dates for the Igbo-Ukwu objects was AD 1445 ± 70, the Ezira date may be credible and the two sites could be related. Unfortunately, the Ezira studies were truncated by the 1967 civil war and most of the objects were lost before any detailed analysis of the material could be carried out. However, one specimen analyzed indicated that the alloy was leaded-bronze, similar to alloys used for Igbo Ukwu castings, but the finish was more exquisite and the decorations consisted mainly of finer line designs than those of Igbo Ukwu, probably a result of improvement in bronze working over the centuries and possibly a later development of the same traditions of the earlier Igbo Ukwu peoples (Hartle, 1980). Also, it may mean that the Igbo-Ukwu Copper Culture belonged to the ancient Nri Kingdom which probably extended to Ezira and is ancestral to the Nri of today, and copper technology continued to flourish in the area (and probably beyond) for around six centuries, contrary to the current belief that it disappeared without trace.

6.6.2 Metallurgy of Igbo-Ukwu artifacts

What is known about the metallurgy of Igbo-Ukwu artifacts derives mainly from the comprehensive work of Shaw (1970) which included emission spectroscopic analyses of drillings taken from a large number of the artifacts. A few were also sectioned and examined by metallography. On the basis of the data obtained, it was possible to draw correlations between chemical composition and the technique of manufacture. The objects divided themselves roughly into two groups: Most of the objects found in *Igbo Richard's burial* site were made from copper, arsenical copper or leaded copper, while most of those found in *Igbo Isaiah's* ritual site were made of leaded copper, tin and leaded copper, or leaded bronze (see Table 6.2).

Table 6.2 Chemical composition of Igbo-Ukwu artifacts *(Shaw, 1970)*

Metal	Copper %	Lead %	Tin %	Arsenic %
Copper	>97.0	<1.0	<1.0	<1.1
Arsenical copper	>95.0	<1.0	<1.0	1.3-2.6
Leaded copper	94.0-97.0	2.0-4.0	<1.0	<1.0
Tinned and leaded copper	<93.8	1.2	2.1	1.75
Bronze/Leaded bronze	<93.0	1.0-17.0	2.0-10.0	<1.0
Leaded bronze (low tin)	<93.0	5.0-13.0	1.0-2.0	<1.0
Leaded bronze (high lead, low tin)	<93.0	>13.0	<1.0	-

Most of the artifacts from *Igbo Richard's* compound contain over 97% copper and were clearly made by smithing and chasing, probably by alternate working and annealing and final light cold work. The few that contained 94-97% copper were probably made in the same way. All the objects have a distinctively high arsenic content of 1.3% to 2.6%. The bronzes from *Igbo Isaiah's* compound all have less than 94% copper content and were clearly made by the lost-wax (*cire perdue*) casting process. The most outstanding of the cast objects is the roped pot on stand, 33 centimeters high, weighing 3.2 kilograms (Figure 6.8).

Figure 6.8 Igbo-Ukwu roped pot produced by complex multi-stage lost-wax technology combined with welding, with several parts having different chemical composition *(Shaw, 1970)*.

Extensive chemical and structural analysis of the object shows that it was produced by casting in a series of complex stages, probably as many as five. Spectrographic analyses also show significant differences in the chemical composition of different parts of the object. Unfortunately, not much metallurgical analysis of the metal objects has been done since the initial work of Shaw although the British Museum also carried out some studies. Most of the analysis has been carried out by surface non-destructive methods which can give erroneous results especially with arsenical copper because of segregation. Also, not much has been done to identify the provenance of the ores, ingots or technologies. Nevertheless a brief discussion of early copper metallurgy and casting technologies at this point may answer some of the questions and throw some light on the intentions of the Igbo-Ukwu metalworkers.

Native copper has been worked by hammering from Neolithic times, from around 8000-6000 BC, and was being melted and cast from around 5000 BC. However, the earliest metallurgical evidence of smelting from ores dates back to about 4000 BC. Many copper ores contain arsenic, lead, zinc, tin in relatively small quantities, and, as discussed in Chapter 5, many deposits are heavily stratified, with lean copper oxide ores near the surface and richer sulphide ores in deeper layers. Copper is a soft metal, easy to cold-work, but small quantities of arsenic or tin as low as 2% improves the hardness of cold-worked copper significantly. This must have been discovered by accident, but it quickly became common practice to mix arsenic-rich ores with copper ores to produce arsenical-copper hard enough for making swords, axe heads, etc. Even when the addition of arsenic is incidental, copper can still be cold-worked extensively but intermediate and final annealing would be required.

The complex copper products recovered from the burial site at *Igbo Richard* compound were made from arsenical alloys, evidently cold-worked by smithing, chasing twisting with multiple intermediate annealing, possibly finished by light cold-working. It is the only way in which the complex designs of twisted copper wire on some of the products could have been achieved. It is unlikely that the objects were made from local ores since no ore deposit with any significant arsenic content has been found in the area. It is likely they were made from imported ingots. The objects had the highest copper content of 95-97% and no lead, and would have been the most expensive of all the metal artifact collections in terms of material and artwork. Clearly they were the objects that furnished the environment of a prominent and wealthy member of the community (probably the Eze), and were buried with him as was the practice in most kingdoms of the early world.

Silver naturally occurs in various ores and minerals, often as sulfides or chlorides or in combination with arsenic or antimony. Ores that contain silver are considered more valuable for silver production and the metal is normally recovered from copper smelting as a by-product. In modern metallurgy, the principal sources of silver are copper, copper-nickel, gold, lead, and lead-zinc ores, commonly extracted from ore by smelting or chemical leaching. The metal is also produced during the electrolytic refining of copper and by application of the Parkes process on lead metal obtained from lead ores that contain small amounts of silver. The amount of silver in Igbo-Ukwu castings was unusually high, and could have come from the copper or, lead ore, or both. Lead ores (PbS, galena) and zinc ores (ZnS, sphalerite) often occur together as lead-zinc ores which have been found in Abakaliki, the most probable source of both the lead and zinc found in Igbo-Ukwu castings. In effect the presence of silver was probably incidental, coming from the lead-zinc ores but its presence in bronze even in very small quantities has a very significant effect on the mechanical properties. The presence of just 0.1% silver increases the strength of cast copper by around 65% and the hardness by 60%.

Bronze is an alloy of copper and tin but tin content of 7-12% is required for true tin bronzes. Tin (or arsenic) content of 7-8% more or less doubles the hardness of cold-worked copper for the same degree of reduction. This explains why bronze quickly replaced copper in the Early Bronze Age once casters had access to tin ingots: it made possible the production of much stronger weapons, in particular, swords, arrow tips, axes. As discussed earlier, tin-bronze was probably discovered by accident in the process of smelting high-tin copper ores. For example, a copper ore found in Cornwall, South Wales in England contained 0.94% tin and 12.3% copper. Smelting of this ore carried out in a laboratory produced true bronze with copper:tin ratio of 93:7. Lead confers fluidity on copper or bronze in the casting process, thereby enhancing the production of complex castings, (although too much lead reduces the mechanical strength of the casting). Again, this must have been discovered in ancient times by accident in the process of smelting lead-rich copper ores, but it soon became common practice from the third to second millennium BC to deliberately mix lead and copper ores in order to produce highly castable copper alloys, as must have happened in Igbo-Ukwu. The bronzes contained on average 6.5% tin and 8% lead and it can be concluded with a very high degree of confidence that lead was added deliberately probably by mixing ores to produce high-fluidity molten copper and bronze (alloy of copper and tin) required for the complex lost-wax (*cire perdue*) process adopted for the castings. Some castings were made in complex multiple casting stages: for example, one bronze bowl appeared to have been made by first casting small decorative items including insects, spirals and other decorative shapes and placing them on the wax model before the main parts of the bowl were made. The vessel itself was then cast in two parts and fitted together by casting a middle band (Shaw 1965).

6.6.3 Quality of Igbo-Ukwu artifacts

The quality of Igbo-Ukwu metal artifacts has been assessed and reviewed by many eminent specialists from different parts of the world and adjudged to be of high technical proficiency, with exceptional surface detail, unique and exotic stylistics not comparable to findings anywhere else in the world, and therefore contradicts the common speculation of a European origin. Furthermore, the very wide range of subjects and objects (ritual bowls, flies, snakes, frogs, eggs, etc., paraphernalia for the dignitary, facial scarifications, were all within the well-known early Igbo culture and also featured in terracotta, pottery and stone carving technologies of the period. The Igbo-Ukwu artifacts have been acclaimed worldwide as exotic masterpieces, evident from the following quotes retrieved from world archaeological literature: *"an exquisite explosion without antecedent or issue"* (Williams, 1974); *"The Igbo-Ukwu bronzes portray a standard that is comparable to that established by Benvenuto Cellini five hundred years later in Europe"* (Frank Willet, 1983); *"Igbo-Ukwu bronzes compare to the finest jewelry of rococo Europe or of Carl Faberge"* (Garlake, 2002); *"The Igbo-Ukwu bronzes amazed the world with a very high level of technical and artistic proficiency and sophistication which was at this time distinctly more advanced than bronze casting in Europe......"A water pot set in a mesh of simulated rope is a virtuoso feat of cire perdue (lost wax) casting. Its elegant design and refined detailing are matched by a level of technical accomplishment that is notably more advanced than European bronze casting of this period"* (Honour and Fleming, 2005); The Grove Encyclopedia of Materials and Techniques in Art describes the castings as being *"among the most inventive and technically accomplished bronzes ever made"* (Ward, 2008).

Although the origin of the lost-wax casting technique is unknown, it was certainly not invented by the Igbo-Ukwu people because it had been practiced in different parts of the world for thousands of years previously. The process has its origins in ancient Indian, Chinese and Egyptian civilizations and there is some evidence that it had been practiced in Mesopotamia by the end of the fourth millennium BC, and in Egypt from the second millennium, but it was only in the Iron Age when inter-regional trade had become well-established that the practice became widespread, used primarily for non-ferrous metals and terracotta. However, many casters infuse considerable local innovations, as evident in some West African practices, for example, the complex multiple-step casting which must have been adopted in producing some of the Igbo-Ukwu artifacts has not been seen elsewhere in the early world. Some of the techniques used by the ancient smiths are not known to have been used outside Igbo-Ukwu such as the production of complex objects in stages with the different parts later fixed together by brazing or by casting linking sections to join them (Willet, 1972; Garlake, 2002). Also, the fine and filigrene surface detail of some of the castings is believed to have been achieved by substituting the traditional beeswax with latex obtained locally.

Archaeologists have questioned the feasibility of Igbo smiths producing such exotic copper/bronze objects, considering they used the simple *cire perdue* or lost wax technique in creating them, and the well-known difficulties of the casting technology. This is erroneous for three reasons: The most important asset of the process is the ability to reproduce the fine details on the pattern and artist in many parts of Africa had demonstrated outstanding capability in earlier works with wood, stone and terracotta work. *Cire perdue* is still a major casting process in modern metallurgical engineering. While the ancient craftsmen used the process mainly for art and craft work, it has found extensive use in the production of precision castings in metals which are usually very difficult or impossible to machine or shape at ordinary temperatures or when exceptionally complex or fine details have to be reproduced. For such components, investment casting is often the only option. It is a high precision process (± 0.05 mm per mm) capable of reproducing the finest details with high dimensional accuracy, often with hardly any need for finishing. Such is the precision and versatility that an adaptation of the basic technique is being used to produce intricate high-precision automobile, aircraft, aerospace and general engineering components which would otherwise entail much more expensive machining. Other modern products of lost-wax casting are fine precious metal jewelry, dental crowns and inlays, automobile engine blocks, jet engine impellers, gas turbine blades, and other complex, exquisite products.

The second reason for the speculation that the objects were not produced locally is the apparent lack of knowledge or sustained practice of metal casting technologies in the area. The most important aspect of metal casting is the production of the pattern which must replicate the desired object as faithfully as possible. Producing a pattern in metal, clay, wood or terracotta is the work of an artist turned pattern maker and the most complex aspect of metal casting technologies. In fact, pattern making is such an intricate work that many modern foundries contract the work out to specialized shops especially for complex designs. In general, the cost of the pattern accounts for around 60-75% of the total product cost depending on the complexity. There is ample evidence that Africans had the artistic competence to produce complex artwork in stone, wood or terracotta, the main skill required for making casting patterns, and were making pots, terracotta figurines and other objects of intricate design from early times, probably from the third millennium BC well before any metal culture in the region. For example, the excavations in Igbo areas carried out in the early 1960s unearthed many items including carved stones, pots and other clay vessels dated between 2555-1460 BC (Hartle, 1966). The terracotta figurines found in the Nok area are believed to be older than the metal objects and much more widespread across many cultures considering the scarifications. It is likely that many of the terracotta figurines may have been produced by lost-wax casting.

The third speculation about the difficulty of casting copper is actually correct: copper is extremely difficult to cast because it oxidizes very rapidly, and microstructure of castings often feature oxide inclusions which are detrimental to mechanical properties and finish. However, copper can still be cast successfully, either by preheating the mould thereby slowing down cooling rate and minimizing oxidation, or by adding fluidity-enhancing alloying elements, such as arsenic or lead. The Igbo-Ukwu castings contain lead, some as high as 8%, (presumably produced by smelting mixtures of copper and lead-zinc ores from Abakaliki area) and it is possible that the casters were also aware of and possibly practiced the option of preheating the mould. Copper casting is certainly a more intricate and expensive process than bronze casting and this may explain why products are usually reserved for royalty or people of means, and why most of the nearly pure copper objects found in Igbo-Ukwu were at the burial site of an obviously eminent citizen, probably an Eze. It should be noted also that most of these objects were not cast but worked, which is typical of nearly pure copper products. The presence of arsenic in the products may have been incidental and a consequence of the copper ore composition but even small quantities could improve the mechanical properties of the worked product significantly.

6.6.4 Ethnography of Igbo-Ukwu

Another puzzling aspect of the Igbo-Ukwu Metal Culture is the apparent lack of typical ethnographic and cultural features that have been found associated with metal cultures in other regions of the early world: archaeological evidence of advanced, complex, hierarchical and prosperous socio-cultural existence that could have hosted, nurtured and funded metal technologies. The origin of Igbo people is hazy, and much of what is known through oral tradition is full of myths. The work of Hartle (1967) shows that Southeastern Nigeria had been occupied at least from around 3000 BC, based on excavated archaeological objects but there is no evidence that the area has been occupied continuously by the same people. No one really knows for sure the ethnography of Igbo-Ukwu in the 9th century AD, or whether the same people have occupied the area from then to date. In fact the date of the Igbo-Ukwu archaeological site seems to have become the only reliable reference for the current occupants. In the course of research for this book, considerable time was spent in the area, interviewing people in Igbo-Ukwu and surrounding towns within about 30 kilometers of the area in order to relate the archaeological findings to the probable early culture. This was inspired by the well-known African practices surrounding location of shrines and burial sites of paramount leaders which were (and still are) off living areas. In effect we should be looking outside Igbo-Ukwu for possible ethnographic data. Perhaps the most interesting was the interview with the Eze Nri, the ruler of Agukwu Nri about 20 kilometers north of Igbo-Ukwu (Figure 6.9b). He claimed that the Nri people arrived in Igbo land in the ninth century AD but he had no idea where they came from. However, the city state soon became very powerful and influential in the region. They were particularly famous and feared for their mystical occultism and ritualistic shrines, with Eze Nri as the spiritual leader; they were also ardent traders with networks inside and outside the Igbo land. The ruler claimed that the land on which Anozie compound was built belonged to Orieri around 5 kilometers north of Igbo-Ukwu, and that Orieri was part of the Nri kingdom. This claim was also documented by Jeffreys (1935), Shaw (1970), and Onwuejeogwu (1981). Shaw speculated that Igbo-Ukwu probably served as the ritual center for Orieri and the wider Nri kingdom, and the burial site was probably that of an Eze Nri. It should be noted also that this region of Igbo land is not strange to metal technology: Nsukka area, around a hundred kilometers north east of Igbo-Ukwu had Early Iron Culture dated 675 BC to AD 75 (Figure 6.9c).

It is likely that the Eze of the ancient Nri Kingdom was the prime driver of local copper/bronze technology and may also have been involved in extensive importation of foreign artifacts, considering the very large number of obviously imported glass artworks. It is also probable that the arsenical copper ingots used for the artwork found in the grave site at *Igbo Richard* compound were imported. The region does not seem to have had any significant inter- of intra-ethnic wars that could have terminated local metal smelting practice like the Yorubas in the Western region, hence the wide speculation that the demise of the Eze may have been the cause. It is also possible that the practice did not disappear suddenly as widely speculated, but continued in the area for several hundred years,

140 *Early metallurgy in Nigeria*

considering the findings in Ezira. Furthermore, in view of the paucity of archaeological studies in the area, important archaeological metal smelting sites and activities in neighbouring areas like Ezira discussed earlier may exist and are yet to be found.

6.6.5 Provenance of Igbo-Ukwu Copper/Bronze Culture

The controversy over the provenance of Igbo-Ukwu metal culture dates back six decades, becoming more political than academic, and there are few signs of abatement. Most foreign archaeologists believe that such exotic castings could not have been produced locally due to lack of evidence of advanced culture that was typical of ancient metal producers, or local sources of raw materials, while their local counterparts have sought relentlessly to prove otherwise. It is not the intention here to get involved in the controversy, but rather to examine the issues critically from the metallurgical point of view. While some items found in Igbo-Ukwu such as glass and stone beads were almost definitely imported from or through the Middle East (most probably Egypt), all the other items were almost certainly produced locally, considering the wide range of subjects that are distinctively symbolic of African culture and art: snake, snails, ritual bowls, staff of office, masks, bronze heads that featured Nri scarifications reserved for important ambassadors of the Nri kingdom, insects, animals that had distinct local symbolism, and many more. The iconography of these objects appears to relate well to present-day Igbo culture (Phillipson 1993).

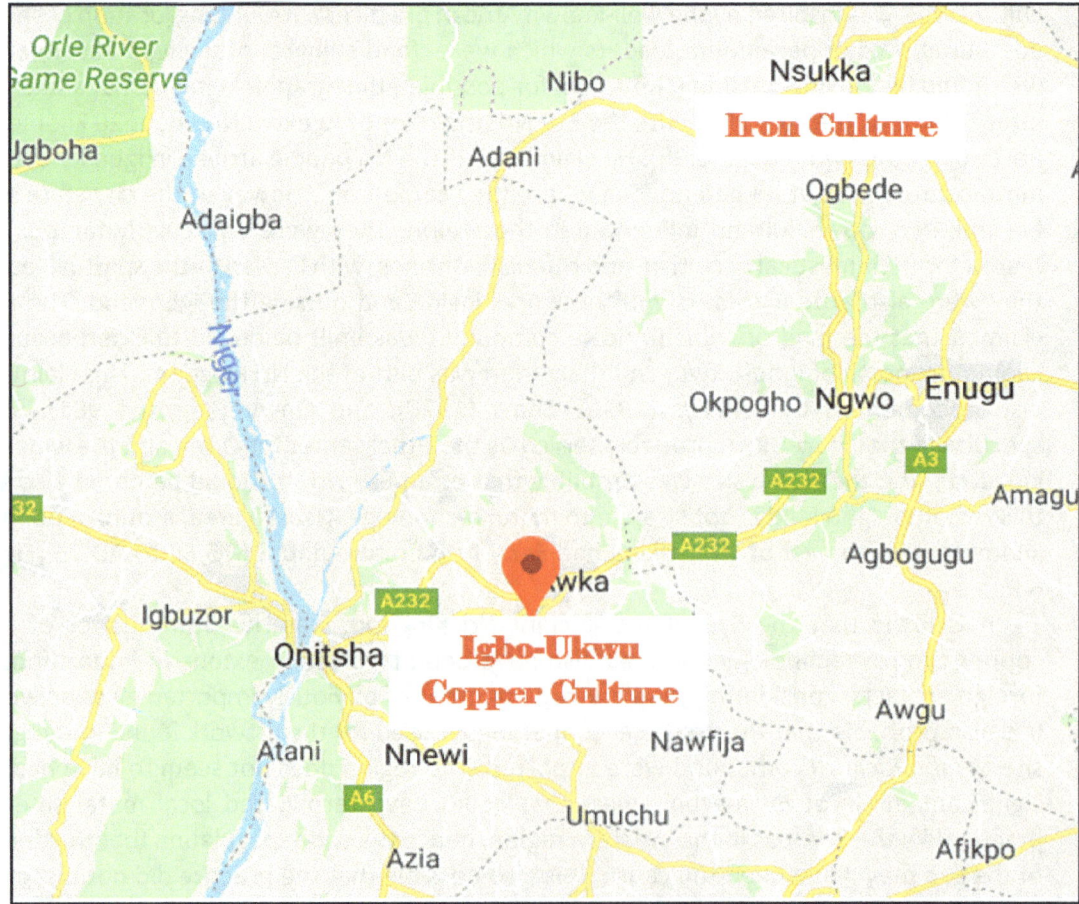

Figure 6.9a Southeastern Nigerian Iron and Copper Cultures around the 9th century AD.

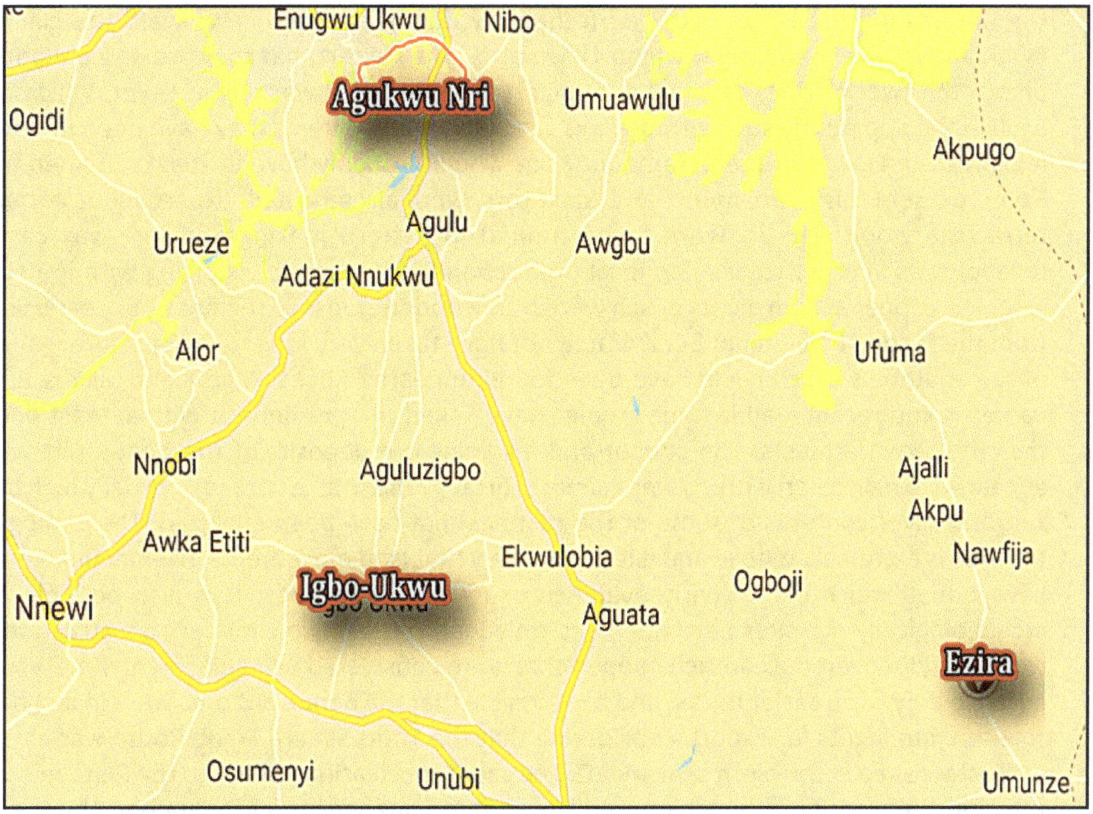

Early iron and copper metallurgy in Nigeria 141

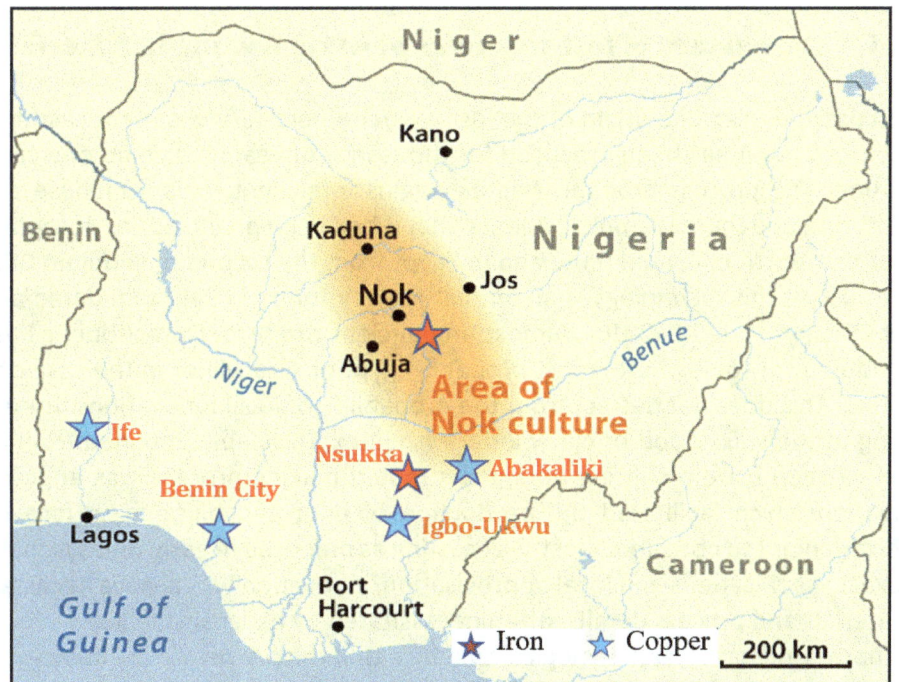

Figure 6.9b Igbo-Ukwu and Ezira in the ancient Nri Kingdom around the 9th century AD.

Figure 6.9c Early/Late Metal Culture areas in Nigeria

142 Early metallurgy in Nigeria

One interesting issue that occurred frequently during the interviews was the claim of Egyptian/Israeli ancestry by the Igbo-Ukwu area. They assert that they are descendants of one of the twelve tribes of Israel and migrated while Israel was still in Egypt, which may explain the apparently strong trade links with Egypt. Some items may have been imported initially from Egypt but the paramount ruler would probably have invited craftsmen from Egypt or sent his craftsmen and sculptors who already had expertise in complex terracotta/wood/clay art work to be trained in pattern making and lost wax casting technologies in order to develop local production facility, possibly starting with imported arsenical copper and tin ingots which were freely traded across all regions of the early world from the second millennium BC. It would not have taken very long to look for local sources of raw materials which could have been found in nearby Abakaliki area and, as discussed earlier, some recent lead isotope studies have linked the ore deposit with at least one of the Igbo-Ukwu artifacts. The copper and lead-zinc ore deposits of the Benue Rift which appeared to have been worked were almost certainly the sources of the unusually high lead, zinc and silver contents of some of the castings that have been analyzed. The geology of the area is extremely mobile and it is not unlikely that land movements, river incursions etc. have buried much of the early evidence of metals technology. It is also possible that archaeologically rich sites have been destroyed inadvertently my modern construction, or remain undiscovered. Lead-rich copper ores were considered valuable in early metallurgy because they were easier to cast and it is possible that the Benue Rift ores were in fact being smelted into ingots for export, considering that the Trans Sahara Trade Route was already well established in the ninth century AD. The same speculation applies to the Plateau's very valuable tin deposits, although no credible evidence has been found to support this theory. However, it is possible that ample evidence remains undiscovered or has been destroyed by extensive opencast mining in the area in modern times.

6.6.6 Provenance of lost-wax (*cire perdue*) casting in Nigeria

As discussed earlier, the origin of the lost-wax/cire perdue/investment casting technology is unknown but it has been practiced for thousands of years hence no one can claim local invention. The process probably has its origins in ancient Indian, Chinese and Egyptian civilizations, and there is ample evidence that it had been practiced in Mesopotamia by the end of the fourth millennium BC, and in Egypt from the second millennium BC. The oldest known use of this technology is an amulet jewelry found in Pakistan, dated around 6,000 years (Thoury, M. *et al.* (2016). Almost any ancient or current practitioner has learnt the technique from somewhere, most probably Egypt or Asia Minor in the case of Igbo-Ukwu smelters. This does not detract from the probability of local innovations: for example, the coating of the wax, wood or clay model with latex, (probably obtained from local rubber trees) to keep it from shifting during the mould making process was apparently a local innovation which facilitated the production of finer and filigrene surface details. One important point to note about lost-wax casting as practiced in early times is that there were no exact specifications and local improvisation/innovation was always necessary, in terms of materials and process details, often necessitated by expensive failures.

There is increasing archaeological evidence that the *cire perdue* technology and possibly the initial supply of copper ingots to Igbo-Ukwu (and possibly Ife and Benin) could have come from the Sahelian region, the area of grassland south of the Sahara that forms a belt around one thousand kilometers long across Africa from the Atlantic Ocean in the west to the Red see in the east (Figure 6.10). New archaeological evidence shows that iron and copper were being produced in many locations and traded across the Sahel from the fifth to seventh century AD, well before the establishment of trade with the north across the Sahara (UNESCO 1992). Metalworking sites have been found in various sites in Senegal valley, Ivory Coast, along the valleys of River Niger, southern region of Niger. Well-organized towns and advanced community life flourished and trade in copper and iron products was vibrant across the Sahel and in the inland Niger Delta. Salt from Awlil mine along the north bank of the Senegal and other local sources was traded by boat on the Nile, Senegal and Niger. Archaeological evidence of *cire perdue* practice has been found in the southern Mauritania dated to the same early periods. Trade between the north-south Saharan route and the Sahel (which was very difficult and needed to involve valuable commodities to justify the risks) began to flourish from around mid-eighth or ninth century AD. The main products which have been identified were exports of valuable gold and, possibly copper, iron and tin ingots from West Africa and imports of precious stones, glass beads, potsherds from the north.

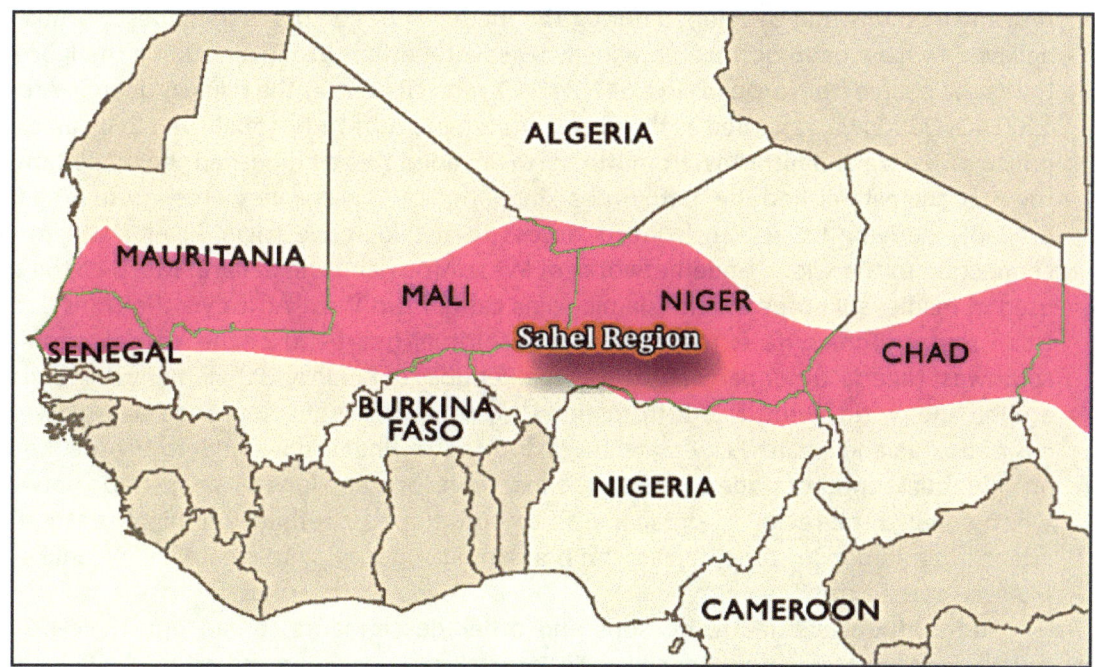

Figure 6.10   Sahel region of Africa

6.7   IFE LATE COPPER/BRONZE CULTURE

Throughout ancient history, metallurgical technologies required significantly advanced cultures to flourish and archaeological metal artifacts tell a lot about the socio-political, hierarchical structure of the early communities in which they were produced. Ile-Ife, an ancient city in Southwestern Nigeria is famous for its bronze artworks from around the 12th century AD. It is important therefore to establish the probable early history of Ife in order to reach feasible conclusions about who produced the copper alloy artifacts, under what

6.7.1 Early history of Ile-Ife

Evidence both oral and written on early human settlements in Nigeria is scanty. The oldest fossil remains found by archaeologists in the south-western area or Iwo Eleru near Akure have been dated to about 9000 BC (encyclopaedia Britanica 2019). There are also isolated collections of ancient tools and artifacts of different periods of the Stone Age, but the oldest recognizable evidence of an organized society was in Nok already discussed above. The oral history of Ife is full of myths: for example, existence of Ile-Ife is believed to date back to around 500 BC but there is no physical evidence to support this. Another myth, claims that Ife was the center of the creation of the world and all mankind but no archaeological evidence has been found to support this claim. The extensive research publications by prominent historians notably from the early part of the last century have been reviewed in depth and the most credible versions are summarized below.

The Ife kingdom first emerged around 700-800 AD, one of several competing West African kingdoms that developed during the medieval period. Ife is the oldest Yoruba city believed to have been occupied originally by several ethnic groups including the Igbo and the Yagba people from around circa 647-747 AD, with Obatala as the ruling monarch. Around 1200 AD, Oduduwa, regarded as the ancestor of the Yorubas who is believed to be an exiled prince of Mecca and his army from the north invaded the city, pushed the inhabitants to the east and established the first Yoruba kingdom. Ile-Ife was a very prosperous kingdom, probably deriving its wealth from its access to the lucrative Niger River trade routes, connecting to the wider trade networks of West Africa and the Sahara. Much of the gold used in medieval European and Islamic coins came from West Africa via the trans-Sahara trade routes. Today, Ife is regarded as the spiritual heartland of the Yoruba people of southwest Nigeria, other parts of Nigeria, the Republic of Benin and their many descendants around the world. From the 12th to the 15th century AD, Ife flourished as a powerful, cosmopolitan and wealthy city-state in West Africa, in what is now modern Nigeria. Ife was an influential center of trade connected to extensive local and long-distance trade networks which enabled the region to prosper. The city developed a refined and highly naturalistic sculptural tradition in stone, terracotta, brass and copper-alloy to create a style unlike any in Africa at the time.

After Oduduwa's death, his sons and other descendants spread out of Ile-Ife and founded other states, with sixteen historic Yoruba kingdoms embraced within the Ife political sphere, which eventually led to the emergence of the Yorubas as one of Africa's largest ethnic groups. Oduduwa brought with him traditional religious and spiritual concepts and practices which rivaled Obatala, the autochthonous deity. Apparently there was incessant conflict between the indigenous communities and the 'foreigners.' It is believed that one of the warring factions contacted Oranmiyan, a grandson of Oduduwa and an ardent warrior who had become the first reigning monarch in Benin. Oranmiyan returned to Ife leaving his son to succeed him and, siding with the Oduduwa faction, sent the reigning monarch Obalufon II who is believed to have reigned in the 13th century into exile. Obalufon II eventually managed to rally support of the indigenous people of Ife and take back power. He was then able to unite the various ethnic factions, and this explains why two dynasties: Obatala and Oduduwa, emerged and have survived to date, with the Obatala group in charge of religious and ritual matters while the Oduduwa group took care of civic and to some extent, political matters. This version of oral history is feasible for several reasons: the well-documented ethnic and multi-cultural diversity of Ile-Ife from pre-historic times has been sustained to date, with groups linked to Obatala dynasty retaining special supremacy on religious matters in the later Oduduwa dynastic era. Both groups still feature prominently in the city's social, political and ritual life today. Furthermore, features and facial marking forms in early Ife sculptures reflect stylistics associated with several ethnic groups. In fact, some historians suggest that the Igbos were the indigenous people of Ife ruled by Orisanla (Obatala) who were subdued by Oduduwa, while others believe that they were of the pre-Oduduwa royal lineage who left Ife as a result of the quarrel between Obatala and Oduduwa to found their own settlements in the eastern parts of the country. It is believed that the reigning monarch Obalufon II played a prime role in unifying the various ethnic factions, giving prominence to the socio-cultural identities of each group and promoting inter-marriages. This is also evident in the very wide range of facial markings on many of the artifacts of the period reflecting different patterns identified today with other cultures: Edo, Igbo, Yagba, Nupe. In some cases, marks from different cultures were displayed on the same face. It is significant also that these various cultures still exist in today's Ile-Ife: the Igbos still feature prominently in modern rituals, and there are Yagba and Igbo-speaking compounds.

Iron culture seems to have arrived in Ile-Ife well before copper/bronze culture. As speculated earlier in this chapter, Nok may have been an industrial park established by people who came from different cultures and directions. They smelted local iron ores using locally produced charcoal, and took wrought iron ingots back to their respective settlements for forging and shaping, and the Igbos who are ardent migrants and prolific traders, with a very long history of competence in iron technology could have been one of the groups. Around the same time or shortly after, the Igbos started smelting iron ores found around Nsukka and, over centuries, acquired strong ironworking skills which they eventually spread to many surrounding cultures including the Edos of Benin area, the Yorubas of Yagba, Ilorin, Old Oyo and Ile-Ife. In fact, some archaeologists believe that the Nsukka Iron Culture predated Nok, starting possibly in the later part of the second millennium BC but this is widely disputed. It is also possible that some of the Igbos who migrated to Ife already had experience in copper alloy artwork from the Igbo-Ukwu Culture which predated the Ife Culture by several hundred years. The Yagbas were prolific traders, boatmen and iron casters who spread trade along the Niger river and into most of southern Nigeria, including Ile-Ife. As we shall see later in this chapter, both ethnic groups may have played a key role in the development of the Ife copper culture. In fact, if the Ife oral history outlined above is correct, Obalufon II who has been credited with the copper culture was probably an Igbo.

6.7.2 Early Ife art history

Ife was undoubtedly a very active center for artwork, considering the very large variety of artifacts that have been found in the area, dated from around the 9th century to 15th century AD. The artists appeared to have excelled in producing artifacts in terracotta, stone, wood before transiting to metals, and many of the artifacts, in particular the stone and terracotta products have bee described in international critiques as '*truly outstanding*' (Figure 6.11). The women excelled in pottery and glass bead production and may also have been involved

146 *Early metallurgy in Nigeria*

in terracotta artwork as well. Some of their products have been found at sites all along the West African coast.

Figure 6.11a Ife terracotta artifacts

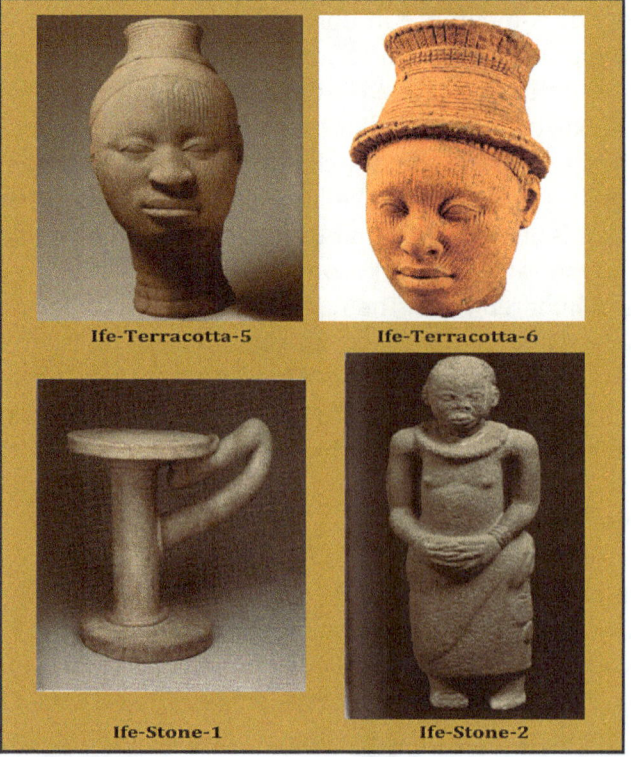

Figure 6.11b Ife terracotta and quartz artifacts

Considering the cosmopolitan nature of Ife city and its wealth, people with different artistic skills probably migrated from different communities that now make up Nigeria, while they traded their products widely and also spread metal technologies over a very wide area of the early Yoruba Kingdom's sphere of influence. However, the tempo was apparently not uniform through out the period, and transition to metals appeared to have occurred in different places between the 13th and 17th century AD, while activities seemed to have declined thereafter.

Several researchers have classified the Late Copper/Bronze Culture of Ife period into three phases under different names but the most recent by Blier (2015) appears the most logical. Blier identifies a *high-fluorescence era* (1250-1350 AD) during which most of the early arts appear to have been made, and provided credible justification: carbon and thermoluminescence dating of most of the artifacts (terracotta, copper alloys) fall in this period; the likely era of Obalufon II who has been identified as the monarch who sponsored Copper Culture was within this period; and this era seems to mark the beginning of Ife's second dynasty - the Oduduwa. Prior to this period (*pre-fluorescence era*) artwork activities were relatively low and less organized, and terracotta, wood, stone and clay were the main media. It is also possible that iron technology was practiced. By around 1400 AD (*post-fluorescence era*), there had been a drastic decline in art production for unknown reasons. Production of artwork, particularly in copper alloys is a very expensive hobby and requires the sponsorship of the rich and dedicated. The demise of Obalufon II may have marked the beginning of the end for the arts and crafts enterprises, just as the same may have happened in Igbo-Ukwu. It has also been speculated that production declined due to the death of the artists by arsenic poisoning. Both theories are credible considering the naturalistic uniformity and strikingly similar and consistent stylistics of most of the outstanding works of this period, giving credence to the suggestion that they may all have been produced in the same workshops by the same groups of artisans over a period of a few decades. Another possible reason is the decline of the Ife empire which started around 1400 AD due to internal unrest and wars with neighbours, a development which gave impetus to the emergence of several new powerful empires, notably the Oyo and Benin kingdoms and shifted political and economic power, and much of the art expertise to these neighbouring city states. This theory is also credible because copper alloy culture spread to other communities throughout the Yoruba kingdom, due probably to the exodus of artisans and artists fleeing from conflict. Most of the artwork found in city states around Ife have been dated post-fluorescence era and the stylistics of many of the products bear substantial resemblance to the Ife artwork (British Museum, 2010).

6.7.3 The high-fluorescence era artifacts

Obalufon II has been acknowledged as the patron of the Ife art culture which flourished during his reign. He is believed to have mobilized and motivated the establishment of art workshops which produced most of the refined and naturalistic sculptures of the high fluorescence era in terracotta, stone and copper alloys. The terracotta sculptures constitute by far the largest group of artworks associated with the era and include sculptures depicting human and animal subjects, vessels, stools, etc. The human heads appear to have been designed to symbolize the diversity of the city state, while most of the animals are prominent cultural and ritualistic symbols. Many of the human heads feature cultural facial striations associated with different cultural groups who probably lived within or around Ile-Ife. The terracotta and copper alloy heads were probably produced for use in the coronation or accession of new rulers of Ife and other Yoruba city states which owed allegiance to Ife, in honour of past rulers, and for use during the numerous ritualistic ceremonies. Some of the male/female figures apparently modeled after high-status people are adorned with crowns, regalia or jewelry. Other products which include facial masks and ritual pots were (and still are) used in many ceremonies including appeasement of various spirits which are believed to reside in Ife. They also serve as objects of worship representing the images of deities and are used for ritual purposes as well as historical objects for personal memory. Ife served (and still serves) as a major center for trado-cultural religion. The city had a large number sacred groves and shrines located in the city forests and some are still in use for rituals to key gods which are performed regularly. The Ife people apparently have a very long tradition dating back around 600 years and most of the artifacts were either in commemoration of passing elites, in particular, the ruler, for adornment of the king's palace or burial site, or for rituals. Most of the terracotta and copper alloy figures were richly adorned with crowns and jewelry. Virtually all the modeled animals had some cultural significance: snakes, snails, elephants, leopards, etc. Some ritualistic artifacts are excavated for use during specific festivals and then buried until the next celebration.

Towards the end of the nineteenth century AD, missionaries and visitors who visited Ife smuggled out artworks which gave Ife sculptures the first exposure to the West, mostly quartz and terracotta artworks. However, it was the work of Leo Frobenius, a German ethnologist in 1913 that led to the discovery of the first copper alloy artwork and perhaps the most famous: the goddess Olokun head Figure 6.12 .

Figure 6.12 Olokun Head

Apparently, Frobenius had heard about the casting from visitors who saw it displayed at a festival to celebrate Olokun the sea god, deity of water, healing, reproduction and commerce. He traveled to Ife and requested that the goddess Olokun head be exhumed (it was normally buried at Olokun grove between festivals). A copper alloy head was exhumed along with seven terracotta heads with attached human hair or beaded veil. Frobenius described the artwork as an exquisite casting made from brass (containing some lead) by the lost-wax casting process. He believed he had found the long-lost Greek Poseidon because he did not think such a high quality casting could have been made locally (Frobenius, 1913). Most of the terracotta heads have rings considered beauty marks on the neck, and some have holes apparently intended for fixture of decorations. All heads have four holes drilled into the neck indicating that they were nailed onto a wooden pole and, as suggested by Willett (1976), borne in a ceremony, probably the second funeral rites. Two other remarkable bronzes were excavated from Ita Yemoo along with the full figure of a past ruler, possibly Obalufon II. One is the intertwined figure of a ruler and his Queen with their hands and feet interlocked in a ritual gesture (Figure 13c, Ife-18). The other is a ceremonial vessel wrapped around by the figure of a queen holding a royal sceptre in her right hand (Figure 13c, Ife-21). The vessel is set on a stool with a looped handle on which the queen's left hand rests. The looped handle of the stool rests on a four-legged foot stool (Ekpo Eyo).

In 1938-39, eighteen more exquisite copper alloy heads and terracotta artwork were dug up accidentally in Wunmonije compound near the Ooni's palace and at Ita Yemoo during construction work. However, from around 1943, the newly established Federal Department of Antiquities organized many excavations which turned up more copper alloy castings and a very large number of terracotta artifacts. Around forty copper alloy artifacts belonging to the fluorescence era have been found and most are designed to convey a wide variety of messages: preeminence, authority, unity, diversity, commemoration, war, peace, disaster, punishment, ritualistics, etc. Many of the artworks feature animals considered as symbols of virtues: ram, elephant, lion, hippopotamus, leopard are all viewed as powerful, alert, protective and commanding in their natural environments (See Blier, 2015). The copper alloy figures produced were sacred and mostly used by the Ife royalty. The figures were mostly heads (revered as crown of body and the seat of the soul) which depict kings and queens, court attendants, sacrificial victims and other religious deities. The portrait-like realism and naturalism of the copper alloy heads, combining technical accomplishment with strong aesthetic appeal, is unique in African art and well-accredited in global arts. In spite of notable individual characteristics of each head, an idealized, naturalistic uniformity is evident. The stylistic similarities of the eighteen almost life-size heads found suggest that they were made by an individual artist or in a single workshop over a relatively short period of time. These heads are believed to be associated with the coronation or the accession rituals of new rulers of Yoruba city-states which owed allegiance to Ife. Some of heads were cast from arsenical copper, a very difficult and dangerous material to work with. These may have been the first set of metal artworks, supplanted by bronze castings either because the artists died of arsenic poisoning, or gave up because of the enormous difficulty of casting copper and switched to newly acquired bronze technology. Since no evidence of copper ore deposit or copper smelting has been found anywhere near Ife, it is safe to assume that copper ingots were imported, remelted and cast into objects, in which case the artists simply used whatever alloy they had access to at a given time. Also arsenical copper which dominated the Early Copper Culture started to be replaced by bronze from the second millennium BC and may have become scarce in the Late Copper Culture era. Most of Ife copper and bronze artifacts are located in British and Nigerian museums and some of the outstanding artworks are shown in Figure 6.13.

150 *Early metallurgy in Nigeria*

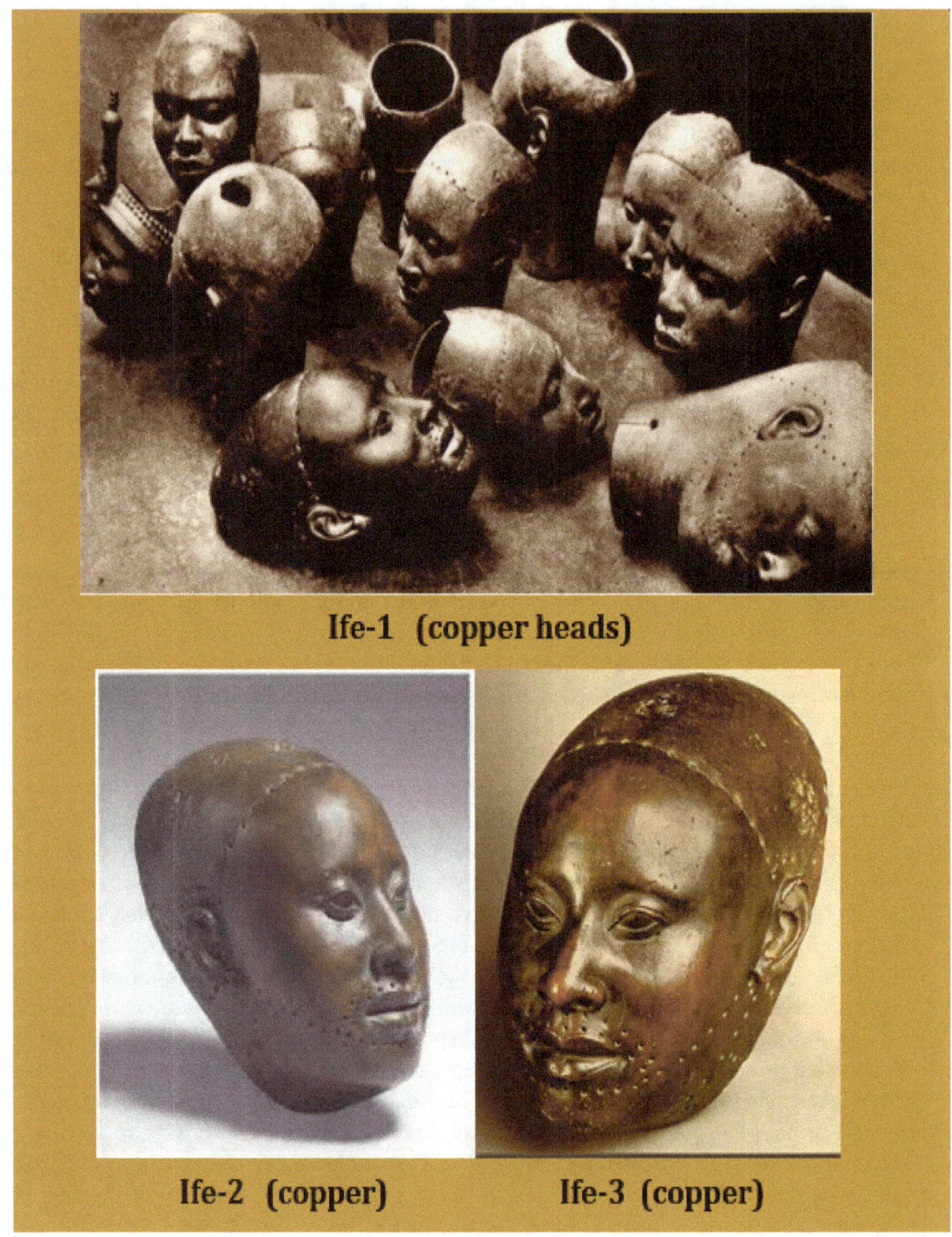

Figure 6.13a Selections from Ife copper/bronze artifacts

Early iron and copper metallurgy in Nigeria 151

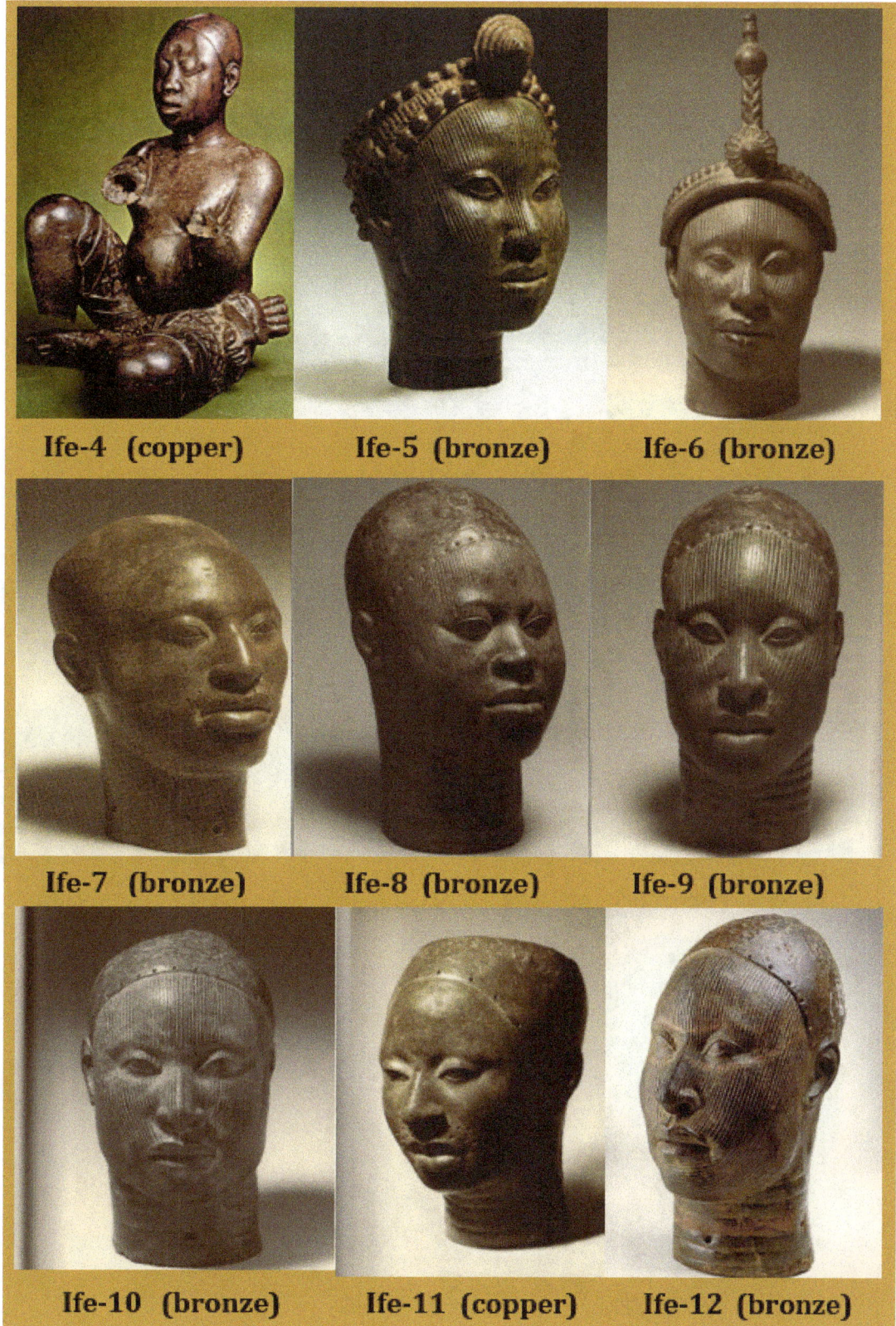

Figure 6.13b Selections from Ife copper/bronze artifacts

152 *Early metallurgy in Nigeria*

Figure 6.13c Selections from Ife copper/bronze artifacts

Early iron and copper metallurgy in Nigeria

Figure 6.13d Selections from Ife copper/bronze artifacts

6.7.4 Quality of Ife artifacts

The Ife artists had clearly mastered stone and terracotta works from the pre-fluorescence era, considering the exceptional quality of their products. The near-life size stone stature is considered a masterpiece, so are the complex and sophisticated stone stools and the fine terracotta heads (Figure 6.11). As explained earlier, production of the model is the most important stage of the lost-wax process which was apparently adopted for the production of virtually all the copper alloy artifacts. Clearly, the high-fluorescent era artists already had the competence to introduce local innovations. The lost-wax process is very basic and successful accomplishment requires considerable personal skills, perseverance, and knack for innovation and improvisation. This explains why the details of the technology were hardly ever the same across regions of the early world. Anyone who has tried the process knows that virtually each beautiful product is achieved only after a series of trials and defective products that had to be re-melted. Therefore, considering the extensive experience which Ife artists already had in working with terracotta, it should not have been difficult for them to master the lost-wax casting technology.

The fluorescence era artwork of Ife has been described in superlative terms in the global modern academic art media: *"superb; unique; distinctive; exceptional; highly naturalistic; portraitlike; humanistic; combines technical accomplishment with strong aesthetic appeal; truly outstanding; comparable to Greek work; the envy of the European Renaissance; abstract art and geometric forms unknown in the West before the 20th century; characterized by a masterful casting technology and an unusually sensitive realism;"* etc. The Obalufon mask, one of the five free-standing heads found in Ife (Figure 6.13a, Ife-3) and the seated figure found on a ritual site on the island of Tada on the River Niger 200 kilometers north of Ife (Figure 6.13b Ife-4) are perhaps the most outstanding and famous of all the copper alloy figures because they were cast in almost pure copper, a process known to be froth with difficulties. Molten copper has great affinity for oxygen and quickly oxidizes as it cools. The oxygen reacts with dissolved hydrogen and the steam formed evaporates as the metal cools, leaving micro-crystalline cavities. Cast products are porous and contain oxide inclusions. Arsenic is a powerful deoxidizer: it reacts with oxygen in the hot metal to form arsenous oxides which vaporize at around 460°C thereby removing oxygen from the atmosphere of the solidifying molten copper alloy. Also, both arsenic and lead in similar quantities increase fluidity by lowering melting temperature of copper. The presence of both elements in quantities as low as 2% should produce good quality castings. However, as discussed earlier, if the cast metal is to be worked, the two elements have opposite effects: while arsenic content of 0.5-2 wt%, can increase the hardness of pure copper by 10 to 30%, presence of lead beyond around 2% will weaken pure copper significantly. The Ife copper mask and head castings are of unusually realistic physiognomy and the quality of the casting is outstanding considering the usual difficulties with casting copper. They are uniformly thin and the founding is almost faultless.

Use of arsenical copper was widespread in the early world from around the 4th millennium BC. Since many copper ores contain arsenic, it is probable that its presence in the early copper products was inadvertent. However, it probably did not take long for copper casters to realize the benefits of arsenic, particularly in copper ingots that are worked to make tools, daggers, arrows, etc. for which pure copper would be too soft. Deliberate addition of arsenic to copper or smelting high-arsenical copper ores had become widespread by the third millennium BC and artifacts containing 7-10% arsenic dated to that period have been found. Copper ingots with different quantities of arsenic and/or lead were being traded worldwide, including sub-Saharan Africa by the first millennium AD and copper casters of the period (which include Igbo Ukwu, Ife and Benin casters) could have imported desired specifications. It should be noted however that arsenic is a highly volatile and poisonous element. As discussed earlier, when arsenical copper ore is smelted under reducing conditions (mandatory for copper ore smelting) most of the arsenic (up to about 7%) is retained in the casting. However, when the ingot is re-melted under atmospheric (oxidizing) conditions as would happen in foundries which import ingots, arsenic volatilizes at 613°C and the boiling point of arsenic trioxide (As_2O_3) is even lower, at 457°C. No credible evidence of smelting copper ores has been found in either Igbo Ukwu or Ife. In any case it would have been counterproductive for Medieval casters to start from tedious ore smelting when copper ingots in a variety of chemical specifications were readily available. It is not unlikely that the copper casters of Igbo Ukwu and Ife melted imported arsenical copper ingots in which case they would have been exposed to arsenic poisoning. Lead which is often present in copper ores or deliberately added to molten copper to improve fluidity also evaporates at low temperature and the fumes are poisonous, although the effect is not as instant as arsenic poisoning. This may explain why almost pure copper castings were so few in both locations, and why activities were so short-lived: most of the competent casters probably died prematurely or switched to safer copper alloys.

Zinc and tin have deoxidizing effect in molten copper that are similar to arsenic without the hazard of arsenic poisoning and the artists may have abandoned difficult copper casting when brass/bronze ingots became available. It may also explain why the Benin casters from around the 14th century have survived for centuries, since they worked mainly with non-arsenical brass. It is possible also that the ingots may have come from different sources. For example, as discussed earlier, there are deposits copper ores and lead-zinc ores in Abakaliki area, and some evidence of early working has been found and many of the artifacts contain minor quantities of lead and zinc. This may well be one of the sources of leaded-brass ingots used by the Benin casters. Also, Mali copper mines were actively trading copper ingots from around the ninth century AD and could have been one of the sources of supply for both the Ife and Benin copper alloy castings.

6.7.5 Provenance of Ife copper/Bronze Culture

There is no doubt that Ife copper and bronze artwork was a local production, considering the local significance and relevance of virtually all the subjects (Figure 6.13) and the distinctive facial striations on many of the copper alloy heads, representing the multi-ethnic groups who lived in early Ife, most of which are still well represented in modern Ife. Furthermore, the Ife artists had proved their competence in earlier work with equally complex terracotta and stone artwork. Copper alloy artwork is expensive and most ancient artifacts have been found in relation to royalty or the rich. There is little doubt that the transition from terracotta to this material in the fluorescence era was made possible by the prosperous and progressive monarch, Obalufon II. What has been the subject of intensive debate is the source of the lost-wax technology. As discussed above, contrary to speculations about local invention, no one knows for sure the source of the technology (although the earliest evidence of practice has been found in Anatolia), but it had been practiced in most regions of the early world for around five thousand years before the sub-Saharan copper culture era. However, as explained earlier, while the basic steps must have been learned from somewhere else, the success of operation depends largely on the ingenuity and capacity for innovation/improvisation of the local artist, usually learnt from a series of failures. In effect, an artist can claim full credit for a successful casting produced by the lost-was technology, which makes the provenance of the technology irrelevant and inconsequential. The fact that the products have been widely acclaimed all over the world as 'truly outstanding', 'unique', 'unusual' 'exceptional' 'distinctive' is proof of significant domestication of the technology and substantial innovation.

No evidence of copper smelting from ore has been found in Ife but ingots were probably imported and remelted, and some crucible melting pots have been found in the area. The ingots may have come through the wide inter-regional trade network, or from Abakaliki area of Eastern Nigeria, which had been exploited a few centuries before, probably by the Igbo-Ukwu casters or metal exporters. Since all available evidence indicates that the Igbo-Ukwu Copper/Bronze Culture predates the Ife Culture and considering the early presence of the Igbos in Ife, It is quite likely that some of the Igbo artists migrated to Ife during or after the collapse of the Nri Kingdom and they or their trained artists may have produced the Ife artifacts. Furthermore, there is substantial evidence that the Igbos were already smelting and working iron in Ife well before the Copper Culture arrived. It is also possible that Obalufon II imported experts from the ancient Middle East which was linked to Ife already by trade, to train local artists. However, the most important conclusion that can be drawn from all the evidences is that the artifacts were produced by local artists and the level of infusion of innovation was outstanding.

6.7.6 Spread of Ife copper/Bronze Culture

The Ife Kingdom appeared to have flourished between the 12th and 15th centuries AD and its influence was widespread, extending eastward to the Niger River and westward to modern day Dahomey and Southern Togo (Figure 6.14). Many metal artworks produced during this period have been found in several locations outside Ife (Figure 6.15). While there is fair consensus that the copper alloy technology was transferred to Benin and many of the early Benin products were copies of Ife artworks, it is unclear how many of the objects found elsewhere got there. Most of the objects found outside Ife are believed to have been sent there for specific purposes. Ancient Ife had many shrines at the perimeters of the city as well as in many of the settlements loyal to the kingdom. It was the normal practice to distribute the body parts of former rulers to various sacred sites around the kingdom for protective, empowerment purposes. It is probable therefore that the artworks symbolized the paraphernalia of a ruler's court, such as regalia, messengers, etc. Tada, a Nupe settlement on the bank of River Niger appears to have served as one of the shrines of Ife, possibly serving Oyo Ile, one of the new city states. The exquisite copper casting of a seated male found there was undoubtedly made in Ife considering its style and metal composition (Figure 6.14a-1). It is also possible that some of the other objects were gifts from the ruler of Ife to his counterparts in several city states that had developed around the kingdom by the 16th century AD: Benin, Oyo Ile, Ijebu Ode, Owo. It is likely that, after the death of Obalufon II, sponsorship of bronze artwork declined and artists migrated to other city states where practice was sustained until around the middle of the 17th century AD.

Early iron and copper metallurgy in Nigeria

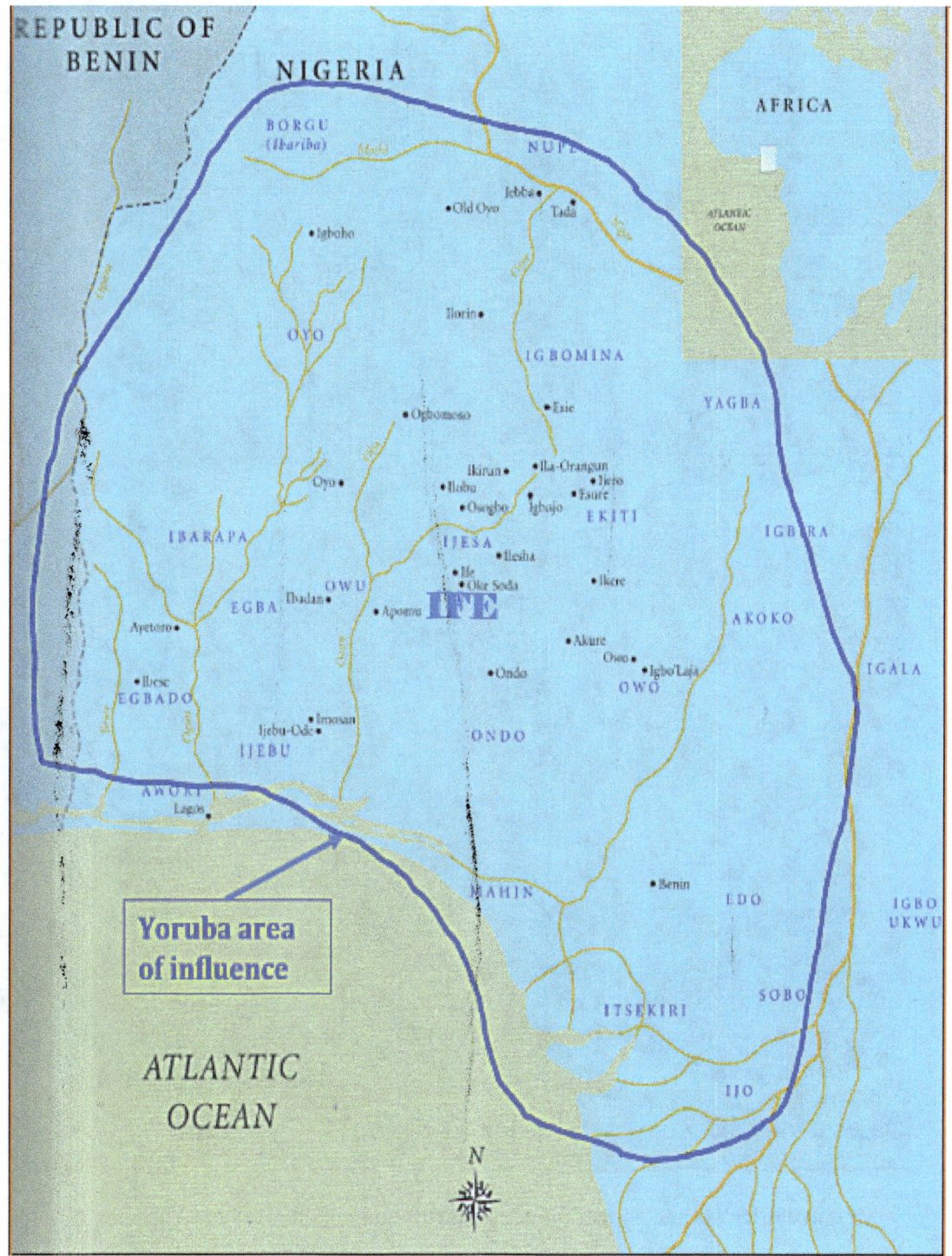

Figure 6.14 Yoruba area of influence, 12th to 15th century AD

Figure 6.15 Some copper alloy castings found outside Ife *(British Museum, 2010)*.

6.8 BENIN LATE BRASS/BRONZE CULTURE

The ancient kingdom of Benin is located about 200 kilometers south-east of Ife. The early oral history of the Benin kingdom is scanty and there are many versions. It is unclear where the Edo and other ethnic groups came from before they settled in Benin area of the West African rain forest from around AD 900, initially in small farming groups but a city state had evolved by around AD 1100, with a series of rulers known as Ogisos, and quickly emerged as a very powerful, highly-developed kingdom. By around 1300, trade links had been established with neighbouring city states and a series of rulers expanded the borders.

6.8.1 Brief history of Benin Kingdom

Most of the written history about the Benin Kingdom is from the records of the Portuguese who made their first expedition to the kingdom in 1485. However, oral history claims that settlers had been in the area for around five hundred years before then and a strong, prosperous city state had emerged by the 14th century AD, with Benin as the administrative center of the kingdom. However, the kingdom remained heterogeneous in terms of ethnicity, language and culture (Edos, Urhobos, Itsekiris, Igbos, Ijaws, Esans) and inter-ethnic rivalry eventually arose. The Edo people, fearing that the city state would descend into chaos, invited the ruler of Ife for help. The king sent his son Oranmiyan who, after restoring order and having stayed long enough to raise a son by an Edo princess, returned to Ife having installed his son Eweka who rapidly developed Benin into a powerful, prosperous multi-cultural kingdom by the late 1400s. That connection to Yoruba dynasty has continued through to the present day Benin. The kingdom was later ruled by a series of prosperous warrior kings who fought wars and expanded its empire in all directions, trading palm oil and rubber. At its peak towards the end of the 16th century, the Benin empire dominated trade along the entire coastline from western Niger Delta through Lagos to present day Ghana. The empire ruled over the tribes of the Niger Delta including the six major ethnic groups which had developed into small city states and many others. With the decline of the Ife kingdom, Benin kingdom extended its influence to the Eastern Yoruba tribes of Ondo, Owo, Ekiti, Mahin/Ugbo, and Ijebu. It also established the first colony of Lagos.

The Benin kingdom reached its peak towards the end of the 16th century and began to decline due to internal strife. The present name 'Benin' is believed to have been coined from the name Ubinu by which the kingdom was known in Ife and called 'Bini' by the Itsekiri. The Portuguese are believed to have made the first trade contact with Benin kingdom in about 1485 by which time the copper alloy artwork was well established and they were probably the first to expose the works to the international art community. A strong trade relationship developed with the Edos trading slaves, rubber, palm oil, ivory, pepper and other tropical products in exchange for western products especially guns. It is on record that the reigning Benin king sent an ambassador to Lisbon while the king of Portugal sent missionaries. The Portuguese may also have been a source for copper ingots used to produce Benin artwork.

6.8.2 Benin artwork

There is ample evidence that the Benin artists were already prolific in the production of exquisite terracotta, wood and ivory artworks well before the copper culture. In effect, the artists already had the expertise needed to transit seamlessly into lost-wax metal casting. The provenance of the Copper/Bronze Culture is disputed: one school of thought suggests that it may have come through the Portuguese who had established trade links with the kingdom in the late 15th century AD and who may have supplied both the lost-wax casting expertise and the copper ingots. However, while this hypothesis is feasible, there is no significant archaeological evidence in support, and the technology appeared to have flourished for over a hundred years before contact was established. It is possible that the copper casters of Igbo-Ukwu in the 9th to 12th century AD migrated to Benin and initiated the technology. This theory is also feasible considering the proximity of the old Nri Kingdom and the well-known migration instincts of the Igbos. The only problem is the apparently long gap of several hundred years between the two metal cultures but this is also questionable since it is unknown when and how the Igbo-Ukwu Copper Culture collapsed. However, evidence is emerging suggesting that it may have continued for a much longer time than currently believed, possibly overlapping with Ife and Benin metal cultures. Ife appears to have been the most probable source for several reasons notably the close ancestral and cultural ties between the two kingdoms, the fact that Ife artifacts predate those of Benin, and the very close resemblance between the early Benin artifacts and Ife castings both in terms of subject and stylistics. There is little doubt that Ife played a prominent role at least in the initial stages of development of Benin Copper Culture. In fact, according to oral history, the Oba of Benin who as an Oduduwa son requested the ruler of Ife to send a copper artist to train his people. Another account claims that he sent his artist to be trained in Ife. Whichever is right, the two copper cultures were clearly very well linked. This may explain the stylistic similarities and the realistic and sensitive representation between many of the initial products from Benin compared with those from Ife (See Figure 6.16).

Benin people have claimed that artists were sent to Ife not to learn but to teach, implying that Benin Copper Culture predates Ife. However, all available archaeological evidences indicate that the Ife copper alloy artifacts antedate those of Benin, most of which have been dated from 15th to 18th century AD. There is no doubt however that there were exchanges and close interactions in copper alloy works between the two cities, although Benin quickly developed a unique identity, with many of the objects made apparently to provide an aesthetically rich record of life in the kingdom, in particular the splendour that surrounded royalty: ceremonial apparel, the king's warriors, and the numerous palace ceremonies. They used artwork to document ancestral images and events for the king, very much like modern royal photographers and historians. Benin artwork, in particular, metalwork was predominantly royal and closely tied to rituals in connection with past and current rulers who were considered to be divine. Many of the artifacts were commemorative head sculptures designed to venerate the achievements and memories of living and dead kings, their Queens and Queen Mothers, and other prominent members of the kingdom. The artisans also made a very large number of plaques which depict royal court activities, historical events, local and foreign personalities, ornate staffs and royal regalia, ceremonial stools, swords, animals (in particular, leopards considered to be the king's counterpart in the jungle), birds, snakes, etc. Apparently, all artwork in the early Benin Kingdom revolved around royalty and the king determined the figures and objects to be produced; crafters were organized into guilds: ivory and wood carvers, bead makers, brass casters, etc., whose

Early iron and copper metallurgy in Nigeria **161**

leaders were prominent members of the royal court. Brass was expensive and considered a precious metal reserved only for royalty and crafters were forbidden from producing for anyone outside royalty or trading in brass artwork. Contravention carried a death penalty until the restriction was lifted in 1914. The brass casters guild was the most prominent of the artisan groups and the craft has survived through generations, still occupying a very prominent position in modern Benin.

Figure 6.16 Stylistic similarities Between Ife and early Benin copper alloy artworks.

Brassworks are now major commercial enterprises in Benin and most of the current brass casters who are descendants of the early artists still use basically the same techniques although their products have become even more exquisite. They are concentrated in Igun Street, Benin in seven groups representing the original ancient families of bronze casters and the street has been recognized by UNESCO as a cultural heritage site (Figure 6.17). Perhaps the main reason why Benin brass/bronze casting has survived for around five hundred years while all other sites in Nigeria collapsed is the sustained interest of the long line of Benin rulers who still control the crafters by issuing licenses, and are still the main patrons. Igun street has become a major tourist attraction and products are being sold worldwide.

Figure 6.17 Modern bronze casters in Igun Street, Benin, Nigeria *(Reuters)*.

The first British expedition to Benin was in 1553 and a strong trade link quickly developed, similar to the links with the Portuguese which were already well developed. For the next three hundred years or so, trade between Benin and Europe flourished until towards the end of the 19th century when relationship between Benin and the British deteriorated, arising from an attempt by the British to annex Benin Kingdom as a protectorate and leading to a confrontation during which Benin was burned down and much of the artwork looted by British troops Figure 6.18). Over four thousand brass/bronze, ivory, terracotta and wooden artifacts mostly taken from the Oba's palace are believed to have been sold by auction to European and American museums as well as private collectors. This explains why most of the important artworks of Benin are scattered all over Europe and the rest of the world, widely duplicated and marketed.

The Benin copper alloy artworks are unique in virtuosity, sophistication and style, well acknowledged by the art world and sought after by art collectors. Almost all the works were created in honour of kings, queens and court members from around the 15th century, decorations and plaques were in commemoration of important events or expressions of the splendour that surrounded the rulers. Although the industry declined with the disruptive events of the late 19th century, production has continued till today, with each sculpture still produced by hand and by the lost-wax process, although styles have changed over the years. Also, the global art market has been flooded with replicas of Benin art and there is considerable uncertainty about the authenticity even of those displayed in museums all over the western world because many were acquired from private collectors. However, most museums have procedures for verifying their art collections. The Nigerian National Commission for Museums and monuments and Benin monarchs have been pressing for the return of as many as possible of these artworks but little progress had been made until a recent agreement with some European museums which includes the construction of a purpose-built museum in Nigeria and display of important pieces on loan from their collections on a rotating basis.

Figure 6.18 British officials seated amidst looted artifacts in the remains of the Oba of Benin's palace after burning it down in 1897. *(Public domain).*

Dating of Benin copper alloy artwork is the most problematic of all the Nigerian copper cultures because, unlike most of Igbo-Ukwu and many of Ife objects, very few Benin artifacts have been found in-situ in archaeological excavations, which means that valuable organic and thermoluminescence samples on which any credible chronological dating could be based are not available. In effect, most published dates have been based on stylistic, morphological, oral and socio-cultural evidences, and some spectrographic surface analysis which can be erroneous because of segregation during casting. However, it is widely accepted that Benin copper artwork flourished between the 14th and 17th centuries AD, probably concurrent with the demise of the Ife dynasty. There is also little doubt that, irrespective of its provenance, the Benin artists excelled in domesticating lost-wax technology, with extensive local infusion of innovations which have given their products unique character and stylistics. They specialized in brass artwork although some bronze and copper/bronze artifacts were also produced and most modern productions are bronzes. Like the Ife and Igbo artists, the Benin craftsmen are acclaimed worldwide for the outstanding quality of their work in every medium. One of the most outstanding works is the 16th century statute of a mounted ruler which is on display in the Museum of Fine Arts, Boston United States (Figure 6.19). The base, the horse and the ornamental caparisons are cast in brass while the horse is cast in bronze, probably with the intention of exploiting the beautiful colour contrast of the two alloys. Selections from Benin artifacts located in many museums all over the world are presented in Figures 6.20-6.22.

Like the Ife kingdom, the Benin empire had great influence on Yoruba communities and many others along the Niger river coastal delta who were under its political trade and influence. This explains why many copper alloy artifacts dated 17th to 19th century AD have been found in many places, for example, Owo terracotta, dress style, style of royal buildings, adoption of Benin titles and rituals (Eyo, 1980). Many copper alloy castings have also been found in lower Niger communities, notably in Jebba and Tada, and in places as far away as Cross River basin.

Figure 6.19 A Benin mounted ruler, 16th century BC. The base, the horse and the ornamental caparisons are cast in brass while the horse is cast in bronze. *(Museum of Fine Arts, Boston, U.S.A).*

Early iron and copper metallurgy in Nigeria **165**

Figure 6.20a Selections from Benin brass and bronze artifacts

166 *Early metallurgy in Nigeria*

Figure 6.20b Selections from Benin brass and bronze artifacts

Early iron and copper metallurgy in Nigeria 167

Figure 6.20c Selections from Benin brass and bronze artifacts

Figure 6.20d Selections from Benin brass and bronze artifacts

Figure 6.20e Selections from Benin brass and bronze artifacts

Figure 6.20f Selections from Benin brass and bronze artifacts

Early iron and copper metallurgy in Nigeria 171

Figure 6.20g Selections from Benin brass and bronze artifacts

Benin-Brass-37 **Benin-Brass-38**

Benin-Brass-39 **Benin-Brass-40**

Figure 6.20h Selections from Benin brass and bronze artifacts

Early iron and copper metallurgy in Nigeria 173

Figure 6.20i   Selections from Benin brass and bronze artifacts

174 *Early metallurgy in Nigeria*

Figure 6.20j Selections from Benin brass and bronze artifacts

Early iron and copper metallurgy in Nigeria **175**

Figure 6.20k Selections from Benin brass and bronze artifacts

176 *Early metallurgy in Nigeria*

Benin-Brass-53 **Benin-Brass-54**
Benin-Brass-55 **Benin-Brass-56**
Benin-Brass-57 **Benin-Brass-58** **Benin-Brass-59**

Figure 6.20l Selections from Benin brass and bronze artifacts

Early iron and copper metallurgy in Nigeria 177

Figure 6.20m   Selections from Benin brass and bronze artifacts

178 *Early metallurgy in Nigeria*

Figure 6.21a Selections from Benin ivory artifacts

Figure 6.21b Selections from Benin ivory artifacts

180 *Early metallurgy in Nigeria*

Figure 6.21c Selections from Benin ivory artifacts

Figure 6.22 Selections from Benin contemporary artifacts

NOTES ON BENIN METAL ARTIFACTS

1. Unlike the Igbo-Ukwu and Ife artifacts, the Benin artworks have never been found in any typical archaeological setting and formally evaluated, hence reliable information, in particular metallurgical analysis, is very scanty. It is unclear which product is from arsenical copper, brass or bronze. Information given about metal type is based on what has been determined by the numerous museums worldwide which currently house the items and may have carried out some non-destructive metallurgical analysis which can be unreliable because surface tests on castings can give erroneous data due to segregation.

2. The Benin metal casters clearly preferred brass probably because of the relatively easy castability and amenability to very attractive surface finish.

3. No evidence of local ore smelting has been found hence it may be assumed that the artisans worked on imported ingots which may have come from Igbo-Ukwu area but it is more likely they were sourced through the well-established intra- and inter regional trade links.

4. Brass was clearly the preferred metal for royalty products but some items may also have been produced in bronze.

5. Brass/bronze casting is a very well-established modern industry in Benin, run by descendants of casters, still organized and patronized by succeeding rulers, and its exquisite products are sold worldwide.

7. BIBLIOGRAPHY

AFS, (1952) "Copper-base Alloys Foundry Practice". American Foundrymen's Society.
Apley, A. (2001). "African Lost-Wax Casting". metmuseum.org.
ASM, Metals Handbook (1948). American Society for Metals.
Awogbade, O. (2016). "Examination of Ife Bronze Casting Culture and its Decline in Maintenance Practice in Contemporary Society". An International Multidisciplinary Journal, Ethiopia Vol. 10(1), Serial No. 40, January, 2016 pp. 225-233.
Bass, G. F. (1967). "Cape Gelidonya; a Bronze Age Shipwreck". Trans. Amer. Phil. Soc., 57, (8), 177.
Bass, G. F. et al. (1984). "A late Bronze Age Shipwreck at Kas, Turkey". IJNA, 13, pp. 271-279.
Beck. C. (2015). *The Value of Art: Studies in the Material Character*
of the Terracotta Figurines of the Nok Culture of Central
Nigeria. PhD thesis, Goethe University Frankfurt/Main.
Ben-Amos, Paula Girshick (1995). The Art of Benin. Rev. ed. Washington, D.C.: Smithsonian Institution Press.
Ben-Amos, Paula Girshick (1999). Art, Innovation, and Politics in Eighteenth-Century Benin. Bloomington: Indiana University Press.
Blier, S. P. (2015). Art and Risk in Ancient Yoruba. Cambridge University Press.
Boullier, C.; A. Person; J.-F. Saliège & J. Polet (2001). Bilan chronologique de la culture Nok et nouvelle datations sur des sculptures. Afrique: Archéologie & Arts 2, 9-28.
British Museum (2010). Kingdom of Ife: Sculptures from West Africa. The British Museum Press.
Burland, C. A. (1957), Lost Wax: Metal Casting on the Guinea Coast. Exhibition catalogue. London: The Studio, 1957.
Breunig, P. & Rupp, N. (2006). Nichts als Kunst. Archäologische Forschungen zur früheisenzeitlichen Nok-Kultur in Zentral-Nigeria. Forschung Frankfurt 2-3, 73-76.
Breunig, Peter. (2014). "Nok: African Sculpture in Archaeological Context: Africa Magna Verlag; Tra edition.
Breunig, P. & Rupp, N. (2016). "An outline of recent studies on the Nigerian Nok Culture". Journal of African Archaeology, Vol. 14 (3) Special Issue, pp. 237-255.
Caldwell, J. R. (1967). "Tal I Iblis". 1967, Iran, 5, 144-146.
Chan, E.K.F. et al. (2019) "Human origins in a southern African palaeo-wetland and first migrations". Nature, 575, 185–189.
Charles, J. A. (1967). " Early Arsenical Bronzes – A Metallurgical View". American Journal of Archaeology, Vol. 71, No. 1, pp. 21-26.
Childs ST. (1991). "Style, technology and iron smelting furnaces in Bantu-speaking Africa". J. Anthropol. Archaeol. 10:332–59.
Childs, T and D. Killick (1993), "Indigenous African Metallurgy: nature and culture". Annual Review Anthropology, 22: 317-37.
Childs, S. T. (2008). "Metallurgy in Africa". In: Selin H. (eds) Encyclopaedia of the History of Science, Technology, and Medicine in Non-Western Cultures. Springer, Dordrecht. Chirikure, S. (2010). On Evidence, Ideas and Fantasy: The Origins of Iron in Sub-Saharan Africa. Thoughts on É. Zangato & A.F.C. Holl's "On the Iron Front" Journal of African Archaeology 8(1):25-28.

Chirikure, S. (2013). "Geochemistry of Ancient Metallurgy: Examples from Africa and Elsewhere". In book: Treatise on Geochemistry Edition: 2nd Chapter: 14.13. Editors: K Turekean Publisher: Elsevier.

Chirikure, S. et al. (2014). Zimbabwe Culture before Mapungubwe: New Evidence from Mapela Hill, South-Western Zimbabwe. PLOS.

Chirikure, S. (2015). " A Global Perspective on indigenous African Metallurgy". In Metals in Past Societies. Springer Briefs in Archaeology.

Cleere, H. (1993). "Archaeometallurgy come of age". Antiquity, 67, 175-178.

Connar, G. (1976). "The Daima sequence and prehistory chronology of the Lake Chad Region of Nigeria". Journal of African History, xvii, 3, pp 321-352.

Connah, G, (2001). *African Civilizations: An Archaeological Perspective.* Cambridge University Press.

Craddock, P. T. (1997). "Metal sources and the bronzes from Igbo-Ukwu, Nigeria". Journal of Field Archaeology, Vol. 24, No. 4 (Winter, 1997), pp. 405-429.

Derry, T. K and Williams, T. I.(1960) A Short History of Technology. Oxford University Press.

Drewal, H. John, J. Pemberton III, and R. Abiodun (1989). Yoruba: Nine Centuries of African Art and Thought. New York: Center for African Art.

Edwards, David N. (2004). The Nubian Past. London, Routledge. pp. 348 Pages

El Gayar, E. S, and P. M. Jones (1989). "Old Kingdom copper smelting artefacts from Buhen in Upper Egypt". JHMS, 1989, 23 (1), 16-24.

El Sayad El Gayar and P. M. Jones (1989). "Metallurgical investigation of an iron plate found in the Great Pyramid at Gizeh, Egypt". JHMS, 1989, 23 (32), 75-83.

Encyclopaedia Britanica (2019). "Ethnographic history of Nigeria".

Eyo, E, and F. Willett (1980). Treasures of Ancient Nigeria. Exhibition catalogue. New York: Knopf, 1980.

Eyo, Ekpo (2014). Masterpieces of Nigerian Art. African Digital Education Series, Vol.3. Google Books.

Eze-Uzomaka, P. I. (2009). "Iron age Archaeology in Lejja, Nigeria". In Dimensions of African Archaeology: Studies in the African Past. Pwiti G. et al. (eds). Dar es Salaam E & D Vision Pub. Ltd. Vol. 7; pp. 41-51.

Eze-Uzomaka, P.I. (2010). "Excavation of Amaovoko: A Further Study of the Lejja Iron Smelting Culture". In Studies in the African Past. The Journal of African Archaeology Network, Vol. 8; 2010. pp 178–191).

Eze-Uzomaka, P.I. (2013). "Iron and its influence on the prehistoric site of Leija". J. Humpris & Th. Rehren (Eds). The world of iron, pp. 3-9. London, Archetype.

Ezra, Kate (1992). The Royal Art of Benin: The Perls Collection. Exhibition catalogue. New York: Metropolitan Museum of Art.

Fagg, B. (1959). The Nok Culture in prehistory. Journal of the Historical Society of Nigeria 1 (4), 288-293.

Fagg, B. (1968). The Nok Culture: Excavations at Taruga. The West African Archaeological Newsletter 10, 27-30.

Fagg, Bernard. (1969). "Recent work in west Africa: New light on the Nok culture". World Archaeology 1(1): 41–50.

Fagg, A. (1972). A preliminary report on an occupation site in the Nok valley, Nigeria: Samun Dukiya, AF/70/1. West African Journal of Archaeology 2, 75-79.

Fagg, B., (1990): Nok terracottas. Lagos: National Commission for Museums and Monuments.

Franke (2016a). Franke, G. 2015. *Potsherds in Time – the Pottery of the Nigerian Nok Culture and its Chronology*. PhD thesis, Goethe University, Frankfurt/Main

Franke, G. 2016b. A chronology of the Central Nigerian Nok Culture – 1500 BC to the beginning of the Common Era. *Journal of African Archaeology* 14 (3), 257–289, this issue.

Furtauer, S. et al. (2013). "The Cu-Sn phase diagram, Part I: New experimental results". Intermetalics, Vol. 34, 142-147.

Garlake, Peter (2002). Early art and architecture of Africa. Oxford: Oxford University Press. p. 120).

Grebenart, D. (1985). "La ré́gion d'In-Gall – Tegidda-n-Tesemt (Niger), II: Le né́olithique final et les dé́buts de la mé́tallurgie". Etudes nigé́riennes 49, Niamey.

Grebenart, D. (1987). "Characteristics of the Final Neolithic and Metal Ages in the Region of Agadez (Niger)". In A. Close, Ed. A Prehistory of Arid North Africa. Essays in Honor of Fred Wendorf (287-316), Dallas: Southern Methodist University.

Grebenart, D. (1988). Les premiers mé́tallurgistes en Afrique occidentale. Paris: Editions Errance).

Haour, A. (2003). "One hundred years of Archaeology in Niger". Journal of World Prehistory, Vol. 17, No. 2, pp. 181-234.

Hartle, D. D. (1965). "An archaeological survey in eastern Nigeria". West African Archaeological Newsletter, 2:4-5.

Hartle, D. D. (1966a). "Bronze objects from Exira, eastern Nigeria". West African Archaeological Newsletter, 4:25-28.

Hartle, D. D. (1966b). "Archaeology in eastern Nigeria". West African Archaeological Newsletter, 5:13-17.

Hartle, D. D. (1967). "Archaeology in eastern Nigeria". Magazine, 93:134-143.

Hartle, D. D. (1968). "Stop Press: Radiocarbon dates form Nigeria ". West African Archaeological Newsletter, 9:73.

Hartle, D. D. (1980). "Archaeology of East of the Niger: A Review of Cultural-Historical Developments". In West African Cultural Dynamics: Archaeological and Historical Perspectives, ed. B. K. Swartz and R. E. Dumett, pp. 195-203. The Hague, Holland: Mouton.

HE (2002).   "Archaeometallurgy". Historic England. HistoricEngland.org.uk

Heine, R. W. Loper, Jr. C. R., Rosenthal, P. C. (1967). Principles of Metal Casting. McGraw-Hill Book Company.

Herbert, E. 1973. "Aspects of the use of copper in pre-colonial West Africa". Journal of African History, 14: 179-194.

Herbert, E. (1984). Red Gold of Africa: copper in pre-colonial history and culture. Madison: University of Wisconsin Press.

Herbert, E. W. (1993). Iron, Gender and Power: Rituals of Transformation in African Societies. Bloomington: Indiana University Press.

Herbert E. (1994). Iron, Gender and Power: Rituals of Transformation in African Societies. Bloomington/Indianapolis: Indiana Univ. Press.

Höhn, A. and Neumann, K. (2016). "The palaeovegetation of Janruwa

(Nigeria) and its implications for the decline of the Nok Culture". *Journal of African Archaeology* 14 (3), 331–353.

Holl. A. (2009), "Early West African Metallurgies: Data and old Orthodoxy". J. World Prehist. 22:415-438.

Holl. A. and ST Childs, (1991). "Style, technology and iron smelting furnaces in Bantu-speaking Africa". J. Anthropol. Archaeol., 10:332–59.

Holl, A. (2000). Iron Metallurgy in West Africa: An Early Iron Smelting Site in the Mouhoun Bend, Burkina Faso. Journal of African Archaeology Monograph.

Jeffreys, M. D. W (1935). "The Divine Umundiri Kings of Igboland". Journal of the International African Institute, Vol. 8, No. 3 (Jul., 1935), pp. 346-354.

Jemkur, J. (1992). Aspects of the Nok Culture. ABU, Zaria.

Jemkur, J. (2014). My adventure with the Nok Culture. In: Breunig, P. (ed.), *Nok – African Sculpture in Archaeological Context.* Magna Verlag, Frankfurt, pp. 93–98.Johnson, J. et al. (1941). African Bronzes from Ife and Benin. Gallery of Sachs, Inc.

Junius, H. (2016). "Nok early iron production in Central Nigeria – New finds and features". Journal of African Archaeology Vol. 14 (3) Special Issue, 2016, pp. 291-311.

Kaufman, B. *et al.* (2016). "Ferrous metallurgy from the Bir Massouda metallurgical precinct at Phoenician and Punic Carthage and the beginning of the North African Iron Age. Journal of Archaeological Science, Vol. 71, pp. 33-50.

Killick, David, et al. (1988). "Reassessment of the evidence for early metallurgy in Niger, West Africa." Journal of Archaeological Science 15.4 (1988): 367-394.

Killick, D. (2001). "Science, speculation and the origins of extractive metallurgy". In D. R. Brothwell A. M. Pollard (eds). Handbook of archaeological sciences, pp. 483-492, Wiley.

Kuper, R. and Kröpelin, S. (2006) "Climate-controlled Holocene occupation in the Sahara: motor of Africa's evolution" in Science 313, 803.

Lechtman, H. and Klein, S. (1999). "The production of Copper-Arsenic Alloys (Arsenic Bronze) by Cosmelting: Modern Experiment, Ancient Practice." Journal of Archaeological Science, Vol. 26(5), pp. 497-526.

MacEachern, S. (2005). "Two thousand years of West African history". In African Archaeology, pp. 441-466. A critical introduction. Blackwell Publishers.

Magnavita, S. et al. (2009). "Crossroads/Carrefour Sahel: Cultural and technological developments in first millennium BC/AD West Africa". Journal of World Prehistory, 22:415.

Melleart, J. (1967). "Catal Huyuk". 1967, London, Thames and Hudson.

Mellink, M. J. (1965). AJA, 69, 138.

Modlinger, M. and B. Sabatini (2016). "A Re-evaluation of inverse segregation in prehistoric As-Cu onjects." Journal of Archaeological Science, 74(2016), pp. 60-74.

Muhly, J. D. (1984). "Timma and King Solomon". Bibliotheca Orientalis, 1984, 3-4, 275-292.

Muhly, J. D. (1985). "Sources of tin and the beginning of bronze metallurgy." American Journal of Archaeology, Vol. 89, No. 2, pp. 275-291.

Neuninger, H. et al. (1964). "Fruhkeramikzeitliche Kupfergewinnung in Anatoia". Arch. Aust., 1964, 35, 98-110.

Norton, M. L. (2011). "Master Sculptors of Benin and Ife". Thames and Hudson.
Onwuejeogwu, M. Angulu (1981). "An Igbo civilization: Nri kingdom & hegemony". Ethnographica. ISBN 978-123-105-X
Pazoukhin, V. A. (1964). "Uber den Ursprung des alten Arsenkupfers". Metallurgija i gornoedelo, I, Moskva, 1964.
Philipson, D. (2005). African Archaeology. Cambridge University Press.
Pringle, H. (2009). "Seeking Africa's First Iron Men". Science, Vol. 323 Issue 5911, pp. 200-2002.
Rapp Jr., G. (1989). Determining the origins of sulfide smelting. In (A. Hauptmann, E. Pernicka & G. A. Wagner, Eds) Old World Archaeometallurgy. Bochum: Selbstverlag des Deutschen Bergbau-Museums, pp. 107–110.
Raymond, R. (1984). Out of the Fiery Furnace - The Impact of Metals on the History of Mankind. By The Pennsylvania State University Press.
Renfrew, C. (1969). "The autonomy of the south-east European Copper Age". Proceedings of the Prehistoric Society, 35, pp 12-47.
Renfrew, C. (1978). "The anatomy of innovation". In D. Green et. al. (Eds). Social organization and settlement: Contributions from anthropology, archaeology and geography, pp. 89-117. BAR International Series, Oxford University Press.
Rhyndina, N .V. (1985). "The earliest copper artefact from Mesopotamia". Soviet Arch., 1985, (2), 155-165.
Roberts, B. W. and C. P. Thornton (2014). Archaeometallurgy in Global Perspective: Methods and Syntheses. Robert and Thornton (eds). Springer.
Ross, E. (2002). "The Age of Iron in West Africa". In Heilbrunn Timeline of Art History. New York: The Metropolitan Museum of Art, 2000-metmuseum.org.
Rothenberg, B. (1966). Bull. Mus. Haaretz, 1966, (8), 86.
Rostoker, W. & Dvorak, J. R. (1991). Some experiments with co-smelting to copper alloys. Archaeomaterials 5, 5–20.
Rostoker, W., Pigott, V. C. & Dvorak, J. R. (1989). Direct reduction to copper metal by oxide-sulfide mineral interaction. Archaeomaterials 3, 69–87.
Rowe, M, (2010). "New method could revolutionize dating of ancient treasures". American Chemical Society Newsletter, March 23, 2010.
Rupp, N.; Ameje, J.; Breunig, P. (2005). "New studies on the Nok Culture of Central Nigeria". Journal of African Archaeology 3, 2: 283-290.
Rustad, J. A. (1980). "The Emergence of Iron Technology in West Africa, with Special Emphasis on the Nok Culture, Nigeria". In eds. Swartz, B. K. et al. West African Culture Dynamics, pp. 227-246. De Gruyter.
Samans, C. H. (1949). Engineering Metals and their Alloys. MacMillan.
Schmidt PR. (1997). Iron Technology in East Africa: Symbolism, Science, and Archaeology. Oxford, UK/Indianapolis, IN: James Currey/Indiana Univ. Press Schmidt PR. 2009. Tropes, materiality and ritual embodiment of African iron furnaces as human figures. J. Archaeol. Method Theory 16:262–82.
Shaw, T. (1967). "The mystery of the buried bronzes". Nigeria Magazine 92:55-74.
Shaw, T.(1968a). "Radiocarbon dates for Igbo-Ukwu". West African Archaeological Newsletter, 4:41.

Shaw, T. (1968b). "Radiocarbon daing in Nigeria". Journal of the Historical Society of Nigeria 4:453-465.

Shaw, T. (1970). Igbo-Ukwu: an account of archaeological discoveries in eastern Nigeria. Vols. I, 2. London: Faber & Faber

Shaw, T. (1973). "The Igbo-Ukwu Bronzes". African Arts, Vol. 6, No. 4 (Summer, 1973), pp. 18-19.

Shaw. T (1977). Unearthing Igbo-Ukwu. Oxford University Press, Ibadan, Nigeria.

Shaw, T., (1981). The "Nok sculptures of Nigeria". Scientific American 244(2): 154-166.

Shaw, T. (1985). "The Prehistory of West Africa". In J. F. Ajayi and M. Crowther eds. History of West Africa. Harlow: Longman, pp. 48-66.

Smith, C. S. (1965) Actes XI Congr. Inst d'Hist. Sciences, Warsaw-Krakow, 237, vol. VI.

Tignor, R. & L. (1990). "W. R. Bascom and the Ife Bronzes". Africa, Vol. 60 Issue 3, pp. 425-434.

Thornton, C. et al. (2002). "On pins and needles: tracing the evolution of copper-base alloying at tepe yahya, Iran, via icp-MS analysis of common place items". J. Archaeol. Sci. 29/12, 1451-1460.

Thoury, M. et al. (2016) "High spatial dynamics-photoluminescence imaging reveals the metallurgy of the earliest lost-wax object". Nature communications. 7.

Torok, Laszlo (1998). The Kingdom of Kush: A handbook of the Napatan-Meroitic Civilization. Brill Academic Pub.

Tylecote, R. F (1962). Metallurgy In Archaeology: a prehistory of metallurgy in the British Isles. London: Edward Arnold, 1962.

Tylecote, R. F. (1970). "Iron working at Meroë, Sudan". Bulletin of the Historical Metallurgy Group 4(2):67–72.

Tylecote, R. F. (1972). Bull. HMG, Vol. 6. .34.

Tylecote, R. F. (1974). "(1974). "Can copper be smelted in a crucible? JHMS, 1974, 8 (1),54.

Tylecote, R. (1975a). "The origin of iron smelting in Africa". West African Journal of Archaeology. 5, 1-10.

Tylecote, R. (1975b). "Iron smelting at Taruga, Nigeria". Journal of Historical Metallurgy 9 (2), 49-56.

Tylecote, R. F. (1975c). "Analysis of Slag Fragments in H. Miles Barrows on the St. Austell Granite, Cornwall". Cornish Archaeology 14,:35-38.

Tylecote, R. F. (1976). A History of Metallurgy. Second Edition, The Institute of Metals, London.

Tylecote, R. F., Ghaznavi, H. A., and Boydell, P. J. (1977). "Partitioning of trace elements between the ores, fluxes, slags and metal during the smelting of copper". Journal of Archaeological Science 4: 305–333.

Tylecote, R. F., and Boydell, P. J. (1978). "Experiments on copper smelting". In Rothenberg, B., Tylecote, R. F., and Boydell, P. J. (eds.), Chalcolithic Copper Smelting, Institute for Archaeo-Metallurgical Studies, London, pp. 27–49.

Tylecote, R. F. (1980). "Summary of results of experimental work on early copper smelting." In W. A. Oddy (Ed.) Aspects of Early Metallurgy. London: British Museum, pp. 5-12.

Tylecote, R. F. (1982). "Early copper slags and copper-base metal from the Agadez region of Niger." Historical Metallurgy. Journal of the Historical Metallurgy Society Oxford 16.2 (1982): 58-64.

Tylecote, R. F. (1992). A History of Metallurgy. Institute of Minerals and Mining.

Tylecote, R. F. (2002). A History of Metallurgy. Maney Publishing, London..

UNESCO (1992) "Africa from the Seventh to the Eleventh Century: Trade and trade routes in West Africa)". unesco.org.

UNESCO (2004). The Origins of Iron Metallurgy in Africa. : New light on its antiquity: West and Central Africa. UNESCO.

Ward, G. W. R, (2008). The Grove encyclopedia of materials and techniques in art. Oxford: Oxford University Press. p. 71.

Wertime, T. A. (1973). "How metallurgy began: A study in diffusion and multiple innovation." In Actes du VIIIe Congress International des Sciences Prehistoriques et Protohistoriques (Beograd) pp. 481-492.

Willet, F. (1967). Ife in the History of West African Sculpture. McGraw-Hill.

Willet, Frank (1972). "The Archaeology of Igbo-Ukwu". The Journal of African History. 13 (3): 514–516.

Willett F. (1986). A missing millennium 7 From Nok to Ife and beyond. In Art in Africa, ed. E.Bassani, pp. 87-100. Modena: F.dizio Panini

Wood, B. (2002). "Palaeoanthropology: Hominid revelations from Chad" in Nature 418, 133-135 (11 July 2002.

Xinhua (2007). "New evidence: modern civilization began in Iran". xinhuanet.com.

Yener, K. A. (1989). "Kestel; an Early Bronze Age source of tin ore in the Taurus Mountains, Turkey". Science, 1989, April 14, 244, No.4901.

Zangato, E. and Holl, A.F.C. (2010). "On the iron front: New evidence from North-Central Africa". Journal of African Archaeology 8 :7-23.

Zwicker, U., Greiner, H., Hofmann, K. H. & Reithinger, M. (1985). Smelting, refining, and alloying of copper and copper alloys in crucible furnaces during prehistoric up to Roman times. In (P. T. Craddock & M. J. Hughes, Eds) Furnaces and Smelting Technology in Antiquity. London: British Museum, pp. 103–115.

Appendix I
Dating of archaeological objects

DATING OF ARCHAEOLOGICAL OBJECTS

One of the primary preoccupations of archaeologists and other researchers working in the field of human history is to construct the chronological events in the history of humankind by searching for evidence of their way of life, the objects they made, the tools and materials they used, etc. The fact that the materials they used by the early people (mainly metals) appear to have to a large extent conditioned their pace of development, has given rise to a very rich area of metallurgy: archaeometallurgy. Archaeologists are unearthing a wide range of metals all the time and detailed studies of these findings promote an in-depth understanding to the development process right from the stone age. One major problem confronting archaeologists and archaeometallurgists is how to put a date on the objects they find. There are two major methods - relative dating and absolute dating. While the first method depends mainly on unreliable oral history, absolute dating dating depends on statistical probability, hence, neither method can be expected to give definite dates. At best they provide the most likely interpretation of archaeological data. Absolute dating involves the use of analytical techniques to determine physicochemical transformation phenomena whose rates are known and can be determined with reasonable precision, thereby helping to determine the actual age of the site/object with an acceptable degree of confidence. There are many methods of absolute dating but the most common are radiocarbon dating, thermoluminescence and dendrochronology.

Relative dating (Anthropo-ethnographic dating)

This method of dating depends on in-depth ethnographic and anthropological study of local traditions, religious and traditional practices, oral history, and how society has changed over centuries. Clearly this is not a precise method of dating archaeological findings. Apart from the fact that local traditions often cut across many centuries, the practice of keeping written records is relatively a recent development in the process of human evolution and oral traditions can hardly have a reliable time depth for placing an archaeological object in a time frame. Nevertheless, this method remained the primary method of dating ancient excavations for many centuries. Relative dating methods rely on the analysis of comparative data relative to the context in which an object or a site is found: geological, regional, cultural. Many techniques of relative dating have evolved but the most common are typology and soil stratigraphy. While it is possible to determine a chronology of events by this method, the absolute age of the site or object cannot be determined. Dates determined by this method are usually given in *number of years before the present (BP), with 1950 standardized as present.* For example an object dated 1000 ± 100 BP was probably made in AD 950 ± 100 (or between AD 850 – 105).

Absolute dating

There is currently no method that can give an absolute date of an archaeological object. However, depending on the material some methods can give approximate dates of when the objects were made. Absolute dating provides a numerical age or range in contrast with relative dating which places events in order without any measure of the age between events.

Radiocarbon dating

Element carbon has three main isotopes: C^{12}, C^{13} and C^{14}. While the first two are stable, C^{14} is unstable and slightly radioactive C^{14} is continually being formed in the upper atmosphere by the interaction of cosmic rays with atmospheric nitrogen. It is rapidly oxidized in air to form carbon dioxide and enters the global carbon cycle. Plants assimilate carbon dioxide and convert to carbohydrates and proteins which animals consume throughout their lifetimes, thereby also assimilating C^{14}. All living organic materials contain Carbon-14 atoms in a constant number and when they die, they stop exchanging carbon with the biosphere and their C^{14} content then starts to decrease at a rate determined by the law of radioactive decay. The isotope has a half life (the time it takes for half of a given sample to decay) of 5730 years. Therefore it is possible to measure the number of these atoms in organic materials to obtain quantified information on the date of an item. In theory therefore any dead object that is excavated can be dated by measuring the amount of carbon 14 left in the object, since this should give a good measure of how long the object has been dead. Such objects include bones, wood, charcoal, shell, leather, textile. The rate of loss of C^{14} is counted over a given period and extrapolated over a period of time. The oldest dates that can be reliably measured by this process date to 50,000-60,000 years ago. The procedure is very complex and requires development of intricate calibration curves from the concentration of the isotope in the air over the last fifty thousand years. The curve is then used to convert a given measurement of radiocarbon in a sample into an estimate of the sample's calendar age. used to convert a given measurement of radiocarbon in a sample into an estimate of the sample's calendar age. The method has a margin of accuracy of a hundred years or more depending on the calibration method. In theory, radio-carbon dating should be precise but in practice it is not, for several reasons. First, the loss of carbon is not determined by weighing but by counting the rate of loss over a given period and extrapolating over a period of time. The carbon is first converted into gas which is passed inside a special counter that is sensitive to particle emissions and records the rate. Since it is not practicable to count over 5700 years, the process of interpretation of data obtained depends heavily on statistical manipulation, and at best yields probabilistic results with varying degrees of confidence depending on the duration of the counting process which may vary from a few hours to many days. A second problem arises from the fact that the rate of carbon 14 decay varies with age. At death, every gram of C^{14} in an object loses fifteen particles every minute, a rate which is expected to reduce to only seven and a half emissions per minute in 5700 years. A much older object would emit at a further reduced rate and radiocarbon dating may become more difficult and less accurate. A third possible source of error is the problem of contamination of an archaeological object. It is possible for example that, between the time of death and excavation, younger carbon sources may have infused into the deposit, for example from a younger plant root or other carbon sources in the more recent overburden of an excavation. In spite of the above limitations, radio-carbon dating has become a potent and the most reliable method of dating archaeological excavations and the process is being refined continuously.

Another limitation of the radiocarbon dating process is the need to take a small sample from the object for gasification to produce carbon dioxide which is the analyzed for C^{14} content. However, even a small damage of the object due to sampling may be unacceptable. A new variant of the method has recently emerged which is non=destructive. The entire object is placed in a special chamber with a plasma, an electrically charged gas similar to gases used in big-screen plasma television displays. The gas slowly and gently oxidizes the surface of the object to produce carbon dioxide for C^{14} analysis without damaging the surface. Test results show accuracy which matches conventional radiocarbon techniques (Rowe, M. 2010).

Thermoluminescence

This method is based on the fact that when a material is heated or exposed to sunlight, electrons are released and some of them are trapped inside the item. Once you heat this item again using high temperatures, the trapped electrons become excited and recombine with the item's material. This process frees energy in the form of light, which can be measured. By making multiple measurements it is possible to determine how much radiation the item was exposed to over the years and can get dating estimates related to when the item was last heated. Two forms of luminescence dating are used by archaeologists to date events in the past: thermoluminescence (TL) or thermally stimulated luminescence (TSL), which measures energy emitted after an object has been exposed to temperatures between 400 and 500°C; and optically stimulated luminescence (OSL), which measures energy emitted after an object has been exposed to daylight. Crystalline rock types and soils collect energy from the radioactive decay of cosmic uranium, thorium, and potassium-40. Electrons from these substances get trapped in the mineral's crystalline structure, and continuing exposure of the rocks to these elements over time leads to predictable increases in the number of electrons caught in the matrices. But when the rock is exposed to high enough levels of heat or light, that exposure causes vibrations in the mineral lattices and the trapped electrons are freed. The exposure to radioactive elements continues, and the minerals begin again storing free electrons in their structures. If you can measure the rate of acquisition of the stored energy, you can figure out how long it has been since the exposure happened. Materials of geological origin will have absorbed considerable quantities of radiation since their formation, so any human-caused exposure to heat or light will reset the luminescence clock considerably more recently than that since only the energy stored since the event will be recorded. Artifacts which can be dated using these methods include ceramics, archaeological objects, burned bricks and soil from hearths (TL), and unburned stone surfaces that were exposed to light and then buried (OSL).

This method has the following restrictions:
a) It cannot be used to date items many thousands of years old;
b) it can only be used in non-organic materials; and
c) the materials to be dated must have been heated to more than 350 degrees Celsius. This method is usually used with carbon dating.

Dendrochronological (tree-ring) dating

New growth in <u>trees</u> occurs in a layer of cells near the bark. A tree's growth rate changes in a predictable pattern throughout the year in response to seasonal climate changes, resulting in visible growth rings. The method is based on the fact that a Each ring marks a complete cycle of <u>seasons</u>, or one year, in the tree's life. It is possible therefore to determine the age of a live tree or wooden archaeological materials and artifacts. It is also possible to determine the rate of change of the environment, notably climate during different periods of history (dendro/paleolclimatology).

Appendix II
Lost-wax (*cire perdue*) casting

LOST-WAX (*CIRE PERDUE*) CASTING

Lost-wax casting, also often referred to as investment casting or *cire perdue* is an ancient technology for making a precise replica of an object in metal, mostly gold, silver, zinc, copper and aluminium alloys. The origin of the process is unknown but it has been used in ancient civilizations of the near East and Asia for thousands of years. There is ample evidence that that is had been practiced in Mesopotamia by the end of the fourth millennium BC, and in Egypt from the second millennium In spite of its long history the process has changed very little and has become a valuable part of modern metallurgical manufacturing processes. While the ancient craftsmen used the process mainly for art and craft work, it has found extensive use in the production of precision castings in metals which are usually very difficult or impossible to machine or shape at ordinary temperatures. For such components, investment casting is often the only option. It is a high precision process (± 0.05mm per mm) capable of reproducing the finest details with high dimensional accuracy, often with hardly any need for finishing. Such is the precision and versatility that an adaptation of the basic technique is being used to produce intricate high-precision automotive, aircraft, aerospace and general engineering components which would otherwise entail much expensive machining. Other modern products of lost-wax casting are precious metal jewelry, dental crowns and inlays, jet engine impellers, gas turbine blades.

The basic technology of lost-wax casting is very simple but the execution can be very complex and calls for a great deal of skill. The process has changed very little over the centuries but has been domesticated through adaptation and infusion innovations in various parts of the world. Archaeological evidence shows that the process was used in many parts of the world for high quality brass and bronze castings of jewelry and artwork in most of the ancient world for six to eight millennia including Mesopotamia, Anatolia, China, India, ancient Egypt Greece, Italy, Japan, Central and South America, and Africa. The basic process involves the production of a pattern made in wax or latex in the replica of the desired end product. If the product is hollow, a clay core made roughly in the shape and size of the end product is made and then covered with wax on which the details of the end product are worked. The model is immersed in a slurry of fine clay, often mixed with cow dung, dried and coated again. This process may be repeated three or four times to produce a thick, strong clay coating. Other materials such as plaster of paris are used in place of clay in modern lost-wax casting. The mould formed by the clay coating is provided with a pouring cup through which molten metal will be poured. Risers are provided for gas expulsion from the mould during pouring, otherwise the molten metal may not flow into all casting spaces evenly and this results in poor casting. Also, risers help to relieve the pressure of expanding gases which may be sufficiently strong to break the mould. The dried mould is heated in an oven upside down, the wax melts and flows out, leaving behind a mould cavity having the desired shape. The technology takes its name from this stage because the wax is 'lost' from the mould but it is usually reclaimed and reused. The mould is now turned with the pourer on top, non-ferrous metal such as brass, bronze is melted and poured into the cup. The casting is cooled, the mould is broken off to retrieve the casting which is then finished. If the clay core can be reached it is broken up and removed from the interior of the casting. The processes are summarized in Figure A-II.1.

Apart from the need to remove sprues, risers and fill up holes, castings hardly ever come out of the mould without defects, the extent depending on the expertise and experience of the caster. Almost every casting needs repairs and delicate reconstructive processes to correct

Appendices **200**

defects, buffing and finishing. Larger sculptures that require assembly of separately cast sections will need chasing to remove weld bumps. Bronze castings are often enhanced by the chemical application of transparent and opaque colours (patination) and each foundry develops its own proprietary water soluble chemicals: ferric nitrate produces reds and browns, cupric nitrate imparts greens and blues and sulphurated potash produces black. The casting may be given a final coat of clear wax to enhance and preserve the patina. Each object produced by lost-wax casting is always unique because the mould is destroyed in the process or retrieving the casting and a new mould has to be made for a new casting.

MODEL MAKING

A model of the original is created by an artist from beeswax, latex or another material with a low melting point. These materials retain their softness and it is relatively easy to reproduce fine details of the original object. Wax sticks are affixed to the wax model with heated tools for different purposes: a gate for pouring the metal, sprues which act as channels for hot metal flow, and risers for the escape of gases during pouring.

SPRUING, GATING AND INVESTING

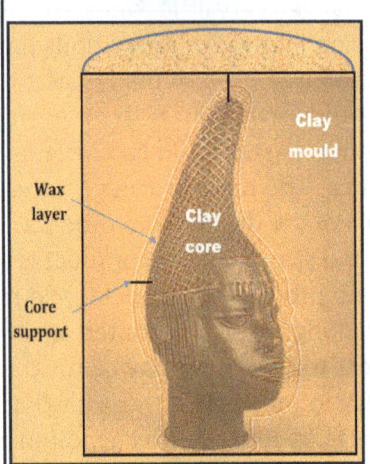

The was sculpture is 'invested' by building a hard shell around it, achieved by dipping into a bath of clay or fine sand slurry, then dried. This process builds a very thin wall of silica around the wax. model. This is repeated about ten times to build a sufficiently thick shell, at least 15 cm. Additional layers of clay are added for support. If the object is hollow, a clay cylindrical core or a slightly smaller version of the model, smaller by the thickness of the ceramic layer is installed and held in place with core supports. The mould is heated in an oven to melt out the wax model, leaving a negative impression of the model in the ceramic layer of the mould for the metal to fill. Moulds are designed in at least two sections held together by fasteners to facilitate easy retrieval of the cast object. Large castings require several sprues and risers or may be made in separate units and assembled by welding.

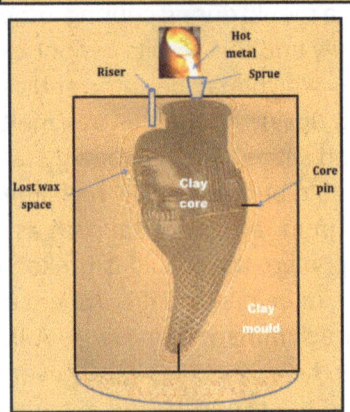

POURING AND FINISHING

The mould is turned upside down, the molten metal is poured and after cooling the casting is extracted and finished by fettling and polishing.

FINISHED PRODUCT

Figure A-II.1 Stages of the lost-wax (*cire perdue*) process.

Appendix III
Basic metallurgy of metals of antiquity

BASIC METALLURGY OF METALS OF ANTIQUITY

Materials have been critical to the survival of humankind through history: they provide tools for all aspects of survival – shelter, clothing, tools for agriculture and hunting. Seven metals known as metals of antiquity have been in use from prehistoric times: gold, silver, lead, tin, copper, iron, mercury. These metals remained dominant in the emerging world until the discovery of arsenic in the 13th century AD, after which the family of metals grew rapidly to the current 86 known metals. However, most were used in small quantities: gold, silver, tin and lead were used for jewelry and ornaments; mercury which forms amalgam with gold, silver and several other metals was used in ointments and cosmetics from early times; lead was used in glazing clayware. The ancient Romans also used lead for making water pipes and lining baths as early as 3000 BC. Copper and iron were the two main structural metals used for a very wide range of applications: tools, weaponry, artifacts, and apart from stone, the two metals form the basis for classifying early periods of civilization: Stone Age; Chalcolithic/Eneolithic Age (transition between Neolithic and Copper Age); Copper Age; Bronze Age; Iron Age. Archaeologists have done invaluable work in documenting ancient cultures and civilizations from pieces and fragments of physical evidence to evolve credible hypotheses on cultures and civilizations from early times. However, their capacity to fully characterize ancient metal objects was rather limited and this has led to the common classification of the Bronze Age as the first metal age because it was originally thought that all early copper-base artifacts were bronzes. Metallurgy evolved as a science towards the end of the eighteenth century and provided new instruments for the study of ancient metal objects using basic physical and chemical science principles, with emphasis on material evidence as a complement to the documentary evidence provided by archaeologists. Archaeometallurgists use scientific methods to study early metal smelting sites including the analysis of ores, slags, pieces of products, from which important information on ores used, smelting and working techniques and probable product composition can be obtained. It is now known that the first metal age was in fact the Copper Age because many artifacts previously identified as bronzes (copper-tin alloys) were in fact coppers containing small amounts of lead, arsenic, antimony, tin, zinc, and this has led to reclassification of many artifacts as well as revision of the metal ages.

    Archaeometallurgists define the beginning of a metal age *as the earliest date of a smelting site and associated widespread use of the metal*. Based on this definition, the metal ages arrived in all places at different times, in some cases separated by over 2,000 years. The Chalcolithic Age dates back possibly to 8000 BC when products were being fashioned from stone, flint, native copper and meteoric iron. The late Neolithic cultures featured limited use of native copper for ornaments but this began to change with the emergence of copper tools in the Chalcolithic cultures. Evidence of exploited copper mines dated 4500-4000 BC has been found in South East Europe but no evidence of ore smelting has been found. The earliest evidence of copper smelting from ore found in Anatolia dates from 7000-6000 BC but use appeared to have been restricted and the true Copper Age did not arrive in the region until after 4000 BC but it spread quite rapidly throughout the region, Europe and Asia. However, Copper Culture did not spread in South America until around AD 500, and even much later in sub-Saharan Africa around AD 900. The smelting of coppers of relatively high purity, or coppers containing substantial amounts of arsenic or antimony persisted for thousands of years in spite of the fact that the first true bronzes (containing at least 7 wt% tin) appeared in Sumeria in Asia Minor around 3000 BC. Use did not spread for a long time largely because of unavailability of tin in the region. Use of bronze only became widespread in most regions from around 2000 BC when tin ingots were traded across regions of the early world. For the same reason, the True Bronze Age did not last long, surmounted gradually by the arrival of much more versatile and plentiful iron from around 1500 BC.

BASIC METALLURGY OF COPPER ALLOYS

Copper is one of the earliest metals known to mankind: native copper was being worked to produce tools and artifacts ten thousand years ago; copper was the first metal to be smelted from ore and cast into a mould five to six thousand years ago; and the metal was the first to be alloyed with tin deliberately to produce bronze. Copper belongs to the group of the three most widely used metals in unalloyed or alloyed condition in the modern industrial world, the others are steel and aluminium. Its properties include high electrical conductivity (second only to silver), high thermal conductivity, high corrosion resistance, good ductility and malleability, and moderate tensile strength.

Copper ores

Copper is a very reactive element and forms complex compounds with many other elements. There are over twenty different types of copper ores but the most common are the oxides and sulphides associated with gangue, in particular, silicon, but there are several other naturally occurring compounds (azurite, malachite, turquoise) which have been used widely and historically as pigments (Figure A-III.1). Most copper ores contain several other elements, notably arsenic, antimony, lead, tin, nickel mostly in quantities below about 1 wt%. Most, perhaps all copper ores were originally in sulphide form but, with time, the surface layers become oxidized and usually contain some oxidized copper minerals, precious metals and possibly native copper. Much of the copper would have been washed down to lower layers which are usually still in sulphide form and much richer in copper (Figure A-III.2). This zone will often contain minerals of the fahlerz type: copper-arsenic-antimony sulphides such as $(CuFe)_{12}(AsSb)_4S_{13}$ or solid solutions of tetrahedrite: $(CuFe)_{12}Sb_4S_{13}$, and tennantite $(CuFe)_{12}As_4S_{13}$. The lowest zone represents the original deposit and contains copper sulphides in low concentration, usually about 1-4 wt% Cu. This is the layer that is currently being worked in most modern copper mines. Most of the early workings of copper ore deposits probably exploited the top oxide layers which are much easier to smelt than sulphides. However, having exhausted these layers, they would have found a way of smelting sulphide ores as well by first roasting the ore over a long period at a temperature not exceeding 800°C to convert both iron and copper sulphides to oxides before smelting, and slagging of the iron oxide with silica sand to form ferrous silicate (fayalite). Archaeometallurgists consider it unlikely that the early copper smelters had the knowledge or expertise to carry out the tedious two-stage smelting of copper sulphide ores. It is more likely that they cosmelted some types of sulphide ores (for example, sulpharsenide) without first roasting. This probability is discussed in some depth in a later section. Sulphide ores are now extracted by pyrometallurgical processes and oxide/carbonate ores by hydrometallurgical techniques in modern copper production.

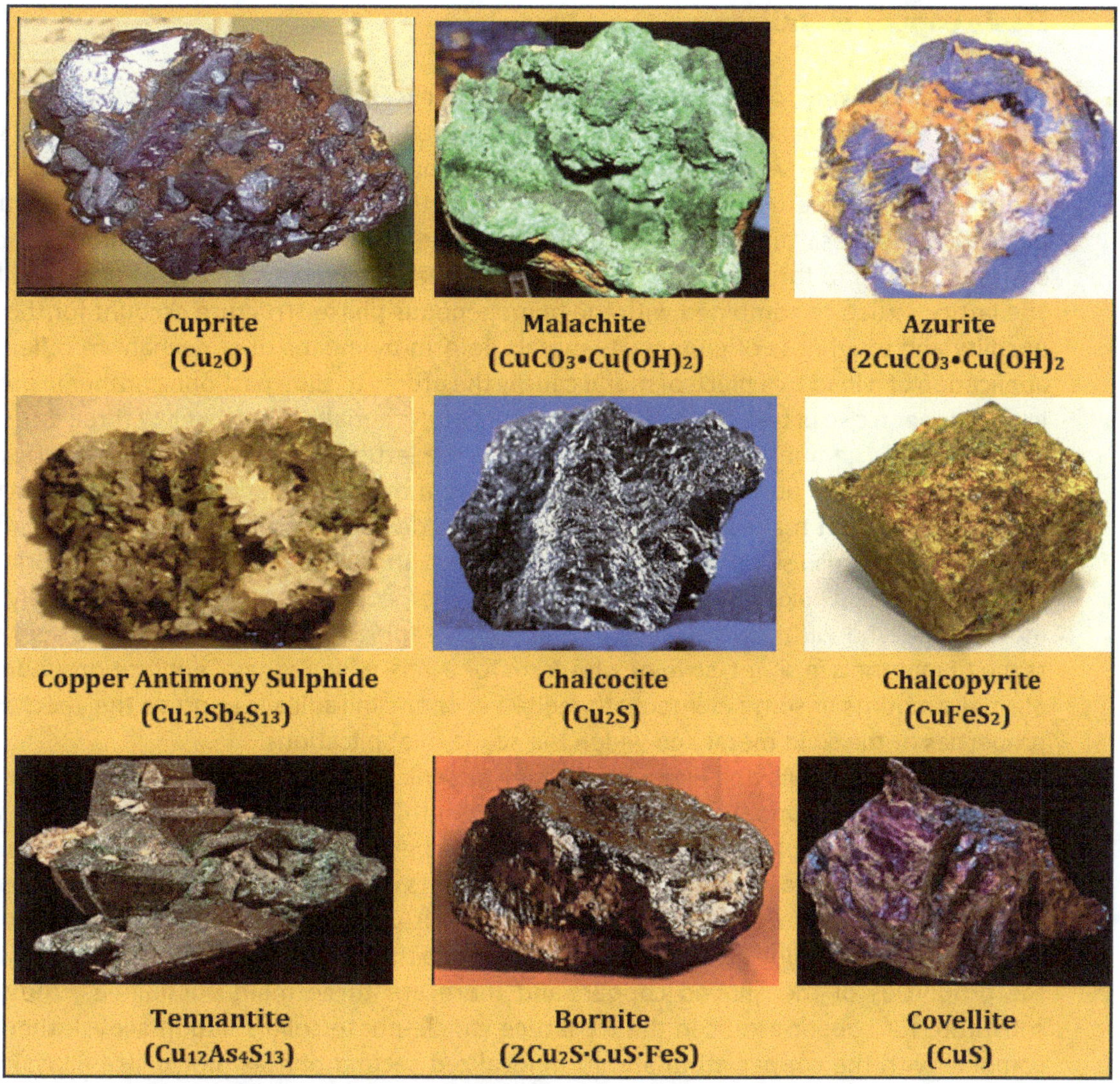

Cuprite
(Cu_2O)
Malachite
($CuCO_3$•$Cu(OH)_2$)
Azurite
($2CuCO_3$•$Cu(OH)_2$
Copper Antimony Sulphide
($Cu_{12}Sb_4S_{13}$)
Chalcocite
(Cu_2S)
Chalcopyrite
($CuFeS_2$)
Tennantite
($Cu_{12}As_4S_{13}$)
Bornite
($2Cu_2S$·CuS·FeS)
Covellite
(CuS)

Figure A-III.1 Some copper ores *(oldcopper.org; Samans 1949).*

1200 m o.d.
old shafts
gossan
25% Cu
secondary enrichment zone
(sulphide)
12% Cu
old adits
4% C
2% Cu
0.3% Cu
70 m
thin oxidized
zone: 2-3% Cu
limit in 1931
primary deposit
level in 1968

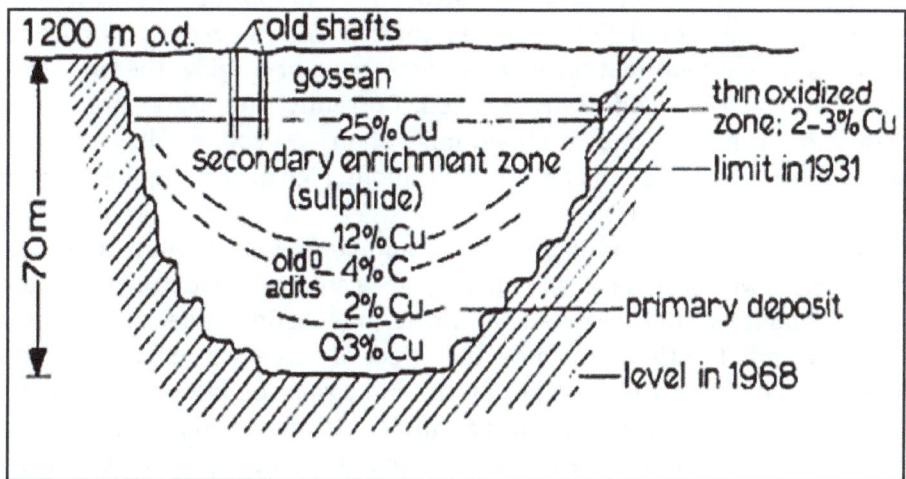

Figure A-III.2 Section through an early Turkish copper ore deposit *(Tylecote 1976).*

Basic copper metallurgy

Copper is a relatively soft and malleable metal with excellent formability because it does not work-harden. This makes it possible to coldwork the metal to produce very thin sheets and micron-sized wire. However, this property makes copper too soft for structural applications and the early people used the metal mostly for artifacts and ornaments. This exceptional malleability derives from the microstructure of copper. Under equilibrium conditions, molten copper solidifies to form a homogeneous (alpha-phase) face-centered cubic (fcc) structure. The lattice structure combined with the homogeneous phase structure account for the high ductility and toughness of copper. All metals deform by means of a mechanism called slip: application of a load to a piece of metal causes the atoms to slide past one another in groups. In the copper fcc structure this movement occurs preferentially in any or all of three directions along a specific geometric plane of atoms within the lattice, and the copper lattice structure offers the maximum number of possibilities for slip movement found in any metal structure. While the excellent malleability and toughness are desirable in many modern applications, these properties also severely limited applications in ancient times because the material was too soft for objects like tools and weapons. However, copper forms alloys more freely than most metals and with a wide range of elements, leading to the emergence of a very wide range of materials in sheet, strip or wire form for a very wide range of applications. Addition of small amounts of some elements to molten copper can radically improve the mechanical properties of the solid metal and widen the scope of applications.

The addition of alloying elements, notably arsenic, antimony, tin, zinc, lead and several other elements to copper increases tensile strength, yield strength and the rate of work hardening. For example, in brasses, the tensile strength and yield strength both increase as the zinc content increases. Different alloying elements vary in their effectiveness at increasing strength and work hardening, thus providing a spectrum of property combinations. The final arrangement of the alloying elements with respect to the parent copper fcc lattice determines the properties of the alloyed copper, and there are three main possibilities: they may substitute for copper atoms in the fcc lattice (single-phase solid solution alloys); they may combine with the copper atom and form localized second phases (polyphase alloys); they may precipitate from the solidifying copper and become trapped as colonies or globules embedded in single-phase or polyphase structures (composite alloys). All three options may be regarded as engineered discontinuities which serve to slow down or pin down dislocation movements during deformation such as hammering or forging, thereby strengthening the alloy, but ductility is significantly reduced. Currently, there are around twenty alloying elements that can be added to obtain more than 400 copper alloys, each with a unique combination of properties to suit many applications, high quality requirements, manufacturing processes and environments.

When cooled slowly and under equilibrium conditions, molten copper containing less than 11 wt% tin will form single alpha-phase, face-centered cubic structure as the temperature falls below about 850°C (Figure A-III.3a). Tin atoms substitute directly into the lattice in place of copper atoms. The tin atoms have the effect of actually strengthening the pure copper because they are larger than copper atoms and strain the lattice, that is, they alter the usual distance between the copper atoms. Under commercial conditions of rather slow solidification, nearly all of the metal will solidify as the alpha phase. This substitutional phenomenon results in a single-phase solid solution of tin in copper. The crystal structure, though stronger than pure copper due to lattice strain, is still fcc. Consequently, the slip characteristics remain very good. Single-phase solid solution alloys of copper known as tin bronzes therefore, retain high ductility despite very significant increases in strength.

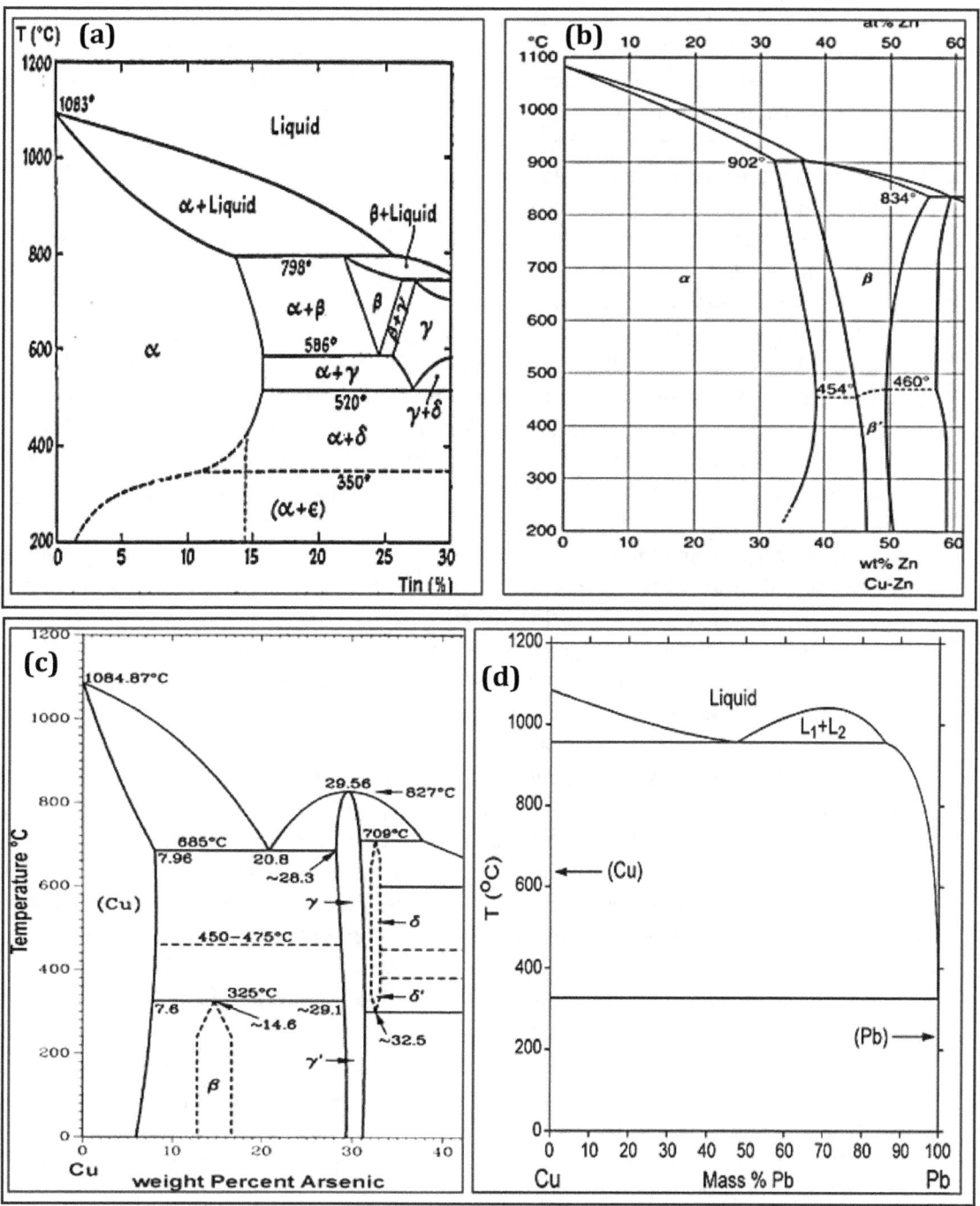

Figure A-III.3 Phase diagrams of some copper alloys.

Tin bronzes, with up 15.8 wt% tin, retain the homogeneous structure of alpha copper. The tin is a solid solution strengthener in copper, even though tin has a low solubility in copper at room temperature. The room temperature phase transformations are slow and usually do not occur, therefore these alloys remain single phase solid solution alloys. If the tin content is increased to 16 wt% or more, some of the alpha phase will transform as the metal cools below 400°C. A new delta phase appears, interspersed throughout the normal fcc alpha crystals. This phase can be preserved in the material with fairly rapid cooling conditions. The delta phase (though still basically fcc) contains much more tin in proportion to copper than is found in the alpha and is very hard and strong but lacks much ductility. It appears under best conditions as finely dispersed islands throughout the alpha microstructure of the material. The influence of this second phase on the slip mechanism is dramatic, having the effect of pinning the slip planes after small degrees of motion thereby restricting their motion. The delta phase also greatly increases the wear resistance of the material, as is indicated by the significant increase in hardness.

Zinc forms homogeneous solid solution with copper when present in amounts no more than about 30 wt% (Figure A-III.3b). This explains why the alloy (brass) is strong and yet retains significant ductility, (substitution of zinc atoms for copper atoms in the copper fcc matrix causes lattice strains that strengthen the alloy but there are no second phases to pin down movement of dislocations) and why it is often preferred to bronze when the object needs to be worked. Aluminium and manganese form polyphase alloys with copper through the dispersion of another much harder and stronger phase in the basic fcc lattice matrix.

Leaded copper castings may contain from 5 to 50 wt% lead. These alloys undergo a two-step solidification process, that is, the copper fraction (pure copper or high-copper alloy) freezes over the narrow solidification range typical of such alloys. The lead solidifies and precipitates only after the casting has cooled to around 700°C (Figure A-III.1d). Lead improves fluidity in casting because it lowers the melting point of copper but it is practically insoluble in solid copper and will precipitate in fine globules distributed throughout the copper matrix as molten copper cools slowly. The effect on the mechanical properties of the alloy depends on the amount of lead as well as the morphology and dispersion of the precipitate in the copper matrix. Fine, uniformly-dispersed lead precipitate in copper matrix enhances machinability and solid/sliding lubrication characteristics of the alloy while decreasing the mechanical strength especially when the precipitate is segregated. Mechanical strength decreases progressively with increasing lead content and the positive effect on sliding friction starts to reduce when lead content exceeds around 35 wt%.

Arsenic is only partially soluble in solid-state copper: 7.8 wt% at 685°C, reducing to 6.9 wt% at room temperature under ideal cooling conditions (Figure A-III.1c). However, the Cu-As system is prone to non-equilibrium cooling as a result of the steep gradient of the solidus-liquidus line (Budd and Ottaway, 1991, 1995, 1996). The higher melting point of copper leads it to solidify first as cored dendrites, leaving behind an arsenic-rich inter-dendritic liquid with a lower melting point. The dendritic structures are preserved during rapid cooling due to the slow diffusion of arsenic ions in solid copper and this results in the formation of a complex eutectic precipitation of copper-arsenic (Cu_3As) which may contain over 20-24 wt% arsenic depending on the cooling rate during solidification. Eutectic precipitations occur over a wide range of chemical compositions and have been observed in alloys with as little as 1 wt% arsenic, well below the expected minimum of 7 wt% suggested by the phase diagram (Budd and Ottaway 1991; Lechtman 1996; Meeks 1993).

Due to its lower melting point, the eutectic phase is usually forced to the surface by the solidifying dendritic network. This inverse segregation of arsenic-rich phases leads to a concentration of arsenic towards the surface of the alloy in contact with the mould where the cooling rate is highest (Charles 1967; McKerrell and Tylecote 1972; Modlinger and Sabatini 2016). This explains why surface chemical analysis of arsenical copper objects may be unreliable due to extensive micro and macro segregation. Arsenic has low melting point and volatilizes mainly as arsenic trioxide when copper is melted or reheated in oxidizing atmosphere. Tin, zinc and antimony harden copper to a similar extent as arsenic but they are not as volatile, hence a greater proportion would be retained in working.

Main copper alloys

Addition of one or more of around twenty different elements to copper can alter mechanical, chemical and electrical properties dramatically. This has enabled the development of around four hundred alloys for different applications. (Figure A-III.4) The main groups are discussed briefly below.

Brasses

Brass is the generic term for a range of copper-zinc alloys with differing combinations of properties, including strength, machinability, ductility, wear-resistance, hardness, colour, hygienic, electrical and thermal conductivity, and corrosion-resistance. Zinc content varies from about 5 wt% for commercial brass to around 40 wt% for Muntz metal. Copper and zinc form solid solution up to about 39 wt% zinc at 456°C giving a wide range of properties depending on the cooling rate which determines the ultimate room-temperature microstructure. Various elements are added to obtain alloy brasses with desired properties, mainly tin, aluminium, silicon, magnesium, nickel and lead. Alpha brasses contain up to 35 wt% zinc and retain a single alpha-phase, face-centered cubic structure at room temperature, while higher zinc content of about 40 wt% will feature a complex two-phase (alpha + beta)) structure (Muntz metal). The presence of the beta phase decreases ductility in cold-working. Annealed brass is extremely ductile (up to around 50 wt% zinc at room temperature but the presence of the beta phase makes the alloy heat-treatable. Nickel-silvers are silver-coloured copper-nickel-zinc alloys containing 10-20 wt% nickel and can be regarded as special brasses. In most respects they show similar corrosion characteristics to the brasses, but the higher nickel versions have superior tarnish resistance and resistance to stress corrosion cracking. They are available in all forms and are used for silver-plated tableware, telecommunication components, food manufacturing equipment, jewelry, model making, tool brush anchor wire and pins, musical instruments, test probes and contact springs.

Tin Brasses are alloys made from copper, zinc (2 wt% to 40 wt%) and tin (0.2 wt% to 3 wt%). This family of alloys includes admiralty brasses, naval brasses and free-machining tin brasses. These alloys are used to make high-strength fasteners, electrical connectors, springs, corrosion resistant mechanical products, marine hardware, pump shafts, and corrosion-resistant screw machine parts. They provide increased corrosion resistance, lower sensitivity to dezincification and higher strength compared with straight brasses. They possess good hot forgeability and good cold formability. These materials have moderate strength, high atmospheric and aqueous corrosion resistance and excellent electrical conductivity. Nickel silvers, also called nickel brasses, are alloys containing copper, nickel, and zinc. Though they do not contain silver, they have an attractive silver luster, moderately high strength and good corrosion resistance. They are used to make food and beverage handling equipment, decorative hardware, electroplated tableware, optical and photographic equipment and musical instruments.

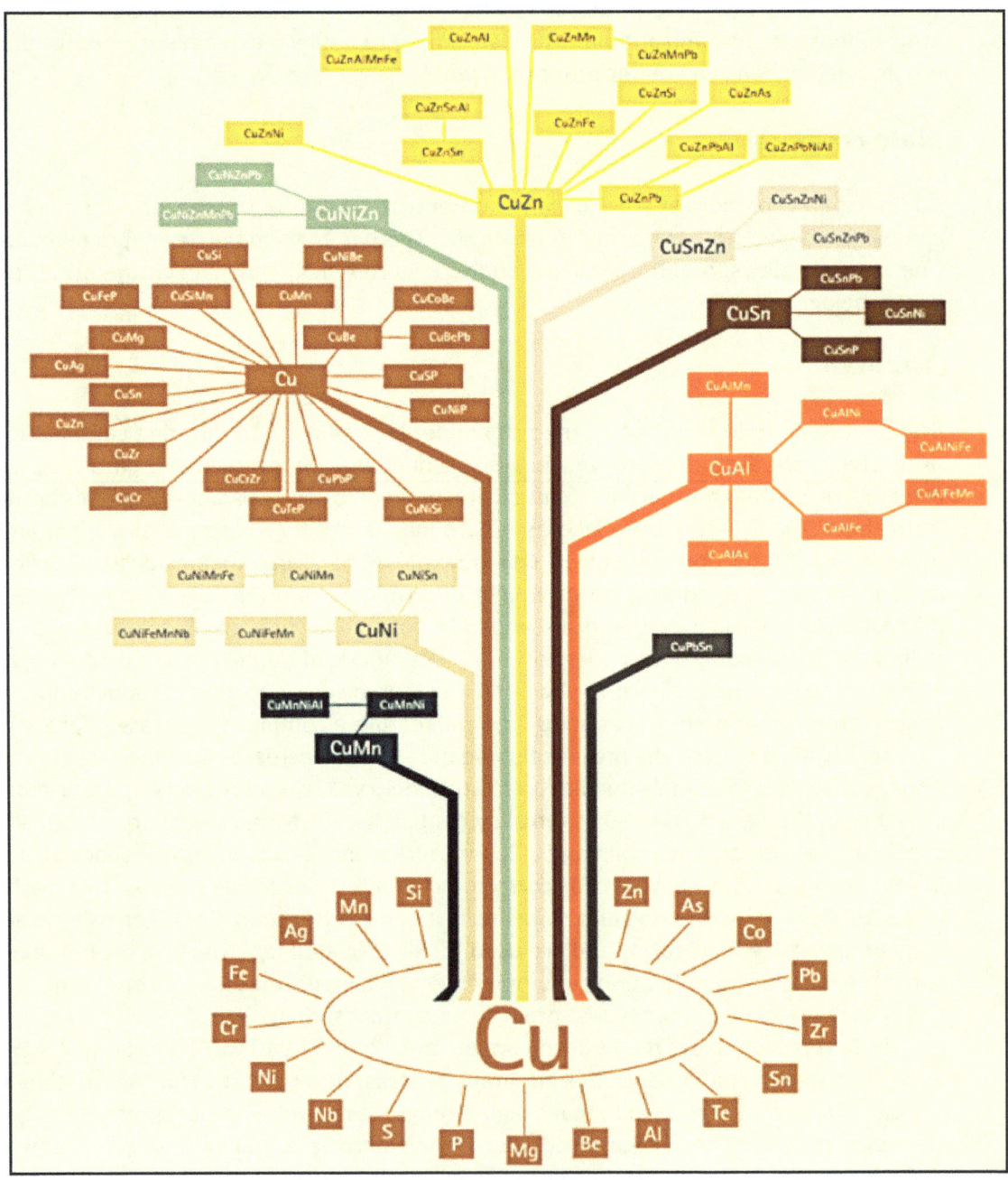

Figure A-III.4 Copper Tree *(copperalliance.eu)*.

Brasses containing between 32 wt% and 39 wt% zinc exhibit excellent hot working characteristics but limited cold workability. Brasses containing more than 39 wt% zinc, such as Muntz Metal, have higher strength and lower ductility at room temperature than alloys with less zinc. Brasses are known for their ease of fabrication by drawing, high cold-worked strength and corrosion resistance. Brasses are routinely blanked, coined, drawn and pierced to produce springs, fire extinguishers, jewelry, radiator cores, lamp fixtures, ammunition, flexible hose and the base for gold plate. Brasses have excellent castability and cast brasses are used as plumbing fixtures, decorative hardware, architectural trim, low pressure valves, gears and bearings. Silicon Brasses are part of the subgroup of high-strength brasses. They contain less than 20 wt% zinc and up to 6 wt% silicon and are solid solution strengthened. Silicon red brasses are used for valve stems where corrosion resistance and high strength are critical.

Tin bronzes

Bronze is an alloy of copper and tin (≥ 7 wt%) and is the earliest metallic alloy to be developed by the ancient people about five thousand years ago, used for a very wide range of products: jewelry and ornaments, weapons, tools, coins etc. Copper and tin form solid solution up to around 16 wt% tin content (lower than that of copper-zinc), forming uniform structure at room temperature when the tin content is not more than about 11 wt% and cooling is slow. This grade of (wrought) bronze is ductile and can be worked into shapes, when tin content is higher as in cast bronze, strength increases but there is a reduction in ductility. This group of bronzes is excellent for high-strength bearings and gears. Addition of about 1 wt% phosphorus deoxidizes copper (phosphor bronzes) and improves castability but excess phosphorus reduces electrical conductivity. Wrought tin bronzes have higher strength and corrosion resistance than wrought brasses, especially in the cold-worked condition. Phosphor bronze alloys containing 20-24 wt% tin have been used for the sand casting of bells (hence the name: bell metal) for centuries. They slowly patinate (develop a thin protective layer by oxidation or other chemical processes), which protects them from further corrosion, leading to a very long service life. Phosphor Bronzes, or tin bronzes as they are sometimes called, contain between 0.5 wt% and 11 wt% tin and 0.01 wt% to 0.35 wt% phosphorous. Tin increases their corrosion resistance and tensile strength; phosphorous increases wear resistance and stiffness. Phosphor bronzes have superb spring qualities, high fatigue resistance, excellent formability and solderability, and high corrosion resistance. They are used primarily for electrical products; other uses include corrosion resistant bellows, diaphragms and spring washers.

Copper-tin-zinc-nickel alloys (gun metal)

Copper alloys containing 2-11 wt% tin, 1-10 wt% zinc nickel up to 6 wt% have been used for more than 2,000 years for statues, artifacts, doors, ornaments. These alloys also known as nickel gunmetal are castable and combine good strength and high corrosion resistance. Addition of lead up to about 7 wt% (leaded gunmetal) greatly enhances castability but reduces mechanical strength. Gun metal derives its name from its main use for weaponry in Medieval times but has been largely replaced by steel. However, they are still used extensively for the manufacture of intricate castings such as high-pressure valves, pipe fittings, pump components, moderate speed/load bearings and modern statues.

Copper-aluminium alloys (aluminium bronzes)

Copper and aluminium form single alpha-phase solid solution up to 9.4 wt% aluminium at 565°C, and solid solubility of the alpha-phase increases with decreasing temperature. Higher aluminium content produces heat-treatable alloys which, when quenched from about 900°C produce hard, brittle martensitic structure but tempering at 400-600°C yields alloys with a good combination of strength and ductility, with excellent corrosion, wear and fatigue resistance. Cu-al alloys containing 5-12 wt% aluminium and up to 6 wt% iron, manganese, nickel and silicon are produced in cast and wrought form, they are stronger than brasses and tin bronzes and have better corrosion resistance due to the formation of a thin, strong protective layer (alumina) as a result of oxidation. They are suitable for a wide range of industrial products such as fasteners, pump and valve components, pipe fittings, heat exchangers, bearings, propellers. Solid solution strengthening, cold work and precipitation of an iron-rich phase contribute to these characteristics. High aluminum-containing alloys can be quenched and tempered. Aluminum bronzes are used in marine hardware, shafts and pump and valve components for handling seawater, sour mine waters, non-oxidizing acids, and industrial process fluids. They are also used as heavy duty sleeve bearings and machine tool ways. Aluminum bronze castings have exceptional corrosion resistance, high strength, toughness and wear resistance. They also exhibit good casting and welding characteristics.

Copper-beryllium alloys

Beryllium has low solubility in copper, only 2.7 wt% maximum at 866°C. However, the alloy is quench-hardenable due to rapid decrease in beryllium solubility. When solution-heat treated at around 800°C alloys with tensile strength up to four times that of pure copper can be obtained due to precipitation hardening, making this alloy the strongest copper alloy. However, it is also the most expensive and use is reserved for special mission-critical applications for which no other copper alloy is suitable.

Copper-silicon alloys (silicon brasses/bronzes)

The maximum solubility of silicon in copper is 5.3 wt% at 843°C. However, most cu-si alloys contain 1-3 wt% silicon and are not precipitation-hardenable, but this level is enough to confer high corrosion resistance particularly in sea water, high strength and toughness. Manganese, iron, tin or zinc are sometimes added to improve properties. The alloy is known as silicon brass when zinc is present or silicon bronze when tin is the other alloying element. Silicon Bronze has improved fluidity which greatly enhances pouring during casting and reduces contraction when cooling. The alloy is less brittle than bronze and has appealing surface finish and superior corrosion resistant properties, even when submerged in liquids and chemicals. This group of bronzes are low-cost substitutes for tin bronzes. Silicon also improves the strength and corrosion resistance of brasses, improves strength but lowers conductivity. Silicon brasses are used to make bearings, gears and intricately shaped pump and valve components.

Copper-lead alloys

Lead is soluble in copper at high temperatures but insoluble at room temperature. Leaded copper alloys solidify in two stages: the copper/copper alloy fraction freezes over the narrow solidification range typical of such alloys while the lead remains fluid and solidifies only after the casting has cooled to around 700°C. This can lead to segregation of lead to the last regions to solidify and unless the casting procedure is such that promotes the uniform dispersion of the lead precipitate, it can cause significant weakness in the casting. Lead increases fluidity and castability of copper/copper alloys at high temperatures, and can also significantly enhance the quality of castings. As leaded copper alloys freeze, the lead remains liquid, trapped in microscopic pools which fill and seal the interdendritic microporosity due to shrinking solidified alloy. The lead seals the pores and renders the casting sound and pressure-tight, and also improves machinability. Lead enhances the casting of high quality, artistic casting of finely detailed objects and featured prominently in many archaeological artifacts of the Copper Age. Eutectic reaction occurs at 326°C, with all the copper in alpha-phase precipitate while nearly all the lead precipitates in beta phase. This reaction occurs in any copper alloy that contains lead. The essentially pure lead precipitate produced in the eutectic reaction will be distributed inter-dendritically in the copper matrix as small globules. Up to about 3 wt% lead will improve machinability of copper/copper alloys and up to around 10 wt% produces globules that fill voids as copper castings cool thereby improving the soundness of castings. However, higher lead content will negatively affect strength largely because of segregation of large colonies of weak eutectic phases.

Copper-nickel alloys (cupronickel alloys)

Copper and nickel can form solid solution irrespective of composition ratio but alloys that contain 10-30 wt% nickel (cupronickels) are the most widely used. Addition of nickel improves strength, oxidation and corrosion resistance, thermal stability, and also greatly increases electrical resistivity. Cupronickels are used for condenser tubes, heat exchangers, chemical process equipment, wound resistance coils for electrical instruments. The addition of iron, chromium, niobium and/or manganese can improve the strength and corrosion resistance of cupro-nickel alloys significantly. They are virtually immune to stress corrosion cracking and exhibit high oxidation resistance in steam and moist air. The higher nickel alloys are well known for their corrosion resistance in sea water as well as resistance to marine biofouling. They are used to make electrical and electronic products, tubes for condensers in ships, on offshore platforms and in power plants, and various other marine products including valves, pumps, fittings and sheathing for ship hulls.

BASIC METALLURGY OF IRON

Iron is the fourth most abundant element in the earth's crust and, because the element is highly reactive, it is very rarely found without being combined with other elements, notably oxygen in a wide range of oxidation states : -2 to +7, although +2 and +3 are the most common. There are seven different types of iron ores but only four are considered important in modern metallurgy (Table A-III.1) of which hematite is the most important. Iron oxides are reduced to iron by reaction with carbon monoxide produced from coke (or charcoal in ancient times) at high temperatures in a series of reactions in different parts of the furnace from feed to tap (Figure A-III.5). When temperatures are above around 800°C but below 1200°C the reactions take place in solid state and the solid product, a mixture of iron and ferrosilicate slag is known as *wrought (worked) iron*. Wrought iron contains less than about 0.1 wt% carbon (unless fuel:ore ratio is high), too low to confer strength through heat treatment. This technology appeared in the second to first millennium BC and spread across the ancient world over the next one thousand years or so. Wrought iron was forged into a wide range of products: tools, implements, weaponry, structures, etc. Carbon is soluble in iron up to 4.3 wt% (Figure A-III.6) and lowers the melting temperature from 1538°C to around 1200°C. However, carbon in iron solution occupies the interstices between very soft alpha-iron atoms because its diameter is smaller. In this position they block dislocation movements of the crystal lattice when external strain is applied, thereby improving mechanical strength but decreasing ductility.

Table A-III.1 Main ores of iron

Iron ore	Formula	wt % Iron
Hematite	Fe_2O_3	70.0
Magnetite	Fe_3O_4	72.4
Limonite	$2Fe_2O_3 \cdot 3H_2O$	59.8
Siderite	$FeCO_3$	48.2

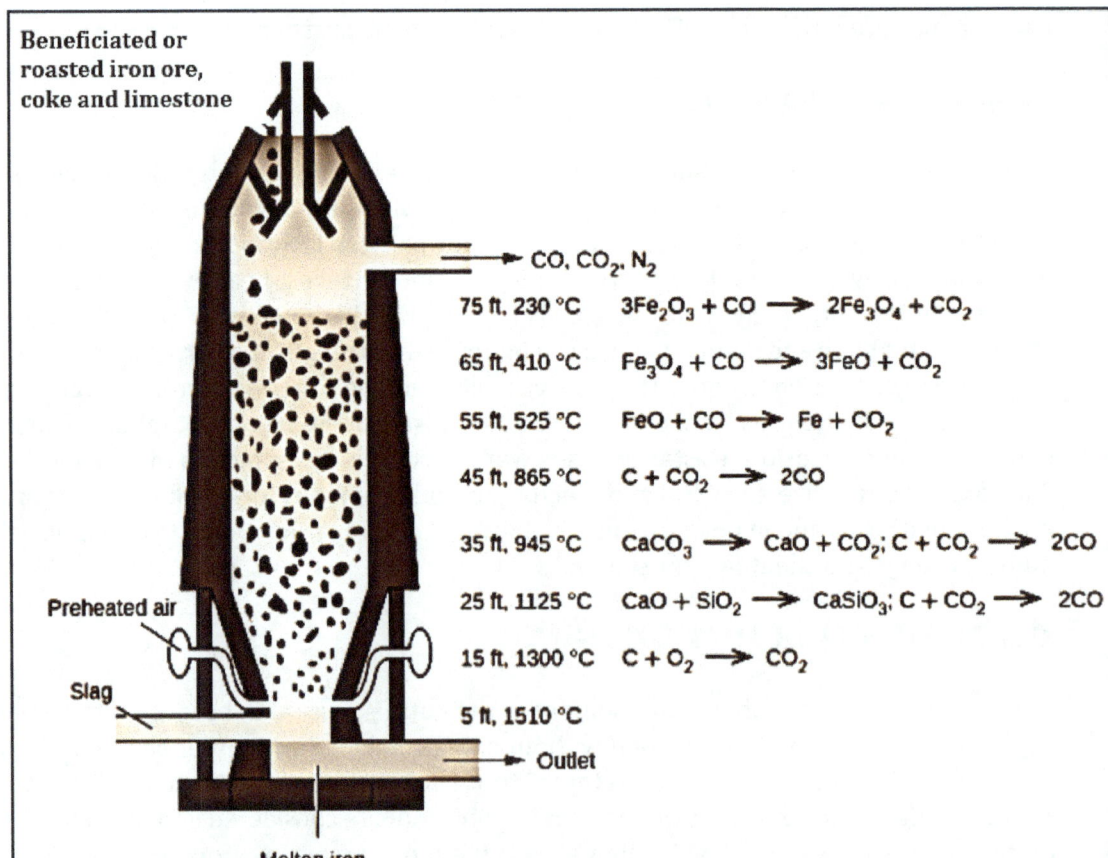

Figure A-III.5 Basic chemical reactions in the iron blast furnace

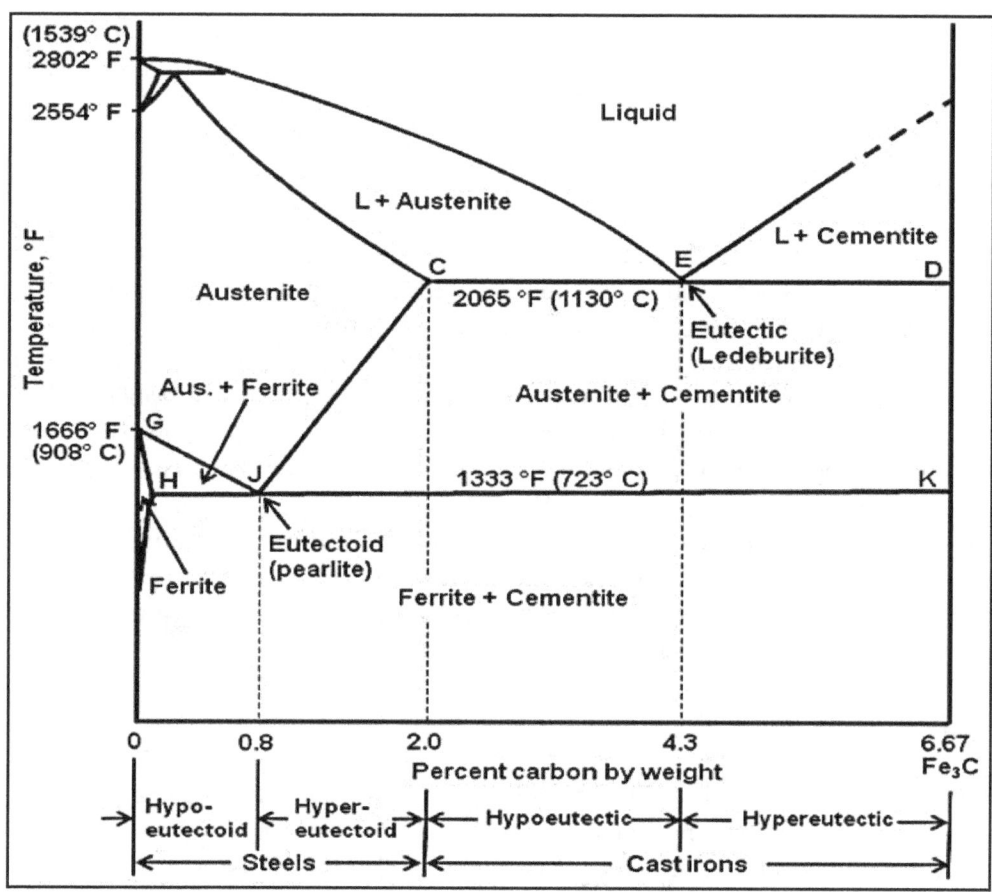

Figure A-III.6 Iron-Carbon phase diagram

Up to 0.8 wt% carbon results in ferrite-pearlite microstructure at room temperature when cooled slowly while higher levels of carbon will result in precipitates of pearlite and cementite (ferric carbide) in varying proportions. However, if cooled rapidly, like quenching from 900°C, the room-temperature microstructure will be mainly martensitic, which imparts high strength but embrittles the alloy. By applying different heat treatment technologies (austenitizing, quenching, tempering, normalizing, etc.), a wide range of combinations of room-temperature microstructures mechanical and physico-chemical properties can be obtained and steel grades suitable for a very wide range of applications can be produced.

The early iron smelters probably started with low-shaft, induced- or forced-draught furnaces similar to those used for copper smelting, which would have been adequate for iron smelting in the solid state if the height:diameter ratio is around 2:1 needed to achieve adequate reducing conditions for solid-state production of iron. Production of molten iron requires around 1200°C and the earliest evidence has been found in China, dated 600-500 BC. This is regarded as the fore-runner of the modern blast furnace, the main differences being the replacement of charcoal with coal and a major increase in size. Modern blast furnaces are fed continuously with beneficiated or roasted iron ore, coke (fuel) and limestone (flux), and molten iron is tapped continuously. Blast furnaces operate non-stop for around five years before they are shut down for relining and production ranges from one million to five million metric tons of molten iron per year. The molten product of the blast furnace is pig iron which has a very high carbon content in the range 3.8-4.7%, and several other impurities, notably silica; it is brittle and has to be processed further to obtain useful grades of iron and steel.

Cast iron

Pig iron is heated with coke in a cupola (shaft furnace) to burn off some of the carbon (reduced to 2-4%) as well as silicon and other impurities. Basic cast iron is brittle and useful mainly for applications that are subjected to predominantly compressive stresses. However, addition of small amounts of alloying elements and suitable heat treatment produces a very wide range of castable, machinable and malleable alloys for many industrial applications including machine bases and automotive components. When silicon content is low, carbon remains in solution, forming white cast iron which is very brittle; higher silicon content forces iron to precipitate in form of graphite which softens the alloy significantly (grey cast iron). Addition of other alloying elements – manganese, chromium, molybdenum, titanium and vanadium, nickel, copper - coupled with suitable heat treatment produces a wide range of multi-phase structures which confer different mechanical and chemical properties required for different types of engineering applications.

Steel

When pig iron is heated in oxidizing atmosphere in an open-hearth furnace or an oxygen converter, much of the carbon, silicon and other impurities are removed and the product is steel with carbon content of between 0.1% (mild steel) and 2% (high carbon steel). Adjustment of the carbon content and addition of alloying elements - manganese, chromium, nickel vanadium, tungsten, beryllium and others - combined with suitable heat treatment produces a very wide range of steels for casting, machining, forging, and for a very wide range of applications that require high resistance to heat, corrosion, fatigue and creep stresses. Plain carbon steel is iron with low-to-moderate content of carbon (around 0.8 to 2 wt% C). The presence of carbon at this level leads to a strong yet ductile room-temperature microstructure which comprises pearlite (compared with soft ferrite in wrought iron and brittle cementite embedded in ferrite in cast irons).

Steel was produced in early times in two different ways: either by carbonizing wrought iron through heating in closed crucibles with carbon) as practiced in India from around 400 BC, or by de-carbonizing molten cast iron through purging with air, a process attributed to the Chinese from 600-500 BC. The Chinese process is still the basic method for modern production of plain carbon steel in open hearth furnaces or oxygen converters. Most plain carbon steels contain small quantities of elements, notably silicon and manganese and are produced in two main grades: mild steels (up to 0.25 wt% C,) and high carbon steels (up to 2 wt% C). Mild steels are machinable while high carbon steels can be quench-hardened. Special alloy steels are produced by adding some elements to molten mild steel: manganese, chromium, nickel, manganese, tungsten, molybdenum, columbium. The primary effect of these alloying elements is to stabilize austenite or ferrite both of which are the predominant phases that form below 908°C. when molten steel is cooled to room temperature. Depending on the alloying element and quantity, this transformation may be delayed right down to room temperature and different microstructures predominantly austenitic, ferritic or mixtures of both with embedded precipitates of carbides of the elements can be obtained, leading to more than two thousand grades of special steels for different types of applications: stainless, corrosion fatigue, creep, high-strength, high-temperature resisting alloy steels. The main groups of irons and steels are shown in Figure A-III.7).

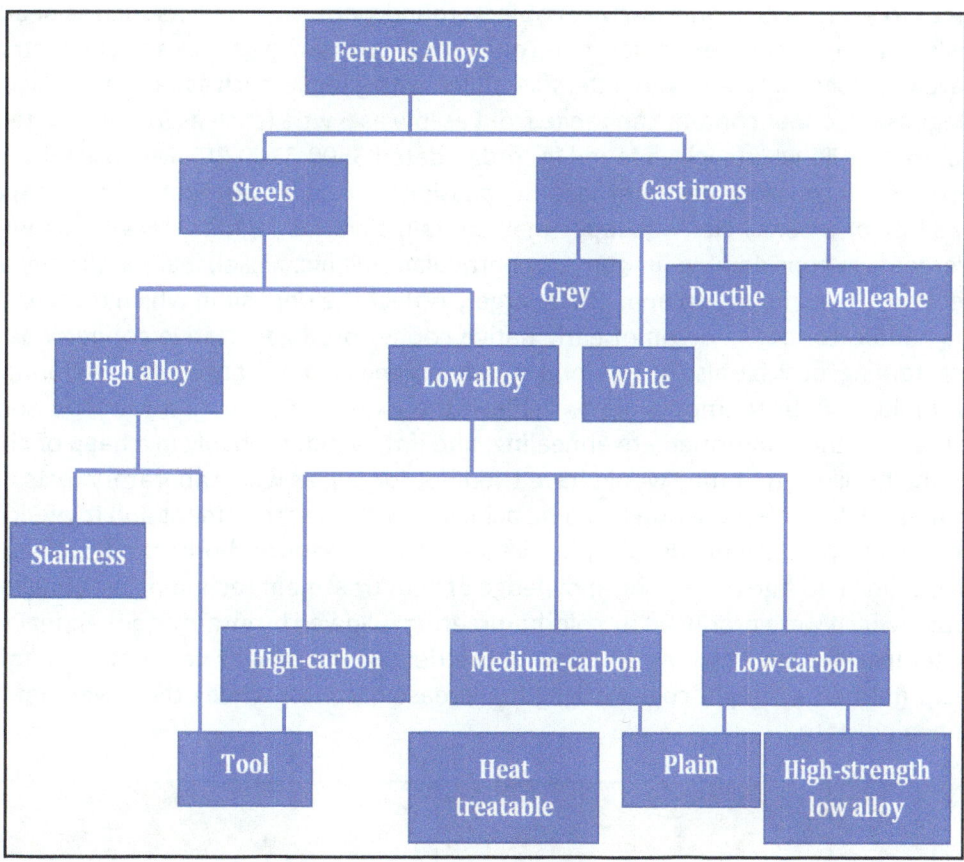

Figure A-III.7 Classification of irons and steels.

NEOLITHIC AGE OF COPPER AND IRON

Copper was the first metal used by humankind in any substantial quantities from Neolithic times. Native copper was worked for thousands of years and used along with stone and flint for tools and weapons. Transition to smelted copper was gradual, starting with melting and casting native copper to smelting ores which became common around seven thousand years ago. During this period different types of copper alloys emerged: arsenical, antimonial, low-tin, high-tin, probably depending on the chemistry of the ore. High-tin copper alloys (bronzes) have the best casting and working properties of them all but use was severely restricted for around two thousand years, until access to very scarce tin deposits was facilitated, probably through intra and inter-regional trade links which had developed by this time. By the second millennium BC, iron technology had emerged and eventually surmounted bronze use because of its superior properties and relatively wide availability of the inputs.

Native copper

Copper occurs in nature in different grades of purity, and has been worked to produce objects from Neolithic times, from around 8000 BC (Figure A-III.8). Most copper ore deposits contain pieces of native copper and the earliest evidences of use found in Anatolia date from the ninth to seventh millennia BC. Most objects found were small objects such as beads, pins and awls. Native copper is extremely heterogenous in terms of grain size and chemistry. They may have large or small grains with interstices filled with gangue such as calcite and silica, alumina, magnesia. Copper content can range from as low as 6 wt% (such as found in Niger dated 800 BC) to over 50 wt% (such as found in Jordan dated 3500-3200 BC). Microscopic examination also reveals considerable heterogeneity possibly caused by segregation due to the presence of silver or arsenic. Native copper may contain silver as high as 0.6 wt% as well as other elements in considerable amounts, in particular, arsenic, nickel, lead, antimony and iron. In general, the composition appears to largely reflect the deposit in which it occurs, and is the main indicator of the origin of early native copper products. Native copper was worked by cold forging, possibly also by hot forging but no significant evidence has been found. However, it would have been impossible to achieve the extensive reduction found in some ancient artifacts without intermediate annealing, and if they did, probably in a heap of charcoal fire, it is highly likely that they would have tried hot forging as well. Laboratory tests have shown that up to 96 wt% reduction could be achieved with heat treatment and it would have been possible to produce beads, pins, or even small axe heads and other tools. Clearly the lithic civilization had a good working knowledge of heat treatment technologies: objects have been found which were produced by cold-hammering followed by intermittent annealing, possibly at temperatures as high as 800°C until the desired shape was very nearly obtained, some were finished with light cold-working to increase hardness while others were left in the fully annealed state.

Figure A-III.8 Native copper and meteoric iron.

It is unclear when the Neolithic people started to melt native copper and cast into objects such as axe heads and hammers, knives, daggers, but it is believed that the process could have led to the discovery of copper smelting from ores. Native copper can be highly oxidized, such as has been found in Niger and several other places. Also, pieces of solid copper oxide may have been picked accidentally or deliberately in the process of picking native copper from copper ore deposits. When melted in a crucible under reducing conditions, such a mix would give more copper than expected and this may have provided the incentive to try copper oxide ore alone. It has been demonstrated that copper oxide mixed with excess charcoal and ground can be direct-reduced in a crucible to produce copper prills at the bottom of the crucible while the excess charcoal is trapped in the slag formed from iron oxide or manganese oxide which was often present in copper ores or may have been deliberately added. Evidence of such practice (large number of used crucibles) has been found in Iran dated 4500 BC. Production of copper by smelting ore became widespread from around 4000-3000 BC mostly in the Near East and South East Europe, marked by the presence of substantial traces of arsenic or nickel in cast objects which would almost certainly have come from copper ores.

Meteoric/native iron

Meteoric (or meteoritic) iron comprises around 6 wt% of meteorites (also known as shooting stars) which are solid pieces of debris from outer space (Figure A-III.8). Meteoric iron contains mainly iron and nickel in mineralized forms and is known as *taenite* when the nickel content is high (20-65 wt% Ni) or *kamacite* when the nickel content is low (5-10 wt% Ni with some other elements such as cobalt or carbon in minor quantities). Native iron occurs as small grains of *telluric* iron in some basalts and there is ample evidence that the metal was being worked in Neolithic times to make tools. However, like native copper, when cold hammered, native iron work-hardens and tends to crack along well-defined crystal planes but by hot-forging or cold-working with intermediate annealing, small tools and artifacts can be made, and many objects (mostly 6-12 wt% Ni) dated as early as 3500 BC have been found in different regions of the early world, mostly in Egypt and ancient Mesopotamia. The use of meteoric iron seems to have remained active well into the Early Iron Age or perhaps even later in some regions.

EARLY METALLURGY OF COPPER AND IRON

Copper and iron dominated the early metals world for ten millennia, although other metals: gold, silver mercury, lead were also used in relatively small quantities mainly for decorative and ornamental purposes. Humanity transited from working stone to native copper and iron; they learnt to melt and cast native copper, and eventually to smelt copper from ore and produce alloys of copper. Finally, they moved to iron metallurgy and produced wrought iron which revolutionized metals production and scope of use. No new primary metals emerged until the seventeenth century AD before copper and iron were joined by other metals, notably aluminium and steel.

Early history of copper metallurgy

As discussed earlier, it is unclear when or where copper was first smelted from ore and use became common, which could be identified as the beginning of the Copper Age, but, based on the dating of the earliest evidence of smelting, it is widely believed it first happened in the Mediterranean area around fifth to fourth millennium BC, possibly in Anatolia, Mesopotamia or Iran, but use appeared to have been very limited for around a thousand years before it spread within the region and to other regions.

Arsenical/antimoniacal copper

Beginning from the late fifth and first half of the fourth millennium BC many of the products of the Chalcolithic smelting, as well as those produced from smelting native copper in most regions of the old world contain high levels of arsenic, as high as 8 wt% As (around the maximum solubility in molten copper), although some contain 14-24 wt% As. However, this may be erroneous because of the well-known segregation issues with arsenical coppers). The dominance or arsenical coppers continued for around two millennia before bronze emerged as a significant competitor. There is extensive debate on whether the presence of arsenic in copper Chalcolithic and Copper Age castings was incidental and a result of the geological co-occurrence of copper and arsenic ores and widespread association of the two ores in the earth's crust, or the early people knew the potential benefits of arsenic in copper castings and deliberately selected arsenical copper ores or mixed the two ores. Unfortunately, most of the published data on arsenic contents of early copper were from surface analyses and arsenic can be segregated into surface layers, therefore surface measurements may not be representative of the casting. This may explain the very wide range of arsenic contents found in ancient copper artifacts that have been published. High arsenic alloys could be made by co-smelting a copper oxide with an arsenical sulphide such as orpiment (AsS). (Metallic arsenic is a relatively volatile substance with a boiling point of 613°C and arsenic trioxide (As_2O_3) is even more volatile, boiling at 457°C. If oxidized arsenical copper minerals are smelted (and this would have to be under reducing conditions), calculations show that most of the arsenic present below 7 wt% will be retained (Tylecote, 1976).

Copper ore deposits are frequently stratified, with the surface layers highly oxidized and relatively easy to smelt with charcoal in closed crucibles. Production remained small in early times and use was restricted to ornaments and artifacts, until pit and induced- and forced-draft shaft furnaces emerged and made possible the smelting of copper ores on a scale large enough to produce material for the manufacture of large castings, tools and weapons. Many copper ore deposits contain arsenic along with several other elements. After exhausting the upper oxidized layers of a stratified arsenical copper deposit (Figure A-3.2), early copper smelters would have had no choice but to use ore from the copper-rich enrichment zone in the middle layers. This is the zone which provides the highest concentrations of copper and, as arsenical and antimonial minerals are relatively soluble, the layer usually contains these two elements in the highest concentrations as well. It seems therefore that the emergence of arsenical copper was incidental initially but it would not have taken long to discover the potential benefits of arsenic in copper, notably as a deoxidant and fluidity enhancer in copper casting, as well as its strengthening effect on worked copper.

When copper is melted in air, for example in a foundry, or at the later stages of ore smelting and refining when an oxidizing environment is produced, considerable quantities of oxygen can dissolve in the molten metal, forming copper oxide which forms a lower melting point eutectic with the copper at grain boundaries of the solidifying metal. Although subsequent forging will close up most of the pores, the presence of eutectic deposits at the grain boundaries makes subsequent working of copper problematic because of its serious effect on ductility and cold-workability. Copper ingots may also be exposed to hydrogen-containing gases during furnace reheating prior to forging. These gases react with the grain boundary eutectic, resulting in blistering, cracking and surface embrittlement. Hydrogen is soluble in molten metal and reacts with oxygen to form steam which is rejected during solidification causing porosity in the casting. However, this is unlikely to happen when the ingot is heated with charcoal in an open fire (Charles, 1967). When arsenic is present in the molten metal, arsenious oxide forms as a separate phase which is insoluble and separates from the liquid, eventually as a sublimate. Arsenic will also reduce any copper oxide formed during the process of solidification to produce discrete particles rather than the eutectic grain boundary network of copper oxide which is detrimental to ductility. In effect, presence of arsenic enhances the structural integrity and surface finish of copper castings but its positive effect is much more significant when the ingot is to be forged to make products such as tools and weapons because of its major enhancement on workability and work-hardenability. Copper that contains as low as 8 wt% arsenic work-hardens very rapidly, nearly doubling the hardness at 60% reduction compared with pure copper. This would have been a major attraction since it meant that tools, axes, weapons, arrow tips and other tools and implements could now be made by cold-forging copper.

Solid copper has a face-centered cubic structure that gives it excellent ductility and toughness, but low work-hardenability, hence it would have been too soft for tools, weapons. Furthermore, molten copper is susceptible to oxidation and it is difficult to produce good quality copper castings. Copper is too soft for working because the face-centered cubic crystallographic structure greatly enhances deformation dislocation movements with few barriers. The early metalworkers probably discovered by accident that small impurities of arsenic, antimony or tin can improve the castability and workability of copper dramatically. These elements are present in many copper ores mostly in small quantities but the amount of arsenic and antimony can be substantial depending on the ore type and degree of weathering. There is little doubt that the smelters eventually selected certain ores deliberately or mixed ores to produce stronger copper alloys. Clearly they were unable to regulate the chemistry of the smelt charge considering the wide variability in the element composition of objects found in the same area or in different regions, consistent with alloying by mixing ores.

Copper forms alloys with many elements: addition of arsenic, antimony, tin, zinc and many other elements even in small quantities can dramatically improve strength of copper. Most of these elements form second phases dispersed in the homogeneous copper matrix and act as inhibitors to free movement of slips and dislocations during working, thereby strengthening the alloy. The main alloying elements that were available in early times are arsenic, antimony, tin and zinc, and they are all present as impurities in many copper ores. When arsenic is present in the molten copper metal, arsenous oxide forms as a separate phase which is insoluble and separates from the liquid, eventually as a sublimate. Arsenic will also reduce any copper oxide formed during the process of solidification to produce discrete particles rather than the eutectic grain boundary network of copper oxide which is detrimental to ductility. In effect, presence of arsenic enhances the structural integrity and surface finish of copper castings but its positive effect is much more significant when the ingot is to be forged to make products such as tools and weapons because of its major enhancement on workability and work-hardenability. However, arsenic has low melting point and volatilizes in an oxidizing atmosphere mainly as toxic arsenic trioxide, causing a significant loss of the element when copper is reheated for casting or forging (this is not a problem in smelting since the atmosphere is reducing). Antimony and tin have similar strengthening characteristics but they do not deplete in reheated copper ingots like arsenic.

Any or a combination of arsenic, antimony and tin, even when present in small proportions of 1-2 wt%, can improve copper workability dramatically. It is probable that, at least initially, the discovery of the potential of these elements was an accidental discovery by the early copper casters since many weathered copper ores contain both elements. The concentrations of both elements in the ore would have increased as the upper weathered layers were exhausted, accounting to the significant increase in excavated objects dated from around 3000 BC. Debate on the intentionality of arsenic addition to copper is intensive but, considering the common geological co-occurrence of arsenic and copper minerals and the wide variability of arsenic content of copper objects it is probable that the ancient metalworkers simply recognized the enhanced properties of copper smelted from certain ore deposits and selected such alloys for specific uses rather than intentionally alloying copper with arsenic or antimony. Alloying copper with arsenic, tin or antimony can happen accidentally through ore contamination or can be intentional. When it is intentional the process is controlled and the chemical composition of the product is predictable. However, the possibility of intentional mixing of ores from different deposits cannot be ruled out, which qualifies to be identified as intentional although poorly controlled.

Arsenic in cast copper has several advantageous effects on both the casting and mechanical properties of copper which early metal casters would have found attractive: a 3 wt% of arsenic lowers the melting temperature of copper by 50°C, enough to delay solidification and enhance pouring during casting. The workability of cast copper is also enhanced significantly. Addition of arsenic sulphide in the form of realgar (As_4S_4) has been found to reduce melting temperature by as much as 250 °C although doing so also introduces significant quantities of sulphur to the final casting (Palmieri et al. 1992). While there is little doubt that the early copper smelters appreciated the potential benefits of arsenic in copper, Arsenic is only present in sulphide copper ores, not oxide ores and it is unclear how the early smelters surmounted the difficulties of smelting sulphide copper ores which require preliminary roasting before smelting. Copper oxides are relatively easy to smelt by heating with charcoal under reducing conditions, in accordance with the following equation:

Direct reduction smelting of oxide ores

$$CuCO_3 + CO \xrightarrow{heat} Cu + 2\ CO_2 \uparrow$$

copper   carbon   copper   gas
carbonate monoxide metal

Some copper sulpharsenide ores (e.g. energite: Cu_3AsS_4) may weather and form copper arsenate, for example olivernite [$Cu_2(AsO_4)(OH)$]. Such ores can also be direct-reduced in accordance with the following equation:

$$CuAsO_4 + 4\ CO \xrightarrow{direct\ smelt} Cu, As + 4\ CO_2 \uparrow$$

copper arsenate   Cu-As alloy

However, sulphide ores require two-stage processing: a long roast at no higher than 800°C to oxidize the ore followed by smelting under reducing conditions in accordance with the following equations:

(1) roast

$$CuS + 1\,1/2\, O_2 \xrightarrow{heat} CuO + SO_2\uparrow$$

copper sulphide + oxygen → copper oxide + gas

(2) direct smelt

$$CuO + CO \rightarrow Cu + CO_2\uparrow$$

copper oxide → copper metal

If the ore is a sulpharsenide containing both copper and arsenic, both elements are oxidized during the preliminary roast to form solid copper arsenate and gaseous arsenious trioxide (As_2O_3) and the following equations apply:

(1) roast

$$8\, CuAsS + 22\,1/2\, O_2 \xrightarrow{heat} 6\, CuAsO_4 + 2\, CuO + As_2O_3\uparrow + 8\, SO_2\uparrow$$

copper sulpharsenide → copper arsenate + copper oxide + fume + gas

(2) direct smelt

$$CuAsO_4 + 4\, CO \rightarrow Cu,As + 4\, CO_2\uparrow$$

copper arsenate → Cu-As alloy

The body of evidence suggests that arsenical copper was produced by direct smelting of arsenical copper ore considering the wide variability in the content of arsenic in early copper objects but this raises another question: Arsenic is rarely found in copper oxide ores which are usually at the top layers of a typical ore deposit because, as explained earlier, copper sulphide and arsenic are relatively soluble and will sink to the middle layers, hence most of the current world's arsenic-bearing ores are sulphides. Therefore, it is logical to assume that the early copper smelters had exhausted the oxidized layers of their copper deposits which would have been relatively easy to smelt and resorted to smelting arsenic-rich sulphide ores. It had been assumed that they carried out either of the two-stage processes outlined above depending on the chemistry of the local ore deposit, and that they produced arsenical copper by roasting sulpharsenide ores and then smelting the oxide products. However, to date, no evidence of copper sulphide roasting has been found. Furthermore, the production of toxic arsenic trioxide fumes during roasting would have posed serious health hazards. It is more likely that they smelted mixtures of copper sulphide and copper or iron sulpharsenide ores in a single process now known as cosmelting, and recent laboratory experiments have shown that this can be done (Rostoker et al 1989, 1991; Lechtman and Klein 1999). In the cosmelting process a mixture of copper sulphide and a sulpharsenide ore of copper or iron is charged into a furnace or crucible. At sufficiently high smelting temperatures, the sulphur acts as a reducing agent and extracts oxygen from the oxide ore, thereby reducing the ore, and is eliminated as sulphur dioxide, thereby eliminating the need for pre-roasting and reducing the possibility of the production of toxic arsenic trioxide. The following generalized equations present typical cosmelting reactions in which the sulphide mineral also contains arsenic. The Sulphur reduces the copper oxide to produce arsenical copper alloy:

Cosmelting

(1) Smelting with enargite

$$8\ CuCO_3 + Cu_3AsS_4 \xrightarrow{heat} Cu,As + 4\ SO_2\uparrow + 8\ CO_2\uparrow$$

copper carbonate + enargite → Cu-As alloy + gas + gas

(2) Smelting with arsenopyrite

$$3\ CuCO_3 + FeAsS \xrightarrow{heat} Cu,As + FeO + SO_2\uparrow + 3\ CO_2\uparrow$$

arsenopyrite, iron oxide

Depending on the chemical composition of the ores, several byproducts may include sulphides of copper or of copper and iron (matte), arsenides of copper and iron (spies), and slag when silica is present in the ore. Lechtman and Klein, (1999) carried out a series of experiments on cosmelting in a crucible and a furnace modelled after ancient arsenical copper furnaces excavated from several early smelting sites in the Peruvian north coast where arsenical coppers were widely used. Copper oxide ore was mixed in different ratios with either copper sulpharsenide or iron sulpharsenide ore, all collected from local deposits that may have been the sources of the early arsenical copper smelting activities. The mixtures were smelted without the addition of fluxes. Charges containing ratios between 2:1 and 4:1 oxide:sulpharsenide ore produced clean arsenical copper metal, fully separated from slag and matte byproducts. The probable chemical and thermodynamic reactions and the phase separation mechanisms were determined from a comprehensive analysis of the metal ingots, mattes and slags by X-ray diffraction and microanalytical methods.

Co-smelting of oxide and sulphide copper ore mixtures in early times may have been deliberate or incidental but it is more likely that the smelters exhausted the fully oxidized, sulphide-free layer of a stratified copper sulphide deposit and now had to smelt ore from the partially weathered lower layers which are mixtures of oxides and sulphides. This would be a natural ore mix for cosmelting. The lowest layers are primarily sulphides, the natural state of copper ores and this explains why most modern copper mines produce sulphide ores. The fact that there is such a vide variability in arsenic content of objects found in the same area is an indication of the inability of the smelters to control the amount of arsenic present in any object. If, as indeed likely, the early copper producers practiced cosmelting, it is not surprising that arsenical copper technology proliferated very rapidly and dominated the early metal world from fourth to second millennia, overlapping with the Early Bronze Age which emerged around 3000 BC when tin began to appear in cast and worked objects in low concentrations with or without arsenic.

Apart from lowering the melting point of copper and acting as a mild deoxidant in copper castings, arsenic significantly enhances the hardness and tensile strength of copper, making it suitable for a wide range of forged products such as tools and weapons. Arsenic content of around 2 wt% improves the strength of copper by around 30%. However, when reheated for forging or remelted for casting, arsenical copper alloys tend to lose arsenic in form of volatile arsenous oxide which is not only toxic but reduces work-hardenability. Tin has similar hardening properties: they both form solid solutions which block the movement of dislocations, thereby strengthening copper (solid solution hardening), but does not volatilize, which explains why transition from arsenical to tin bronzes in many places was rapid. However, there was a significant overlap between the arsenical copper and low-tin bronze eras particularly in areas which had access to suitable ores, because arsenical copper was excellent for cold forging with intermediate annealing, making it suitable for the production of thin plates. Furthermore, tin was rare and expensive compared with arsenical copper ores which were much more common.

Antimony is also present in some copper ores (fahlerz ores) and some ores have high concentrations of copper and antimony, for example a Hungarian mine worked around 2000 BC had 17.4 wt% Cu and 16.6 wt% Sb and many copper alloy objects containing the element in proportions as high as 15 wt% have been found in different regions of the early world. A large number of copper-based metal objects excavated in the Judean desert of the Early Middle East and dated to the Chalcolithic Era (fourth millennium BC) were apparently made of a ternary copper-arsenic-antimony alloy. Some of the objects contain more antimony than arsenic and the combined content reaches 20 wt%. There is little doubt that they were made from weathered tetrahedrite-type ore [$Cu_{12}(As,Sb)_4S_{13}$]. Such ores would normally weather to malachite, azurite and complex oxides of copper, arsenic and antimony, and have been found in several locations in the Early Middle East. Since antimony hardens copper to the same extent as arsenic it would be just as desirable and because it is not so volatile, a greater proportion would be retained in working (arsenic is lost in appreciable rates when arsenical copper is hot-forged) but antimony-rich copper ores were not common.

Zinc also imparts good work-hardening characteristics on copper although the product is softer and more malleable than bronze but, like arsenic, zinc is also volatile. Throughout the Bronze Age, zinc appeared in some copper and bronze objects in small quantities no more than 1-3 wt%. The element is an impurity in some copper alloys and this may have been the source in some regions where zinc occurred in some bronze objects. Most of the objects have been found in areas which also had zinc-rich copper ores, notably Cyprus, Palestine, Ireland, China, India. There is no credible evidence that true brass was produced in the Early or Late Bronze period whereas many castings were gunmetals (ternary alloys of copper, zinc, tin, lead), with zinc contents varying from 1 to 9 wt%. Full (alpha) brass (20-30 wt% zinc) did not appear until the beginning of the Roman Empire around 30-29 BC produced by the calamine process in which additions of zinc carbonate (calamine) or oxide were made to copper and melted in a crucible under the cover of charcoal which created reducing conditions. In the process, some of the zinc was reduced before copper was molten. The zinc vapour produced entered the copper and lowered its melting point to about 900°C. Use appeared to have been restricted to a few objects, notably coinage. Even then, gunmetal gradually replaced brass in coinage and by second century AD it had become the metal of choice. It is unclear why full brass never displaced bronze or gunmetal for around two millennia considering the relative scarcity of tin. In all probability, the early smiths considered the alloy too soft for anything but artifacts, musical instruments and ornaments. Even the Romans used brass almost exclusively for coinage while gunmetal was preferred for cast products. The main reason may have been because most objects were produced by casting and gunmetal has superior castability compared with brass or bronze. On the other hand, coins were produced by stamping and the relatively superior malleability of brass would have been an asset. Furthermore, brass objects can be polished to a high degree of surface finish and this would have made is very suitable for such products as coins, buttons, musical instruments, artifacts, etc. For some reason brass seemed to have been considered more valuable than bronze by the Romans but this may have been a result of relative scarcity of zinc compared with tin ingot which was being traded very widely across regions.

Archaeologists often divide the Bronze Age into Early, Middle and Late. The Early Bronze Age (EBA) is actually a period when low-tin copper alloys with non-bronze compositions were in extensive use. This persisted for around two millennia before the Middle Bronze Age (MBA) which could be regarded as the beginning of the True Bronze Era, when tin-copper alloys began to feature tin contents as high as 7 wt% or more. As would be expected, there was an overlap with the EBA in many places for a long time. The main difference between the MBA and the Late Bronze Age (LBA) is one of scale and proliferation. Production of bronze metal increased in batch size and areas of practice in the Mediterranean area and had spread to most countries of Asia, Europe and the Americas by the LBA. While there was no marked change in technique which prevailed in the MBA, the appearance of ingots weighing 30-50 kilograms in many places from around 1600 BC was a clear evidence of substantial scale-up of production practice and evidence that casting technology had reached a high degree of sophistication, probably because tin ingots were now widely traded across regions. There was now more attention to detail, with the production of finer objects and more accurate castings. Addition of lead to increase the fluidity of the metal is believed to be an innovation of the Late Bronze Age. Furnaces were bigger and featured complex design of tuyeres and the technology for casting large objects in multiple stages had clearly been mastered. Objects which required large amounts of molten metal, as much as 1500 kg were produced in China, presumably in piece moulds and assembled.

Tin/zinc copper

Tin and zinc enhance the strength of copper in a manner similar to arsenic but, up to a level of concentration, they form homogeneous solid solutions with alpha copper, hence they are uniformly dispersed and do not segregate or volatilize like arsenic. The very long preeminence of arsenical coppers in virtually all regions of the early world for thousands of years must have been due to the relative abundance and wide distribution of arsenical copper ores. In regions where these ores were readily available, use of arsenical copper remained extensive until the arrival of the Iron Age. This very long period of early metallurgical history is often classified as Early Bronze Age although true bronzes were not in use. In spite of the relative superiority of tin coppers, use was severely restricted for millennia probably because of the scarcity of tin ores. Even today, there are less than ten significant tin deposits in the world: Malaysia, China, Bolivia, Cornwall, Saxony-Bohemia, Nigeria. Most of the tin copper objects found and dated prior to around the third millennium BC had very low tin concentrations mostly less than 2 wt%, which apparently must have come as impurity in the copper ore, whereas tin contents of the Full Bronze Age objects were consistently high, mostly above the minimum of around 7% required for a true bronze. If tin oxide is mixed with copper ore and smelted in reducing conditions under charcoal in a crucible, molten tin can be produced which would combine with copper to form an alloy. However, it would be near impossible to control such a process and this strengthens the speculation that tin in most copper alloys in the Copper/Early Bronze Age were incidental, coming from copper ores as impurities, especially because many early copper-base alloys from widely-separated areas of Eurasia contain small amounts of tin, often together with arsenic (see Tylecote, 1975) Table 11). Published analyses show that the smiths of the True Bronze Age were capable of producing true bronzes with 7-10% tin with astonishing regularity, a consistency that could only have been achieved by the direct addition of tin to molten copper. However, no evidence of tin smelting in the period has been found in the Mediterranean area where the earliest true bronze objects have been found. A few tin-rich copper ores deposits have been found in the world: in Saxony-Europe and Cornwall-England. Depending on the chemical composition, copper ores with low tin contents can be smelted to produce true bronze. For example, the copper deposit in Cornwall has a tin content of tin content of only 0.7-1% compared with 12.3% copper content. However, smelting this ore would produce true bronze giving a copper:tin ratio of 92:8. Cornwall also has a tin deposit at St. Austell where the earliest evidence of tin smelting has been found dated 1600 BC (Tylecote 1975b, 1975c) and this has led to speculations that bronze technology could have been invented independently in Cornwall and this area may have been one of the earliest sources of traded tin ingots.

Arsenical and antimoniacal coppers fizzled out with the arrival of the Full Bronze Age and are no longer of interest in modern metallurgy for two main reasons: arsenic has a low melting point and a strong tendency to oxidize and volatilize. Under reducing conditions as is the case in smelting copper ores, arsenic content of up to 7 wt% is retained but any excess will volatilize (Tylecote 1976, 1991; Lechtman and Klein 1999). However, under oxidizing conditions which normally prevail during melting and casting of copper, up to 70 wt% of arsenic can be lost. The second reason for the decline of arsenical copper is the toxicity of arsenic trioxide which is released during re-melting and casting of copper. In modern metallurgy, small quantities of arsenic (less than 1 wt%) are still added to certain copper alloys to improve scaling resistance, corrosion and wear although other less hazardous and equally competent alloys have emerged. Small amounts of arsenic are still used in the manufacture of gallium arsenide semiconductors for use in electronics. Some arsenic is also used in glass-making. However, in general, the element is now considered a toxic impurity which must be reduced to less than 0.5 wt% in copper ore concentrates.

Provenance of arsenical/antimoniacal copper technology

One of the great puzzles of archaeometallurgy is determination of the provenance of tin that launched the Full Bronze Age. Tin is a very rare ore, present as cassiterite (SnO_2) within veins or quartz running through the granite rock. Ore particles are freed by degradation of the quartz and granite through weathering or by the force of a flowing river, hence, the particles often settle as concentrate in the bed of the stream and is recovered like gold by panning of the gravel in the stream bed, and separating the small black nuggets of cassiterite from sand and gravel (cassiterite is normally white in the pure state but is more often contaminated with iron which renders it brown or black). It is possible or even probable that many civilizations across all regions had access to tin-rich copper ores, the fact that they have not been found does not mean they did not exist. They may be waiting to be found or evidence may have been obliterated by land movements and river/ocean incursions. However, it is likely that low-tin copper metallurgy incubated in many areas of the early world possibly simultaneously but practice remained small and did not flourish until tin ingots became available in substantial quantities probably through trading. It is important to note that this development coincided with the practice of tin smelting on a significant scale in Cornwall and possibly several other locations in other regions. Apparently, the rapid development of intra- and inter-regional trade starting from around the third millennium BC facilitated access to imports of tin ingots and marked the arrival of the Late/Full Bronze Age.

Early history of iron metallurgy

The oldest evidence of significant iron smelting and use from about 2000 BC has been found in Asia Minor and this is widely regarded as the beginning of the Early Iron Age (EIA). Archaeometallurgists believe that iron technology was incubating in the Anatolian-Iranian region during the period 1500-1000 BC and spread to parts of Europe, Asia, North and West Africa in the following five centuries. It is believed that the invention of iron technology may have been accidental in the process of smelting copper ores with iron oxide fluxes either present in the copper ore or deliberately added. There is a distinct possibility of iron oxide being reduced in the bottom of the furnace, causing the furnace bottoms to contain much slag and reduced iron. Evidence of such an occurrence has been found in some more recent copper smelters in Central Iran (Tylecote 1972, 1976). The possibility could have occurred anywhere in the Late Bronze Age, in several places independently, even before the Anatolians, except that the Anatolians had a longer experience with copper smelting, and it was in this area that the earliest iron daggers have been found. It is also possible that development of copper furnaces in some areas reached a point at which temperatures as high as around 1150°C could be obtained, high enough for the solid-state direct reduction of iron oxide by carbon monoxide produced from charcoal, thereby producing significant amounts of almost pure iron at the bottom of fluxed-ore copper furnaces. This would have encouraged the smelters to try smelting iron ores which were more common than copper ores. The practice of iron smelting was apparently small and spasmodic for several hundred years until around 1200-1000 BC when it was being used on a large scale for weapons. In effect, bronze use remained prominent and extensive for a long time. The higher strength and ductility of iron compared with bronze must have been a major incentive for extensive experimentation which eventually let to the emergence of the Full Iron Age in the Mediterranean by the beginning of the first millennium BC, proliferating to most other regions over the next five hundred years or so. Greece had the technology by 900 BC and it probably spread to Europe, Asia, North Africa and West Africa in the following few hundred years.

Wrought iron

The early technology of iron involved heating iron oxide mixed with charcoal at about 1150°C. Carbon monoxide released from the charcoal reduces the iron ore and the product is a spongy, nearly pure iron mass known as sponge iron. The reduced iron, a mixture of solid iron, slag, and pieces of unburnt charcoal was removed as clod or bloom, heated in a smith's fire followed by hot hammering. The product was a strong, ductile iron-slag elongated structure. In some cases, the blooms were broken, sorted and the small iron pieces were then welded into larger pieces of purer iron by heating them and hot-forging. The product known as wrought iron quickly became a choice material for a very wide range of applications but it would have been too soft for tools and weapons because of the low carbon content which would have been around 0.08 wt%. The product of the bloomery process can be very heterogeneous, with non-uniform distribution of important elements, in particular, iron and arsenic. It is also possible that the common process of quenching forged blooms may have induced martensitic structures in areas where the carbon content was sufficiently high. There is no doubt that the early iron smiths were aware of the potential benefits of martensitic precipitation and that the harder, high-carbon areas could be separated from the softer iron, smithed separately and used for making tools and weapons. Also, there is substantial evidence that the Asian smiths found a way of carburizing wrought iron by heating an object buried in a mass of charcoal in a smith's fire. Carbon would diffuse into the outer layers of the object (carburization), making it possible to give swords and arrow tips a hardened edge by water-quenching.

If the fuel to ore ratio is high and the air bellows are efficient, furnace temperatures could reach 1150-1200°C, high enough to make the iron absorb so much carbon that it forms a molten alloy of iron and carbon known as cast iron which contains 4-4-5 wt% carbon, has a melting point of 1150°C and can be cast like bronze. This could have occurred in different places around the same time but it was the Chinese who seemed to have appreciated the enormous potential of cast iron and developed furnaces with powerful, water-driven blowers, and produced molten cast iron regularly in substantial quantities. The Chinese cast iron technology is widely regarded as the forerunner of the modern pig iron blast furnace.

It is unclear who first made molten iron or where it occurred but it is quite likely that some of the iron furnaces of the Anatolians, Europeans or Asians reached around 1200°C in which case some of the iron would melt and settle in a pool at the bottom of the furnace. The solidified lumps could have been remelted in a crucible and cast like bronze. The process of making wrought iron was tedious and labour-intensive, and supply could not cope with demand. It is not surprising therefore that the metalworkers (probably the Chinese around 600-500 BC) quickly found a way of making wrought iron from cast iron by stirring molten cast iron while blowing air through. Much of the carbon in the object would be expelled as carbon dioxide, leaving softer iron similar to wrought iron (de-carburization). Also, around 500-300 BC, the Indians are believed to have invented a method of carburizing wrought iron by heating high-purity wrought iron mixed with charcoal, other carbonaceous materials and glass in a forced-draught for several hours, producing a homogeneous, heat-treatable steel with carbon content of about 1.8-2 wt% carbon, known as *wootz* or *Damascus* steel. This process, the forerunner of the modern carburization, is solid state carburization of wrought iron in an atmosphere which promotes diffusion of carbon into the iron and prevents oxidation. The product, a complex mixture of iron, some trace elements, precipitates of carbides and cementite which had been flattened into fine fibers through hammering, was then annealed to reduce the carbon content to about 1-1.6 wt%, compared with around 0.08 wt% for wrought iron, then hammered into bars from which a wide range of finished products were made. The quality of the steel produced was outstanding and products were widely exported to all regions of the early world including Europe.

Not much else happened in early iron metallurgy for nearly two millennia, except that the furnaces got bigger and more efficient, complex blowing systems were developed, and slagging became common. Much of these developments have been attributed to the Roman Empire which flourished from 29 BC, an era often referred to as the Late or Roman Iron Age. Whereas the pre-Roman iron production was in kilograms, the Romans quickly developed large facilities capable of producing tonnes of iron which they needed for their military arsenal. Also, iron was traded very widely to conquered territories and the technology was disseminated to the surrounding tribes who also produced weapons for the Roman military effort. This monumental mistake is believed to have led to the downfall of the empire because the weaponized surrounding settlements rose against the Empire. The Romans also developed large-scale production facilities for brass which they used extensively in coinage.

Cast iron

Molten iron contains excessively high carbon and several other elements, notably silicon which make it too brittle for structural use. Heating with charcoal in a cupola reduces carbon and silicon contents to acceptable levels and enhances the engineering properties of the iron significantly. Also, addition of other alloying elements, notably manganese, chromium leads to the production of a wide variety of irons (cast irons) with different engineering properties. Cast iron quickly displaced bronze and wrought iron for the manufacture of tools, agricultural implements and weapons. The alloy became a major structural metal in applications requiring high compressive strength such as building structures, bridges and machinery components, while wrought iron was used in applications that required malleability, ductility and high tensile strength. Further advances in cast iron technology produced malleable (ductile) cast iron by heat treatment which transforms the microstructure into spheroidal aggregates of graphite embedded in ferrite or pearlite matrix. This microstructure confers significant ductility and the development opened up a very wide range of applications for spheroidal cast iron beyond cast products. Malleable cast iron is believed to have been produced in China as early as 4th century BC, based on worked cast iron artifacts discovered in the region and dated between 4th century BC and 9th century AD. However, production was probably limited to small quantities because of the rigorous technology involved. A French scientist took out a patent in England for malleable iron in 1720 produced by a method similar to the Chinese technology. However, the real breakthrough came in the United States in 1826 when a foundry was established by industrialist Boyden that produced malleable iron in large quantities. Today, different types and grades of malleable (nodular) cast irons are produced for different applications, notably small castings that require some ductility: machine components, hand and bench tools, structural and powerline fittings, etc. The cast iron technology has changed very little over time, the most important being the development of coke-fired cupolas capable of producing large volumes of molten metal for casting large shapes in foundries.

Steel

The modern blast furnace technology has changed only in size and charge composition since the Chinese iron era (apart from substitution of charcoal with coke, use of more powerful electrical blowers and injection of supplementary fuels). Most furnaces produce 5 million metric tons or more of pig iron a year and coke is charged instead of charcoal or coal. Blast air is pre-heated and supplementary fuels such as coke breeze and natural gas are injected to optimize production parameters. The product, pig iron is too impure for any engineering application and is either refined into cast iron or steel which is basically decarbonized cast iron (reduction of carbon content from over 4 wt% to 2 wt% or below). Technologies emerged in Europe in the 17th century for processing molten cast iron produced in the blast furnace by heating and stirring in an oxidizing atmosphere. The emergence of mild, low-carbon steel marked the beginning of the demise of wrought iron as a material of choice in any but ornamental applications such as gates and fences. A very wide variety of alloys of cast iron or steel may be produced by varying the level of carbon content of molten pig or cast iron and addition of small quantities of some elements (manganese, nickel, chromium, molybdenum, tungsten, columbium, etc.) and thermochemical heat treatment to achieve desired microstructures (some elements may remain in solution, some form new chemical compounds, while others form hard precipitates). The emergence of alloying technologies has extended the range of steels to around 3000, including corrosion, creep, fatigue resistant alloys, high-temperature alloys, high-strength alloys, as well as a wide range of cast irons for different applications. Steel now accounts for about 95 wt% of all metals used by modern industrial society. Iron and steel became widely available beyond Europe by the 18th century AD and marked the beginning of closure of the Early Iron Age in some regions, although it persisted in some developing nations until around 1900 when scrap steel became widely available.

www.ingramcontent.com/pod-product-compliance
Lightning Source LLC
Chambersburg PA
CBHW060419010526
44118CB00017B/2286